TARGETING
THE FOREIGN DIRECT INVESTOR

TARGETING THE FOREIGN DIRECT INVESTOR

Strategic Motivation, Investment Size, and Developing Country Investment-Attraction Packages

Edward J. Coyne, Sr., C.D. *(Hon.)(Jamaica)*
B. Sc., M.I.B.A., Ph. D.

School of Business & Entrepreneurship
Nova Southeastern University

Kluwer Academic Publishers
Boston/Dordrecht/London

Distributors for North America:
Kluwer Academic Publishers
101 Philip Drive
Assinippi Park
Norwell, Massachusetts 02061 USA

Distributors for all other countries:
Kluwer Academic Publishers Group
Distribution Centre
Post Office Box 322
3300 AH Dordrecht, THE NETHERLANDS

Library of Congress Cataloging-in-Publication Data

A C.I.P. Catalogue record for this book is available from the Library of Congress.

DEDICATION

To the people of Jamaica.

TABLE OF CONTENTS

TARGETING THE FOREIGN DIRECT INVESTOR
Strategic Motivation, Investment Size and Developing Country Investment-Attraction Packages

LIST OF FIGURES

LIST OF TABLES

ABBREVIATIONS

CARICOM	Caribbean Economic Community
CBI	Caribbean Basin Initiative
CR	cost reduction
F	financial restrictions
FDI	foreign direct investment
FTZ	free trade zone
GDP	gross domestic product
GSP	Generalized System of Preferences
H	Hypothesis
HCM	host country market
H-O	Heckscher-Ohlin Theory (Factor Endowment)
I	investment & ownership
IAP	investment attraction package
IMF	International Monetary Fund
IPLC	International Product Life Cycle Theory
LDC	Lesser Developed Country
LG	large investment ($1,000,000 or more)
MNC	multinational corporation
MNE	multinational enterprise (synonymous with MNC)
NAFTA	North American Free Trade Agreement
Oa	Asset advantage
OECD	Organization for Economic Cooperation and Development
OPEC	Organization of Petroleum Exporting Countries
Ot	transaction advantage
RM	raw materials (natural resources)
SM	small investment (less than $1,000,000)
T	taxes & incentives
TNC	transnational corporation (synonymous with MNC)
U.K.	United Kindgdom
UN	United Nations
UNCTAD	United Nations Conference on Trade and Development
UNCTC	United Nations Centre for Transnational Corporations
U.S.	United States of America
USDOC	U.S. Department of Commerce
WWII	World War II

FOREWORD

Foreign direct investment in less developed countries remains a concern for those interested in improving the lot of the economically disadvantaged. Report after report (notably those from the Division on Transnationals at UNCTAD) bemoans the paucity of stocks of direct investment in the world's poorest regions and the levels of current flows of investment hold little immediate hope that this will change. Attention is frequently drawn to spectacular (and sometimes short lived) booms in flows to one particular country or region; currently China and India attract the spotlight. Overall though, less developed countries find themselves competing to attract a relatively small share of world direct investment.

Clearly, it is necessary to pay attention to the decision processes of the investing companies and in particular to their motivations to invest. Broadly, three motives stand out: raw material seeking investment, market seeking investment and efficiency seeking investment. Countries well endowed with raw materials (oil, copper and the bauxite deposits which have attracted much inward investment to Jamaica) attract multinationals in the extraction industries. These ventures are often subject to extensive regulation and are often the focus of political tensions. Market seeking investment, of course, tends to be targeted at large, rapidly growing markets and those with at least a segment of high income earners (India is a prime example). Efficiency seeking investment is to a large degree seeking cheap labour and may, initially at least, have very low spill over benefits. It is also highly "footloose" in that it can often be shifted to an alternate location if the conditions in its original host country choice deteriorate.

The following study by Ed Coyne tackles these issues by dividing foreign direct investment by motive, by investment timing and by size. The three motives outlined above, the amount of investment and the initial investment versus expansion dichotomy provide a basis by which policy makers can begin to target potential investors and re-investors. This attempt to improve policy targeting is welcome and Coyne has produced a simple, yet powerful framework for the design of policy. This enables progress to be made in identifying and creating an optimal Investment Attraction Package for each less developed country's needs.

Ed Coyne brings a vast amount of high level managerial experience to bear on his subject and this, combined with a great deal of insight from the academic literature, has produced a valuable and thought provoking study which takes us forward in the practical and theoretical issues of modelling appropriate investment attraction packages.

Peter J. Buckley
Professor of International Business
Director, Centre for International Business
University of Leeds

PREFACE

Time, funds and age may work against any individual researcher but the depth, breadth, and immediacy-of-need in the developing countries cries out for facts, ideas, and solutions. Small-economy, developing countries have very limited resources to spend for attracting foreign direct investment (FDI). Yet their need and their goal is capital inflow - including FDI - for stimulating economic growth to increase the quality of life for their people.

In today's post cold war environment, developed country direct assistance to small-economy developing countries is evaporating about as fast as the geo-political usefulness of the developing countries vanished with the collapse of the former Soviet Union. Foreign aid has not enjoyed broad popular support for quite some time. Throughout recorded history, the more energetic and daring of the poor have consistently shown a strong propensity to make Herculean efforts to improve their lot. When the opportunity doors were closed at home, the path of immigration has most often been the chosen channel of those efforts. Modern experience does not indicate any lessening of the energy and daring of the disadvantaged. The nightly T.V. pictures of Cuban nationals accepting enormous risks to escape severe deprivation haunt the mind.

Coinciding with the lessening of the willingness to support foreign aid has come the lessening of the "tolerance" of the developed world for accepting the "invasion" of individuals from the developing world. The final decade of the 20th century has borne witness to European efforts at implementing a "closing of the door" strategy, the U.S. internal struggle with the wisdom of its immigration policy continues its divisive dialogue, and the Japanese historical preference for protection of its inhabitants against incursion from outsiders continues unabated. The T.V. images protesting "illegal immigration", "$1.00-a-day labour", and the "giant sucking sound" also haunt the mind.

At the heart of the "economic refugee" immigration conundrum for the developed world is the underdeveloped world's lack of economic growth and its by-product - the lack of an improving standard-of-living for its residents. When the broader population senses the future to be less desirable than the present or recent past, emigration historically has been the option of choice for the adventurous. With the developing countries becoming less comfortable in opening the "immigration door", it is clear that alternate doors-of-opportunity must be vigorously pursued. The UN's Paul Streeten has put the case more somberly:

"Unless global production finds ways of engaging these poor (countries) in productive and remunerative work, the outlook for global peace is dim."

The need for increasing FDI into developing countries is particularly acute as FDI is private sector investment, does not add to the already crushing burden of government debt, and is generally of a more entrepreneurial, productivity-enhancing character than state-owned investments. Developing countries need is for inward bound FDI of virtually all descriptions - market-seeking, raw material-seeking, cost reduction-seeking, large investment, small investments, first-time investments, expansion investments.

It is a truism that a target cannot be hit with any acceptable level of efficiency unless the target is identified, the appropriate missiles selected, aimed, and launched. Modern warfare allows us to add the post-launching phase: "guided". Modern warfare has also taught the efficiency of the surgical strike over the general-area bombardment strategy.

Just as modern warfare has many different type of missiles in its armory, so too does the developed world have many different avenues available for pursuing a mission of assisting the developing world to achieve an increasing standard of living for its current inhabitants. Foreign direct investment is one such avenue or missile. It is in the task of aiming and in the lessons afforded by the surgical strike that the body of this work has sought to make a contribution to the world's armory for attacking the unacceptably large gap in living standards that exist within our global village.

I would like to record his deep appreciation to Professor Peter Buckley for contributing the Foreword and for his unfailing encouragement, support and advice. I am particularly grateful for the most helpful suggestions of Professors Jeremy Clegg of the University of Bath, Allen Gart of Nova Southeastern University, Hafiz Mirza of the University of Bradford, Falih Alsaaty of the University of District of Columbia, Fred Ricci of Georgetown University, Dr. (Hon) Carlton Davis, O. J., C. D., Permanent Secretary/Cabinet Secretary, Government of Jamaica and my editor, Julie M. Kaczynski. Ms. Joi Soto was most generous in giving both time and talent for accomplishing the model drawings. Overriding all, of course, has been the unfailing support and encouragement of my wife, B.

Edward J. Coyne, Sr.
Ft. Lauderdale, Florida

Chapter I

INTRODUCTION

> *"But in spite of all the progress that has
> been made the greatest problem in the
> world today remains the gap between rich
> and poor countries and we shall not begin
> to close this gap until we hear less about
> nationalism and more about
> interdependence"*
>
> *Queen Elizabeth II*
> *Christmas Message to*
> *Commonwealth, 1983* [1]

Works published by the World Bank (1989)[2], William Lewis (1991)[3], Lester Thurow (1992)[4], and others point to the same conclusion - the gap in living standards between developed countries and developing countries (excluding Southeast Asia) is widening and likely to continue doing so for the next century. Over the next 50 years, the world's population is likely to double to approximately 10 billion people. At the end of that period, the prospects are that 10% of the world's population will have a standard of living that satisfies their reasonable material needs and desires. The remaining 90% - 9 billion people - may be living somewhat better in real terms than they are today but most of them will be living near the economic margin with no real hope of participating in the life of the industrial world - except by migrating. (Lewis, 1991).

The literature reflects that little dispute exists over such unattractive projections and the accuracy of the projections are not disputed herein - if things continue in the future as they have in the recent past. An underlying assumption of the this study is that fulfillment of the above projections is simply an unacceptable result for the world and its people. As such, the world is presented with a "defining moment". Without research into potential avenues for changing the projections, the projections will prevail by default. If the projected results are unacceptable, some change(s) must occur that act to inhibit the projected results or the projections must be found to be inaccurate.

This study advocates the "change" approach and focuses on one area of economic development - foreign direct investment (FDI). FDI into developing countries represents one avenue for making a contribution to the required changes. Its incremental and cumulative effect can be of assistance in positively shaping the economic growth trajectory of developing countries.

At the Tokyo Round Table Conference of the Organization for Economic Cooperation and Development (O.E.C.D.,1989)[5], the observation was made that while prior to 1981 the developing countries' share of direct investment inflows had been growing, investments had since declined in both absolute and relative terms. The situation was further exacerbated during the period by the sharp fall in bank lending. At the beginning of the 1980s, bank lending was four times the level of direct investment. By 1989, it was half the level of investment inflows. Further, there had been an important shift in investment patterns toward Asia at the expense of Latin America and the Caribbean. Africa continues to lag the inward FDI attraction field. Robert Cornell, Deputy Secretary of the O.E.C.D., advised the conference that a trend toward liberalizing investment policies was growing among both developed and developing countries. He detected "Some disenchantment...with the policy rationales that were provided in the 1970s and early 1980s for the more restrictive regimes"[6], although he added that those developing countries with severe debt burdens may have felt more pushed than led into the relaxation of FDI-discouraging policies. The late 1980s-early 1990s trend toward investment policy liberalization has continued and accelerated. (Wallace, 1990[7], Streeten, 1992[8], The World Bank, 1993[9]). It is a trend that has been established one-country-at-a-time as each individual country struggles with the circumstances and pressures that are peculiar to it. Weekly and Aggarwal (1987) point out that the essence of MNC activity is the transmission of resources from country to country and that the ways in which countries respond to MNCs is likely to be determined by whether the nation is a net contributor or net receiver of the resources being reallocated by the MNCs.[10]

THE NEED FOR THIS STUDY

Host developing country governments are struggling to find solutions to their capital inflow shortages. Lack of foreign direct investment into these countries is playing some role in retarding the economic growth needed to raise the standard and quality of life in the developing countries.

Governments and international lending institutions are likely to be fashioning their actions and recommendations to developing countries for attracting FDI based on the best available evidence as supplied by researchers in the field. Review of currently available research in the field indicates that urgings and recommendations being made to host developing countries by influential international bodies may be being based, in part, upon findings formulated from overly-aggregated data that masks the needs of identifiable and substantial subgroups. Should such be the case, adoption of recommended actions could lead to the risk of overpayment for attracting some investors and missing other investors by not providing sufficient enticement. Incentives given to those whose intended behavior has not been favorably altered represent a squandering of assets by the provider and a windfall profit to the receiver. Valued incentives withheld or onerous restrictions applied to specific investor groups can represent missed opportunity for the overly-cautious provider and force second-best locations on the would-be recipient. Developing countries, especially small developing countries with very limited resources to spend on investment attraction programs, can ill-afford unnecessary risk.

This study looks to the multinationals themselves as being suppliers of clues for the development of a process for identifying fundamentals of attracting FDI into developing countries. In reality, investments are made - and attracted - one investment at a time. The potential for segregation of foreign direct investors into reasonably homogeneous and discrete groups can lead to a closer "up front" approximation of fitting the needs of the individual investor into a framework of "equal particulars/equal treatment" or "right things for like people". Such a policy does not eliminate the need for individual case bargaining to "fine-tune the fit", but it can reduce the scope of such bargaining which leads to the benefits inherent in increased transparency.

The study presented here attempts to respond to the growing call for research that segregates FDI by strategic objectives (motivation), by investment timing (initial and expansion) and by investment size (quantum). Policy makers must rely on the best available research and advice to assist them in shaping effective future plans. Poor developing countries - and the policy makers attempting to assist them - require improved knowledge-tools to assist in the task of effectively focusing the limited resources of developing countries for attracting FDI.

The objectives of the study are:

    1. to construct a model - based upon recognized economic theories - for identifying discrete units of foreign direct investors possessing relatively homogeneous attributes, and,

2. to utilize the model to identify location-determining investment attraction preferences desired by identified MNC investor groups from those developing countries seeking FDI .

3. to propose a model for future research into developing country FDI attraction.

The model used in the study gives evidence that these homogeneous groups of investors (labeled as "micro-groups") can be identified. The proposed model for future research extends the two dimensional model utilized in the study (motivation and quantum on the single plane presented by the initial investment decision) to a three dimensional model that incorporates the additional investment-timing dimension presented by the expansion investment decision. Once identified, variation in the importance attached by individual micro-groups to the individual elements of the Investment Attraction Package (IAP) presented by developing countries can be studied and addressed. Host developing countries, multinational corporations, and/or both, may benefit from this targeting of focus.

Areas for further research specifically highlighted in the text include expansion investment versus initial investment, cost reduction investment, key variables in the investment attraction package, examination of home country tax laws, quantum of investment and attraction parameters, effectiveness of attraction elements to both MNC and to the host country, and applicability of indicated findings to other groups of countries.

FDI ATTRACTION RESEARCH - EVOLUTION OF FOCUS

Since the mid-1970s the world's deliberative bodies have been stalled in an abortive debate between the "haves" and the "have-nots" on the subject of FDI and its sponsor - the MNCs ("Transnational Corporations" in U.N. nomenclature). The issues have been many and complex - "law" versus "voluntarism"; who needs control of whom; cultural differences; philosophic differences; ideologic differences; "block" solidarity and interests; political positioning; ad infinitum. What has not been disputed is the enormous growth in MNCs. By the early 1990s MNCs numbered some 37,000 world-wide, having over 174,000 foreign affiliates. 24,000 (65%) of the MNCs were located in 14 developed countries, up from 7,000 in 1970. The developing countries account for about 8% of all MNCs. (Gold, 1993).[11] The U.N. Committee on Transnational Corporations (now the Transnational Corporations and Management Division of the Department of Economic and Social Development of the United Nations) has not been able to put together an effective code governing the activities of MNCs in its almost 20 years of existence. The Organization for Economic Cooperation and Development's (O.E.C.D.) "Guidelines for Multinational Enterprises"[12] is a minimal, voluntary code that has not been revised since 1976. While the world awaits the unreconcilable-to-date, the economic growth of the developing countries (with a few notable exceptions, such as, Southeast Asia) has continued to languish and the gap between the developed countries standard of living and that of the developing countries continues to widen.

The "gridlock" over MNCs and FDI codes occurring at the official level of discourse between the developed and developing nations has not derailed all progress in the search for ideas that may alleviate the lack of developing world economic progress. Far from it. Much progress has been made in the international arenas, such as the U.N., on matters like information exchange, the strengthening of the bargaining skills of developing countries and the search for workable solutions to economic development. In reaction to the void of unattainable international agreement on MNCs and FDI, a realism appears to have been spawned based on the recognition that each country and each corporation has its own set of criteria that an investment must meet before it is allowed to come into fruition and that such criteria is rarely arbitrary but stems from specific variables impinging upon each of the entities.

As the recognition of the potential for MNCs to play a positive role in the economic development of developing countries has spread, so too has research accelerated for determining what attracts the MNCs to make investments into a developing country. The correlated research for determining how to insure that the investment nets a positive return for the host country has also received much attention.

Research into what attracts MNCs to invest into developing countries appears to have followed a discernible path that broadly corresponds to the predominant thrust of FDI being experienced during the period of the research effort. Such a focus is not surprising, given the needs to be met and the urgency for meeting them. Given the slow/no progress evident in the attempts to find holistic solutions for accelerating economic growth at the inter-governmental levels of international institutions, concerned individuals and organizations continued the search for solutions to the practical problems presented. Although the basic motivations for MNCs to conduct FDI into developing countries essentially have remained fixed - host country market, raw materials, cost reduction (Buckley, 1989[13]) - over time, the major motivations appear to have gradually rotated in their importance.

Stage I (Mid 1960s - mid1980s)

Representative of FDI-attraction research in its awakening stages are such distinguished researchers as Aharoni, (1966)[14], Reuber, et al. (1973)[15], Usher, (1977)[16], Root and Ahmed (1978)[17], Shaw and Toye (1978)[18], Lim (1983)[19], Group of Thirty (1984)[20]. The days of new, major raw material investment were fading, the great majority of FDI was being conducted for purposes of gaining access to the markets of the host country, and cost reduction motivated FDI was in relative infancy. Responding to the need for practical direction and answers, research appears to have focused on the overpowering majority motivation of the MNCs - host country market - and the effective mechanisms/conditions for attracting FDI so motivated. The other motivations for FDI, if mentioned, were treated as an aside. Toward the end of this period, researchers began pointing out that incentives for attracting FDI could indeed be different for different motivations and commenced speculating that incentives would also differ in their effect between original and expansion investment. In the main, however, the research into the subject of attracting FDI was reported in the conglomerate - FDI as a single entity.

Stage II (Late 1980s & continuing)

With the late-1980s and early-1990s rapid rise of cost reduction motivated FDI (frequently referred to as export-oriented FDI), the need to differentiate the attraction-requirements of cost reduction investment from the more numerous host country market motivated investment has become urgent. The globalization of the manufacture of product components has mushroomed as MNCs urgently seek ways and means to increase or maintain product competitiveness. Advances in communications, transportation, and strategic thinking have awakened the searchers to the potentials of world-wide locations. Initial responses to the challenges and uniqueness of cost reduction motivated FDI have been suggested by researchers such as Guisinger (1985)[21], Evans and Doupnik (1986)[22], Cable and Persaud (1987)[23], Wells (1986)[24], Austin (1990)[25] and Contractor (1990[26], 1991)[27]. Recently Rolfe et al (1993)[28], Woodward and Rolfe (1993)[29], and Kumar (1994)[30] have published conditional logit models and/or empirical research findings focused on the cost reduction FDI motivation. Rolfe et al (1993) introduced the variable of investment size as a further potential differentiating indicator of attraction requirements.

Stage III. (The Current)

The study reported here focuses on original investment of MNCs into three developing countries of the Caribbean and on the MNC'S' evaluations of the proffered Investment Attraction Package (IAP) presented by these developing

Investment Attraction Package

countries. The IAP examined in this study is a selection of actions and conditions of developing countries known or believed to positively or negatively effect MNC investment-location decisions. The study utilizes a matrix approach anchored on the one side by the strategic motivations (reasons) for conducting FDI and on the other by the dominant capital risk element of transaction cost theory - non-triviality of investment (quantum or dollar-size of investment). The study was restricted to the initial investment decision made by country-investing MNCs and the MNCs' evaluation of the impact that stated elements of the IAP made on their decision to make their original investment into the host country. The inquiry was restricted to original investment on the premise that without original investment expansionary investment could not be made in that country by that MNC.

Figure 1.1, titled "Foreign Direct Investment Research Stages", sets out pictorially what could be considered as stages in the evolution of the focus of FDI-Attraction research.

To-date, researchers appear to have not responded to the oft repeated speculations of previous researchers that original investment and expansion investment are likely to require different Investment Attraction Packages (IAPs).

Setting the stage for the discussion of the who, what and why for attracting FDI into developing countries is Chapter II, which provides a definition of terms and a discussion of some of the key theories affecting FDI, MNCs and international trade. While researchers have long made a prefunctory bow in the general direction of the idea that governments can influence market behavior, it is only in recent years that this influence has been more formally acknowledged as a major factor to be included in the search for more relevent trade theories.

The research published to-date concerning the value of FDI for developing countries is oftimes contradictory and not infrequently partisan. Background to this on-going debate is found in Chapter III. No less contradictory is the research published on the value of investment attraction conditions, policies and practices required or expected of those developing countries that choose to participate in the FDI process. There seems to be little accepted wisdom or consensus surrounding the key issue of the priorities utilized by investors when accessing potential locations for FDI nor is there agreement as to which policies and incentives, if any, are the more helpful.

Chapter IV reviews the strategic motivations of MNCs for conducting FDI into developing countries and reviews the differences existing among researchers concerning the effectiveness of host country general conditions and incentives for attracting FDI. Researchers such as Aharoni, (1966); Usher, (1977); Shaw and

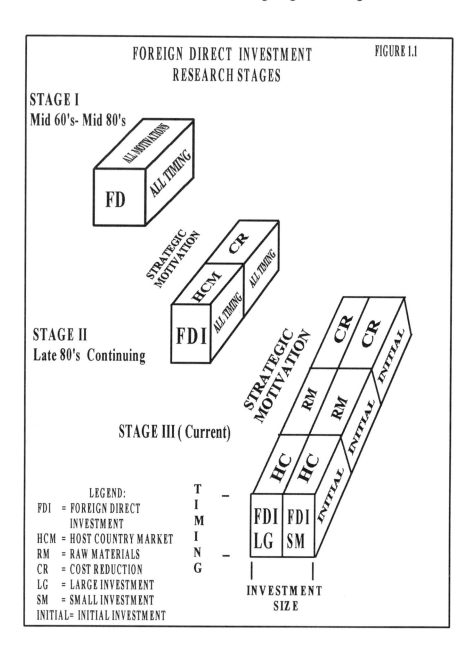

FOREIGN DIRECT INVESTMENT
RESEARCH STAGES   FIGURE 1.1

STAGE I
Mid 60's- Mid 80's

STAGE II
Late 80's Continuing

STAGE III (Current)

LEGEND:
FDI   = FOREIGN DIRECT
           INVESTMENT
HCM = HOST COUNTRY MARKET
RM   = RAW MATERIALS
CR   = COST REDUCTION
LG   = LARGE INVESTMENT
SM   = SMALL INVESTMENT
INITIAL= INITIAL INVESTMENT

TIMING

INVESTMENT
SIZE

Toye, (1978); Lim, (1983); Rolfe and White, (1992), among others, have concluded that investment incentives have little impact on the location of FDI. These researchers generally take the view that incentives are unnecessary as the key attractors are such things as market size, GNP growth and country stability. Others like Rueber, (1973); Root and Ahmed, (1978); and Group of Thirty, (1984) agree that market size or GNP and stability factors are probably more important . Evans and Doupnik (1986) state profit repatriation as #1 priority. Still others, including Cable and Persaud, (1987), partially agree but express unwillingness to write off the value of incentives . Yet Guisinger (1985), Wells (1986), Contractor (1991), Woodward & Rolfe (1993) point out that the effectiveness of incentives may depend upon the specific investor's situation. They draw particular attention to the probable positive benefits of incentives in export-oriented investments and to the potential that expansion and initial investment may have differing reactions to the investment attraction elements.

Although the differing investment attraction requirements of initial investment and expansion investment has received speculation by researchers, evidence of empirical study of either investment timing group appears to be rare. The norm appears to be to lump both timing sequences together. Beamish et al (1991)[31] and Miller (1993)[32] predict that fewer and fewer foreign investments will be motivated by market seeking behavior and note that the strategic interests of investing firms is to build plants whose output will be internationally competitive in cost and quality. Brewer (1993) has observed that the distinction between market and cost reduction motivation for investing has been largely overlooked in the internationalization literature. He advocates that the distinction becomes important in analyzing the effects of government policies on FDI because "government subsidies and restrictions that effect market imperfections and FDI flows vary according to the strategic nature of the FDI projects."[33]. The present study is an attempt to respond to the growing call for research that separates FDI by strategic objectives (motivation), by investment timing (initial) and by investment size (quantum).

In order to bring the position of the small, developing country into focus, Chapter V concentrates on the three English-speaking Caribbean countries of Barbados, Jamaica, and Trinidad-Tobago. As independent island-states of the Caribbean, they represent the populations of the small (264,000), the large (2,469,000) and the mid-size (1,265,000) nations of this sub-region. By any standard, even the largest is considered small among the global village of countries - small in terms of their economies as well as their population and land mass.

Small economies present minor targets to the most prolific reason for FDI - host country market. All three host countries present small economies with a limited range of export alternatives and a large diversity of import requirements. Not all small-economy developing countries are small in size and/or small in population. The common denominator of smallness of economies lends potential generalizability to the findings of the study. However, it is the parent Corporations who have conducted the FDI in the focus countries. The overwhelming majority of the parent corporations surveyed have conducted (and are conducting) FDI in developing countries. It is the MNCs themselves that hold the real key to the potential generalizability of the study findings.

Given that MNCs have choices and make choices according to an individual MNC's predetermined scale of desirability, the substantive question is: what is important, to whom, and under what circumstances?

The methodology for the study is reviewed in Chapter VI. The study utilizes transaction cost theory and FDI motivation theory in a search for discrete "investor micro-groups" whose preferences for elements of the IAP may depart from the preferences of FDI investors as a whole. The identification of such micro-groups is a condition-precedent for maximizing the effective use of the limited resources available to small developing economies for attracting FDI from the maximum range of potential sources. The information needed to fulfill the objectives of this study was secured by primary research as the need was for information concerning the perceptions and evaluations of individual companies on selected elements thought to be of major import in corporate location-decisions.

Chapter VII sets forth the propositions to be examined. There are three basic propositions, each with appropriate sub-parts designed to add confirmation, clarity and illumination to the base proposition. An objective of the study is to construct a model based on recognized economic theories. To be useful in further research, the model must be replicable. The capital risk elements of transaction cost theory are examined for determining their interrelationships and for evaluating their use in a novel application of their power. The search for the location-determining preferences of the micro-groups identified by the research model is conducted on both the macro basis of MNCs motivations for FDI and the more micro basis of quantum of investment within and between the identified motivations for FDI.

The study is limited to data supplied by MNCs of the focus countries and who registered their preferences for elements of the IAP which affected their original investment decision. Key assumptions of the study are that (1) MNCs review potential FDI locations against a set of corporate desires in a reasonably consistent fashion; 2) the investment attraction preferences of MNCs domiciled in the U.S. and the U.K. are essentially similar; 3) the response of U.S. MNCs investing in one of the individual host countries is not significantly different from the response of the U.S. MNCs to the other two subject countries.

Chapters VIII reviews the data and presents study findings and interpretations. Chapters IX takes the discussions of the findings and compares the findings with those reported by other researchers. Although the differences in the findings of this study with those of previous researchers could be attributed to the uniqueness of the subject countries, the uniqueness of the responding MNCs, or other uniqueness that could tend to invalidate the results, the more likely explanation for differences in the findings of this study from those of prior researchers is that similar questions were addressed to dissimilar audiences. While the questions put to the respondees appear broadly similar to those of prior studies, the harmony with prior researchers began to dissolve as the responses were segmented into unique MNC/FDI micro-groups of reasonably homogeneous identity. Chapter X looks at the micro-groups identified by the study model and offers interpretations for some of the unique investment attraction preferences identified.

The Conclusion offered in Chapter XI summarizes the key findings of the study. At minimum, the evidence from the study, taken in conjunction with other studies of other researchers, suggest that:

* FDI investors constitute a market for host developing countries seeking to attract FDI.

* Host developing countries are offering a product to the market.

* Identifiable market niches of FDI investors DO exist.

* These niches have unique needs to be met.

* The over-agglomeration risk in FDI research to-date is unnecessarily high.

* The two-dimensional research model used in the study is incomplete, especially in the scope of the timing dimension.

A three dimensional model for FDI research into developing countries is proposed as the basis for future research. The findings of the two-dimensional model maintain their validity for investigating the attraction preferences of initial investment by MNCs into developing countries but the additional dimension of expansion investment is required to determine those unique micro-group preferences that reflect the needs of this powerful investment option. The chapter addresses the concerns of researchers for the potential generalizability of the findings for other developing countries and outlines additional areas of suggested research.

Policy recommendations areas suggested by the research are raised in Chapter XII. The recommendations are framed around the belief that knowledge of the differing needs and preferences of unique groups of FDI investors may permit developing countries to target specific groups whose unmet needs have been masked by their inclusion in larger groups of investors. Marketing theory suggests that targeting enhances the effectiveness of market penetration efforts.

Governments can and do "distort" the market (via laws, policies, practices and incentives) in attempts to alter the distribution of the gains. (Brewer, 1993).[34] The business theories propounded to-date have explained production, costs and income generation but they have not attempted to explain the distribution of costs and benefits between firms and governments. In fact, the theories have provided explanations and behavior prediction - assuming the absence of government intervention and yet it is this very government intervention that is a necessary quid quo pro for the MNC to gain entry permission. What is known, however, is that FDI is made by individual firms interacting with the total attraction package offered by host countries. It is at the point of interaction - small market host countries desiring FDI interacting with MNCs looking for best locations for FDI - that this study seeks to make a contribution to the existing body of knowledge that surrounds the subject of investment attraction.

Much of the heat has gone out of the storm over MNCs. Streeten (1992) proclaims that all developing countries now welcome FDI and that relations between governments of host countries and MNCs have moved from ideological heat to pragmatic light. "Transnational corporations are considered by many observers and by host countries as wholly benign agents".[35] However, Ostry (1992) of the U.N.C.T.C points out that globalization creates a growing pressure for convergence of policies which increases the risk of conflict because pressure for convergence raises the issue of sovereignty. Ostry reminds that the globalizing world has a low tolerance for system-divergence.[36] The implication of this observation is that the world may not have heard the last of the clash between sovereignty, interdependence, globalization and the MNC.

In a reminder to the developed world, Paul Streeten (1992) penned this warning: "Unless global production finds ways of engaging these poor (countries) in productive and remunerative work, the outlook for global peace and prosperity is dim."[37] To engage the poor countries in productive and remunerative work requires that investment in productive assets be aimed at these countries. What attracts FDI into developing countries? The study reported here reviews the evidence that a more focused analysis produced differing replies from those heard in the past and proposes a new research model for more accurately targeting the Foreign Direct investor.

[1]Elizabeth, Regina II. 1983. "Christmas message to the Commonwealth". *The London Times*, 27 December, 1983, p.1.
[2]The World Bank. 1989. "The World Bank, the IFC and MIGA". *The World Bank Annual Report. 1989.* Wash. D.C.
[3]Lewis, W. 1991. "Free market and the prosperity gap". *The McKinsey Quarterly*, No. 4, pp.116-132.
[4]Thurow, L. 1992. *Head to head. The coming economic battle among Japan, Europe, and America.* N.Y.: William Morrow & Co. Inc.
[5]Organization for Economic Cooperation and Development (1989*). "International direct investment and the new economic environment: Tokyo Round Table.* Paris France: OECD, p.3.
[6]Cornell, R. (1989). *International direct investment and the new economic environment: Tokyo Round Table.* Paris: OECD, p.10-11.
[7]Wallace, C. 1990. *Foreign direct investment in the 1990s. a new climate in the 3rd world.* Dordrecht, Netherlands: Martinus Nijhoff Publishers, p.177.
[8]Streeten, P. 1992. "Interdependence and integration of the world economy: the role of states and firms". *Transnational Corporations*, Vol 1, No 3, (December), p.132.
[9]The World Bank (1993). *The World Bank Annual Report 1993.* Wash. D.C.: p.36.
[10]Weekly, J. and Aggarwal, R. 1989. *International business operating in the global economy.* Orlando, FL.: Dryden Press, p.316
[11]Gold, D. 1993. "World investment report 1993: Transnational corporations and integrated international production. An executive summary". *Transnational Corporations*, Vol.2, No.2, Aug., 1993. p.99.
[12]Organization for Economic Co-operation and Development. 1986. *The OECD guidelines for multinational enterprises..* Paris: OEDC: pp. 11-16.
[13]Buckley, P. 1989. *The multinational enterprise.* London: MacMillan Press, p. 13.
[14]Aharoni, Y. 1966. *The foreign investment decision process.* Boston: Harvard University Press.
[15]Reuber, G., Crookell,H., Emerson, M., and Gallais-Hamono, G. 1973. *Private foreign investment in development.* Oxford: Clarendon Press, p. 131.
[16]Usher, D. 1977. "The economics of tax incentives to encourage investment in developing countries". *Journal of Development Economics.* June, pp.119-61.
[17]Root, F.R and Ahmed, A.A. 1978. "The influence of policy instruments on manufacturing foreign direct investment in developing countries". *Journal of International Business Studies.* Winter 1987, pp. 81-94.
[18]Shah, S.M.S. and Toye, J.F.T. 1978. "Fiscal incentives for firms in some developing countries: Survey and critique", in *Taxation and Economic Development.* J.F.T.Toye,(Ed.). London: Frank Cass.
[19]Lim, D. 1983. "Fiscal incentives and direct foreign investment in less developed countries". *Journal of Development Studies.* Jan. pp.207-12.
[20]Group of Thirty . 1984. *Foreign direct investment 1973-87.* N.Y.: Group of Thirty, p. 31.

[21]Guisinger, S. 1985. *Investment incentives and performance requirements: patterns of international trade, production and investment.* Westport, CN: Greenwood Press, p.48.

[22]Evans, T., and Doupnik, T. 1986. "Foreign exchange risk management under standartd 53.83". Stamford, CT.: Financial Accounting Standards Board. .

[23]Cable, V. and Persaud, B. 1987. "New trends and policy problems in foreign investment: The experience of Commonwealth developing countries". *Developing With Foreign Investment.* The Commonwealth Secretariat. Kent: Croom Helm Ltd., p.8

[24]Wells, L. 1986. "Investment incentives: An unnecessary debate". *CTC Reporter.* Autumn, 1986, pp. 58-60..

[25]Austin, J. 1990. *Managing in Developing Countries.* N.Y.: Free Press.

[26]Contractor, F. 199). "Government policies towards foreign investment. An empirical investigation of the link between national policies and FDI flows". A paper presented to Annual Conference, Academy of International Business, Miami: p. 21.

[27]Contractor, F. 1991. "Government policies and foreign direct investment". *UNCTC Studies.* Series, No. 17, N.Y.: United Nations, p.23.

[27]Cable and Persaud (1987). op cit ", p.11.

[28]Rolfe, R.; Ricks, D.; Pointer, M.; and McCarthy, M. 1993. "Determinants of FDI preferences of MNEs". *Journal of International Business Studies.* Vol 24, No. 2, Second Qt., 1993.

[29]Woodward, D. and Rolfe, R. 1993. "The location of export oriented foreign direct investment in the Caribbean basin". *Journal of International Business Studies.* Vol.24, No.1, p. 121.

[30]Kumar, N. 1994. "Determinants of export orientation on foreign production by U.S. multinationals: an inter-country analysis". *Journal Of International Business Studies.* Vol.25, No.1, 1st Qt 1994. p.148.

[31]Beamish, P.; Killing, J.; Lecraw, D.; Crookell, H. 1991. *International management, Text and cases.* Homewood, IL.: Irwin, p. 95.

[32]Miller, R. 1993. "Determinants of U.S. manufacturing abroad". *Finance and Development.* March, 1993. p. 118.

[33]Brewer, T. 1993. *op cit,* p. 105.

[34]Brewer, T.; David, K.; Lim, L. 1987. *Investing in developing countries. A guide for executives.* Lexington, MA.: Lexington Books, D.C. Heath & Company, p.105..

[35]Streeten, P. 1992. *op cit,* p.133.

[36]Ostry, S. 1992. "The domestic domain: The new international policy arena". *Transnational Corporations,* Vol.1, No. 1, p. 7.

[37]Streeten, P. 1992. *op cit,* p.135.

CHAPTER II

WHAT'S WHAT

Definitions & Theories: FDI, MNCs, International Trade

"Those who cannot remember the past are condemned to repeat it."

George Santayana
The Life of Reason

An overview of Foreign Direct Investment (FDI) and its hand maiden, the Multinational Corporation, together with a summary look at the economic theories impinging these activities, is in order as a prelude to examining the what and why of effective mechanisms for attracting FDI into developing countries.

FOREIGN DIRECT INVESTMENT (FDI)

Foreign Direct Investment (FDI) literally may not be "as old as the hills" but many of its vestiges date back to beyond recorded history. The fabled merchant caravans of antiquity have continued though the ages to incite exotic visions of the roving merchants "from afar". It is but a small step from fabled caravans to the establishment by those merchants of "regular" or even "permanent" way stations for conduct of daily business in the most lucrative cities along the roving merchant route. Permanent way stations suggest "investment" - maybe in buildings, certainly in inventory. If we equate "from afar" with some distant land, it requires no leap of the imagination to suggest that the roving merchant was investing in some country other than his home country. In truth, foreign investment has been with us for a long, long time. So long, in fact, that the countries of the world are in general agreement as to its definition - even if similar agreement does not surround its proper functions and value.

Definition of FDI

Foreign direct investment is "investment that is made to acquire a lasting interest in an enterprise operating in an economy other than that of the investor, the investor's purpose being to have an effective voice in the management of the enterprise." (International Monetary Fund. 1977).[1] There are multiple definitions of FDI. Each tends to utilize varying degrees of particular emphasis, yet most embrace the essential elements outlined in the foregoing. For the purposes of this study, the simple, yet inclusive, definition of the IMF will be used throughout.

Foreign investment can be divided into two primary components: portfolio investment and direct investment. Portfolio investment is the purchase of stocks and bonds solely for the purpose of obtaining a return on the funds invested, whereas direct investment enables the investors to participate in the management of the firm in addition to seeking a return on the funds invested. Foreign direct investments are defined as investments that give the investor effective control and are accompanied by managerial participation.

The distinction between portfolio and direct investment might be difficult to draw, since it is not always clear at what point a holder of foreign assets may begin to assume a managerial role or what share of ownership of an enterprise is required to exert managerial control. The intent of the investor with respect to participation in management is usually apparent from the size or nature of the investment. Building plants or buying substantial shares of the voting stock or real assets of a foreign company could generally be assumed as indicating the intent to become involved in the management of facilities or business. Purchase of debt instruments or purchase of a small amount of the common stock of a foreign company would normally not enable the investor to take part in managing the company that issued the securities.(Weekly and Aggarwal 1989).[2]

The U. S. Department of Commerce, which is the U. S. Government agency chiefly responsible for reporting on American investment abroad, includes under direct investment any situation where a U. S. investor (defined to include an associated group of investors) owns ten percent or more of a foreign business enterprise. This figure is obviously an arbitrary one as managerial control might be affected with less than 10 percent ownership in some instances and might require a greater share in other cases.[3] The origin of the ten percent was the U. S. Treasury, who used it as an aid in deciding the definition of "direct investment" as opposed to "portfolio investment" for tax purposes (Behrman, 1974).[4] OECD (Organization for Economic Cooperation and Development) also urges its members to use the ten percent rule. The application of the "rule" is purely for the purpose of standardizing "classifications" of investment for statistical reasons and has no bearing whatsoever on the actual determination of management and/or control in any given case. Such determinations are the province of the individual corporation.

Perhaps the most succinct statement of the function of FDI was supplied by Alan Rugman (1981) when he wrote: "FDI is the method which allows the MNC its best chance of monitoring the use of its firm's specific advantage".[5]

MULTINATIONAL CORPORATIONS (MNCs)

Although FDI may or may not have accompanied the caravans of old, (depending upon how finely the point is drawn), the focus of this study is FDI by relative new comers - multinational corporations (MNCs). Specifically, the study concerns MNCs domiciled in the U. S. and the U. K. and the making of their investments in the Caribbean nations of Barbados, Jamaica, and Trinidad-Tobago. It follows that a straight-forward definition is suitable for a straight forward purpose.

MNC relative new comer

Definition of Multinational Corporation

True to the contentious history that has followed these corporate entities, there is little agreement on their proper title. Some use the term "Multinational Corporations" ; some refer to Multinational Enterprises (MNEs) and international bodies seem to prefer Transnational Corporations (TNCs). However, Ball and McCulloch point out that business people use the term "transnational" to refer to a company formed as a result of a merger of two firms of about the same size from two different countries .[6] There is difference of opinion over the origins of the MNC - some refer to trading companies of older colonial times; some refer to relationships between parent and subsidiary of the more recent colonial mining companies. According to Vernon (1971), the emergence of multinational firms is often traced to the sourcing of raw materials, such as oil, copper, and alumina.[7] However, there does not appear to be great debate that the concept denoted by the term "multinational" is fairly new.[8] American University's Professor Howe Martyn traced the origin of the term to a 1958 speech made by David Lilienthal, who was head of the Tennessee Valley Authority at the time.[9] The definitions of the entity - in spite of the confusingly different names - are similar, albeit not uniform, and generally refer in a recognizable manner to the same form of corporate organization. Throughout this study, the term MNC will be used - in the face of contention, seniority seems as good a yardstick as any.

The definition used in this study is a simple one: multinational corporations are business enterprises that own and manage affiliates located in two or more different countries. It is essentially the definition of Weekly and Aggarwal.[10] However, whereas operation in two countries (home country and at least one other) satisfies the criteria for this study, Weekly and Aggarwal argued for the non-specific "several different countries" and Buckley and Casson (1976) used "owns and controls activities in different countries".[11] Given the limited number of MNCs available in the Caribbean countries chosen for this study, the definition chosen is the "threshold" definition, associated with firms that own or control income generating assets in more than one country. Buckley (1985)[12] identified additional definitions used by various authors. A perusal gives a glimpse of the range of characteristics being included within the term multinational - be it MNC, MNE, or TNC: a "structural" definition, where multinationality is judged according to the organization of the firm; a "performance" definition, incorporating some relative or absolute measures of international spread; "behavioral" criterion based on the corporation's degree of geocentricity.

Sturdivant reports that Lilienthal identified the key element in qualifying for the MNC label as foreign direct investment (FDI) involving deployment of corporate assets in other countries. Using such criteria, Lilienthal held that companies who only exported or licensed technology for use by others in other countries were not multinationals.[13] Robuck and Simmonds' definition "cluster of corporations controlled by one headquarters but with operations spread over many countries"[14] is not discordant with the one used for this study but they point out that there are many definitions. Some simply point to the behavioral characteristics of top management, i.e., thinking globally.

David Teece (1980) has provided a rationale for the emergence of the MNC as being a response to one of three groups of incentives: circumventing or minimizing taxes and controls; monopoly; and efficiency.[15]

SOME KEY THEORIES AFFECTING FDI & MNCs
Two International Trade Theories

Whether it started with the fabled caravans of an earlier or later time, international business activity commenced with international trade - the satisfaction of demand for goods not available domestically. Demand increased, markets grew, and government policies arose and were debated on the basis of who was winning and why. Moral and political philosophers supplied the underpinnings of the early debates. As the body of knowledge grew, the discipline of economics arose as a branch of moral philosophy to specialize in the investigations of the serpentine labyrinths of international trade. In Mercantilist Theory, a country was wealthy when it had a large reserve of gold and silver bullion. To obtain the bullion, a favorable trade balance was required and government sought to insure this via policies of support for home industry. (Schnitzer 1991).[16] The win/lose philosophy of mercantilism was the first to claim the field. (Fusfeld 1990).[17] This "beggard thy neighbor" philosophy has not entirely been vanquished and periodically enjoys its nostalgic reruns, particularly during periods of low or no world economic growth. Of more recent times, there is ample evidence of a growing re-emergence of merchantilism as the chosen international trade strategy of those countries who are either emerging from national catastrophic events (i.e., Japan) or from a lengthy period of underdevelopment (i.e., South Korea, Taiwan, etc). The re-emergent forms have attracted many names, such as, "developmental capitalism" (Johnson 1992)[18], "non-capitalist market economy" (Sakaibara 1992)[19], "network capitalism" (Nakatani 1992)[20], and "catch-up capitalism" or "the capitalism of the late-comer" (Okita 1992).[21]

Comparative Advantage

With his theory of Absolute Advantage, Adam Smith, a moral philosopher, commenced the exposure of the mercantilist short sightedness of accumulating ever increasing gold reserves (foreign exchange) for the nation at the expense of the national quality of life. Ricardo, the economist, accelerated the earlier demise of mercantilism with the Theory of Comparative Advantage. David Ricardo (1772-1823) might be termed the "Father" of international trade theory. Although born in a simpler time and utilizing many assumptions that have long since been supplanted, Ricardo's "law of comparative advantage" still maintains enough directional validity to be frequently invoked by wide-audience vehicles such as "the Economist" as well as by the less widely read scholarly works of our times. Whereas Adam Smith had earlier brought forth the theory of Absolute Advantage (each nation should produce that good of which it produces the most with the least amount of input), Ricardo showed that, in a two good exchange, even if a nation held an absolute advantage in the production of both goods, trade could still take place between two countries, to the advantage of both, so long as the less efficient nation was not equally less efficient in the production of both goods (Ball and McCulloch, 1993)[22] , i.e., relative rather than absolute cost advantage. Recast in simpler form, comparative advantage states: let each produce what he (she) does best, trade the surplus, and all will have a higher level of consumption. Ricardo showed that international specialization and division of labour would help all nations and that restrictive trade policies enacted to protect local producers would injure the country imposing them.(Fusefeld, 1990).[23] Although the theory has many limitations, stemming from both its overly simplified assumptions and the constant march of business progress, and although modified and further developed over the years, the concept of comparative advantage retains its wide acceptance.

From Ricardo's time forward, the focus has been for seeking, finding, explaining and predicting the causes and effects of comparative advantage and the role each player (government, industry, individual firm) plays in the search for competitive advantage in international trade. The search has led to discoveries of theory inadequacy, restatements, additional revisions, etc., but the fundamental posture of comparative advantage as the beacon of revealed truth remains the corner stone of the study of international trade.

Factor Endowment

Flowing from the concept of comparative advantage there arose an explanation to account for the cost differences between nations. Ricardo had concentrated on labour to explain the differences in comparative costs and assumed labour was immobile. In 1933, the Swedish economist, Ohlin, introduced the theory of Factor Endowment, which states that trade occurs because nations have different relative endowments of the factors of production. Later, Ohlin was joined by Heckscher and together they produced the Heckscher-Ohlin Theory (H-O), which states that a nation's comparative cost advantage will be determined by its domestic factor (resource) supply, and indicates that a nation will specialize in and export those products that make the greatest use of the productive factor(s) with which it is (in relative terms) most abundantly endowed (Flam and Flanders, 1991)[24] i.e., trade between regions of a country and between countries is caused by difference in their factor endowments. The theory holds that each country will export that factor (land, labour, or capital) of which it has the most. Though helpful, the theory also has its limitations and, again, the limitations start with the assumptions upon which the theory is predicated. The basic assumption - price of the factor depends only upon factor endowment (supply and demand) - is known to be untrue (Kreinin, 1991).[25] Factor prices are not set in perfectly functioning supply and demand markets. Additionally, Ohlin assumed technology was universally available, transportation costs were ignored, etc. Although Wassily Leonitief attacked the heart of the Heckscher-Ohlin Theory when he uncovered that the U.S. , a capital-rich country, was actually exporting more labour intensive products than American products that competed with imports,[26] the H-O Theory has contributed to moving forward the understanding of international trade and factor endowment has continued to be recognized as having a role in international trade.

Key Theories of Foreign Direct Investment

Trade theory was advanced by the Factor Endowments Theory. However, international business theory remained focused on countries and their imports or exports - the "trade" conducted by "their" national companies in the aggregate. Yet the very market imperfections introduced by governments "in their national interest" ultimately spawned the phenomenon of FDI. Generally, government sponsored market imperfections creates threats or opportunities initially in those markets for goods and services that here-to-fore have been met by importation.

FDI (investment to obtain ownership and control of productive facilities by foreign domiciled companies) had existed for some time in the raw material extraction industries, was of relatively low total volume, and - apparently - relatively easily explainable as it attracted little academic attention or demand for causal explanation. (Lack of demand for causal explanation, however, is not synonymous with lack of controversy over appropriateness or benefits of FDI/MNC existence - especially in developing countries during the post World War II period). FDI, which at the time was focused primarily on serving the host national market, attracted little need for causal explanation of the investing entity - possibly because of the polycentric orientation of the companies and the resultant non-differentiation by government in the perception of conduct of foreign versus domestically owned companies. (Harris and Moran, 1991).[27]

Rapidly improving communications and transportation technologies provided the means by which MNCs could capitalize on the market efficiency opportunities that flowed from the general lowering of global tariff barriers following WWII. The here-to-fore "enclave" national markets became susceptible to centrally directed strategic management concepts and the potential for globally located, least-cost manufacturing became evident. The emergence of a critical mass of foreign-owned firms investing outside of their "home" territory for other than the presumed easily understood reasons of raw materials or national "enclave" markets brought the activity of the MNC into sharper focus and called forth the need to examine, explain, understand and project the role of the firm in FDI.

International Product Life Cycle

Introduction of the International Product Life Cycle (IPLC) commenced the expansion of the theorists vision of international business . (Grosse and Behrman, 1992).[28] The IPLC point of departure was that the country (importer or exporter) did not make FDI decisions - individual businesses did and they did so for reasons of survival in a cost competitive production environment emanating from the market growth of a non-standardized product into a standardized commodity. In

1966, Raymond Vernon, in search of better explanations for shifts in international trade and international investment, concluded that any theory which did not include the roles played by innovation, economies of scale, ignorance and uncertainty was incomplete. He postulated that the roles of ease of communication and geographical proximity effectively force the abandonment of the standard economic theory assumption that knowledge was a universal free good and, in lieu thereof, introduced it as an independent variable in the decision to trade or invest (Vernon, 1966).[29] Adding the foregoing to knowledge of locations of high income, relatively unlimited capital, and high labour costs, plus standard product life cycle behavior, Vernon arrived at an International Product Life Cycle theory. Paralleling the life cycle of the product itself (introduction, growth, maturity, decline), the International Product Life Cycle attempts to explain the international trade and the international investment decisions flowing from the maturing of the product from non-standardized product stage to standardized commodity stage. Commencing with product introduction (non-standardized product, developed country, strong R & D, low price sensitivity, quick market feedback, local production, low priority for manufacturing cost), International Product Life Cycle Theory moves the product to:

> (1) Export Stage (Producer gains economies of scale by exporting to other developed countries with similar needs and purchasing power. Product being improved and commences early stages of standardization).

> (2) Foreign Production Stage (As local competitors enter the market, producer invests in foreign production facilities to protect market position and to counter real or potential trade barriers. Continues to export to other regions).

> (3) Foreign Competition in Export Markets Stage (Product is becoming ever more standardized. Developed country competitors are increasing. Market may be becoming saturated).

> (4) Import Competition for Producer in Home Country, (Domestic and export sales of foreign producers reach economy of scale, product has become a standardized commodity, only low cost producers survive - question becomes who enjoys the advantage in factor endowment - capital, raw material or labor cost?).(Weekly and Aggarwal, 1987).[30]   At this stage, production costs have taken over from market considerations as determinant of location. (Lane and DiStefano, 1992). [31]

Although the International Product Life Cycle has its critics and the march of time and pace of change has amended some of its original thrust, the IPLC is particularly pertinent to at least one major aspect of this study. The IPLC connects standardized products (and by implication, sub-products and components) with low cost-based globalized production competition. In that game, the survivors are likely to be those who have invested in facilities in country locations enjoying advantage in one or more of the factor endowments. Given the internationalization of the capital markets that currently exists, developed country differences in the costs of capital are narrow. Depending upon the product, delivered raw material costs can still be substantially different in different regions of the globe, although technology is continuing to lessen the ratio of raw material consumed to finished product produced. Few raw materials today qualify for the benefits bestowed by global scarcity.

Buckley (1992) references Casson's (1985) suggestion that factor substitution has a very limited role in the location of production and observed that, if capital is mobile, the only significant margin would be that at which labour is allocated between industries. (Buckley, 1992).[32] The developing countries are overly endowed low cost sources of the labour factor. One of the basic reasons for MNCs making an FDI is cost reduction and the prominence of this reason is increasing rapidly as firms seek least-cost component manufacture in their worldwide integrated system of manufacturing. The IPLC helps explain the attention producers of highly standardized products and components are giving to cost reduction locations. A goal of this study is to help focus that attention onto the developing countries.

Market Imperfection Theories

Heretofore, classical and neoclassical theory of foreign direct investment concentrated on the country and/or the external market yet neither are the entity that makes the actual investment. The firm's involvement was generally assumed to be virtually an automated response and readily explainable as an exploitation of a monopoly situation. As Coase observed, monopoly power is often imputed to many poorly understood business phenomena.[33] Teece (1981) has commented that " it was not surprising that some scholars have missed important features of the multinational enterprises as they were obsessed with the market power considerations". Teece felt that the efficiency consequences of the organization of economic activity by MNCs were more interesting, possibly more important and less understood than market power considerations.[34] An examination of the firm itself had begun and the search was instituted to discover what was going on within the firm itself that motivated it to make an FDI. "Market imperfections, in general, are impediments to the simple interaction of supply and demand to set a market price." (Rugman, 1981).[35]

Monopolistic Advantage Theory

Monopolistic Advantage Theory focuses on the concept that during the course of the firm's evolution and operation in the home market, it will have acquired certain firm specific advantages, i.e., advantages possessed by the individual firm rather than by all members of the industry. These firms' monopolistic advantages (firm specific advantages) enable the firm to successfully compete with local firms in a foreign market. (Stephen Hymer, 1976).[36] In spite of the advantages that local firms enjoy - such as market proximity, familiarity and local experience - the MNCs' specific advantages or unique capabilities are deemed to result from market imperfections, i.e., variance from the purely competitive market structure in which all firms in the industry have equal access to the factors of production (including managerial and technical know-how) and produce identical products. It is this variance from the purely competitive market structure which gives rise to the monopolistic advantage reference. (Weekly and Aggarwal, 1987).[37] Having gained unique capabilities and advantage in the home market (such as producing a differentiated product which others have difficulty duplicating or achieving superior managerial, organizational, marketing or technical skills), the advantage can usually be extended to foreign locations at little incremental cost plus it can potentially achieve a competitive edge in the foreign market.

Internalization Theory

Internalization Theory holds that markets external to the firm frequently do not provide an efficient avenue for the firm to profit from resources, capabilities and/or technologies that it has developed over time (Buckley and Casson, 1976)[38], i.e., external market imperfections exist. Buckley and Casson maintain: "when markets in intermediate products are imperfect, there is an incentive to bypass them by creating internal markets".[39] In creating an internal market, the firm brings under its ownership and control the activities which are linked by the market. Thus, internalization across national boundaries generates FDI and MNCs. The benefits of FDI (internalization) arise from the avoidance of the inefficiencies of imperfections of the external market. The incentive for internal coordination of activities of a firm's intermediate products lies in the potential that the external market offers such products to the firm on an exchange basis which leaves the firm under compensated vis-a-vis the cost to the firm of undertaking the activity itself. Such FDI will continue until the costs associated with the FDI become equal to the savings (benefits) expected of the FDI. Buckley (1989) [40] points out that the higher the volume of trade between two plants of the same firm producing in the intermediate market, the greater will be the tendency for the firm to internalize. However, he observes that such will be the case if the higher volume is associated with high frequency of transactions but warns that the incentive to internalize is lowered if the frequency is lowered since long term contracts or bulk buying can become more attractive alternatives. (Buckley, 1989).[41]

Transaction Costs Theory

A transaction is said to occur when a good or service is transferred across a technologically-separable interface. (Commons, 1934).[42] The decision required to acquire the good or service is essentially a "make or buy" decision. Williamson (1986) states that transaction cost economics adopts a contractual approach to the study of economic organization and likened transaction costs to be the economic equivalent of friction in physical systems.[43] If transaction costs were trivial, there would be no advantage in one mode of organizing a transaction as against another mode as all such advantage would be nullified by costless contracting. Transaction costs have been defined by Kenneth Arrow (1969).[44] as the "costs of running the economic system" Transactions costs are the costs of governance. Either decision - make or buy - entails costs over and above the costs associated with the purchase or production of the good/service itself. In accomplishing a commercial transaction, the criterion of cost economizing comes in two parts: economizing on the production expense and economizing on the governance costs of making and completing the transaction itself. Teece (1981) comments that transaction costs embrace all the costs associated with organizing the economic system.[45] Coase (1937) proposed that firms and markets be considered alternative means of economic organization i.e., whether transactions were organized within a firm (internalization) or between arms length firms (across a market) was a decision variable. In which manner the transaction was organized depended upon the transaction costs that attended each.[46] (For a detailed discussion of the transaction costs theory, see Oliver E. Williamson, 1986, "Economic Organization, Firms, Markets and Policy Control".)

Pertinent to this study, transaction costs theory highlights the following: (1) The two principal governance structures for organizing transactions are markets (external organization) and firms (internal organization). A firm will choose that structure for conducting its business (market or internal) that it anticipates as returning the greatest rewards (principally by having the least transaction costs). (2) The market method of providing a governance structure for a transaction relies upon contracts to both detail the transaction and secure the enforcement of the transaction. The internal firm method of providing a governance structure relies upon hierarchical organization to perform the transaction definition and enforcement functions. When the internal firm method of transaction governance is chosen for conducting an international business venture the result is a FDI.

The form of governance utilized tends to be a function of the three critical dimensions (attributes) for characterizing transactions: (1) Uncertainty: the greater the uncertainty, the more difficult for the parties to specify agreed actions in advance. (2) Frequency: the more frequent the transactions, the more dependent the relationship of one or both parties can become. (3) Durable transaction - specific investment: the greater the specificity, the greater the investment risk that must be served. The interaction of each characteristic on the others produce a variety of situations where choice between market (contracting) and internal governance are clarified. This interaction necessitates a case-by-case examination of the specifics of any given transaction in order to arrive at the estimate of the transaction cost exposure for the anticipated transaction and the appropriate structure for governing the transaction. In classical economic theory, these critical dimensions are efficiently dealt with by the market, which is presumed to be in perfect competition, endowed with perfect knowledge, etc. Transaction-cost economics relies on another set of assumptions: broadly described as the conjunction of bounded rationality, opportunism, and asset specificity.

Bounded rationality and opportunism are both human behavior traits. Transaction cost economics makes the assumption that human beings possess bounded rationality and although their behavior may be intended to be rational, it can only be rational up to a limited degree (Simon, 1982).[47] It is a assumed that no human can know all things at all times. In addition, transaction cost economics assumes that human beings are given to opportunism, which Williamson (1986) has defined as "a condition of self-interest-seeking with guile." Finally, transaction costs theory holds that the most critical dimension for describing a transaction is the condition of asset specificity. If any one of the three assumptions is absent, then contracting is likely to be the most efficient, least cost vehicle for governing the transaction, i.e., if rationality is unbounded, then all (present and future issues) are known in advance and the parties' agreed-desires can be specified in the contract. If opportunism is absent, then any unforeseen circumstances can be covered by the general clause that each seeks only a fair return and, thus, the contract clause becomes self-enforcing. Even if opportunism and bounded rationality are both present but asset specificity is absent (either insignificant investment or generalized assets not requiring investment to enable transaction completion) the parties have no continuing interest in the identity of one another.

The two human behavior traits can be taken as a given. Knight (1965) referred to "human nature as we know it"[48] supplanting the classical assumption of "economic man". Empirical evidence and human humility argue persuasively that human rationality is not unbounded. Empirical evidence and mental integrity also argue persuasively that self-interest is an integral part of human behavior. Consequently, it is the condition of asset specificity that holds the key to the appropriate governance structure for business transactions. If it were not for asset specificity, each party to a contract could go his/her separate way after the completion of each contract without costs to the other party. (No economic value would be sacrificed if the ongoing relationship between the two parties were terminated.) Asset specificity is critical because once an investment has been made, it represents a "sunk cost" for one of the parties, usually the seller. An expectation for the exchange relationship to continue for some period is required to induce the investment. In addition, the other party (usually the buyer) cannot easily and economically turn to other sources of supply if the item required by the buyer requires specialized investment. Accordingly, both parties will have an interest in securing the least cost governance structure for their relationship that nets the required level of continuity and certainty. (Hennart, 1989).[49]

Asset specificity is a function of the capital risk undertaken. (Williamson, 1988). The transaction costs relating elements of capital risk are (1) non-trivial investment (2) redeployability of assets (3) transaction-specificity of assets, i.e., how much cost is "sunk", and how "sunk" is it (both in place and in function).

To review, in international operations, FDI is undertaken by MNCs. MNCs are hierarchically organized in some fashion. FDI is undertaken to gain management and control of the operation (or have an effective voice in same.). Therefore the MNC has concluded that the combined acquisition cost of good/service (production function costs) plus its transaction costs (governance costs) associated with the FDI are less than the cost to the MNC of obtaining the same good/service plus cost of governance via the market (contracting) structure. This study seeks to determine if the quantifiable elements of transaction costs (the capital risk elements of non-triviality, redeployability and transaction specificity assets) are indicators (and hence predictors) of investment attraction package requirements for inducing investment into developing countries, such as Barbados,

Jamaica, and Trinidad-Tobago. A fundamental question of this study is: do companies differ in their perception of the host country's total investment attraction package depending upon the degree of asset specificity accompanying the investment?

Internationalization Theories

A number of theories of internationalization have been put forward and, as the phenomenon continues to grow and expand in ways limited only by the imagination, newer theories and revision of older theories continue to evolve. Perhaps it is more accurate to label the efforts as process descriptions rather than as theories which normally possess some predictive power. By whatever name, however, the operative feature of all such attempts has been to enhance our ability to view the dynamics of international expansion with greater clarity and thus a major contribution to our understanding continues to unfold. Even the meaning of the term "internationalization" is undergoing continual updating as our perspective continues to widen. Welch and Luostarinen (1988) have enlarged and clarified the term from being essentially a description of outward movement in an individual firm's or larger grouping's international operations to "the process of increasing involvement in international operations", i.e., the process has both inward as well as outward links to the dynamics of international trade.[50]

Commencing with Vernon and his International Product Life Cycle theory, which included two of the three strategic motivations for FDI - host country market and cost reduction -, his process of reducing decision-making to sequential steps had great influence on internationalization theory and focused much of the ensuing empirical literature on international marketing. A major contribution was made by Jan Johanson and Finn Wiedersheim-Paul in their work with four Swedish firms. Although a small sample work, they established that international firms gradually and incrementally progress from a position of no regular exports to exports, to independent representatives, to the establishment of sales representatives, to the establishment of production facilities.[51]

There is, of course, no single path to internationalization for all firms and the literature is indebted to Buckley, Newbould and Thurwell (1988) for charting the various paths to internationalization as well as for performing an analysis of the relative success of small U.K. firms who utilized the various paths in their initial international FDI.[52] The Buckley et al. diagram, which graphically portrays the firm's potential routes to FDI and which appears in one form or another in most of the literature advocating the sequential approach of internalization, is shown below.

Figure 2.1

PATHS TO INTERNATIONALIZATION OF FIRM

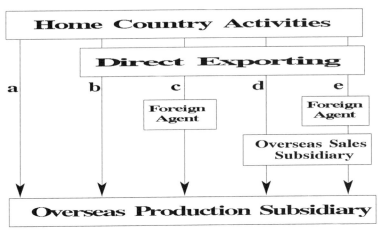

As is customary and healthy in the struggle for better understanding of on-going processes, there are opposing views to the gradual stages of internationalization. Peter Turnbull (1987) powerfully argues that an orderly and progressive sequence is inconsistent with the empirical and theoretical evidence. He suggests that operating environment, industry structure and a company's own marketing strategy will determine a company's "stage" of internationalization.[53]

Internationalization theory to-date is still unfolding. Most investors search for ways to minimize risk. Gradualization, with its obvious ability to educate management, follows the risk-reward spectrum from lowest (exporting), through foreign agent, to overseas sales subsidiary, to licensing / technical and management service contracting / and turn-key contracts, to FDI (joint venture to wholly-owned subsidiary). However, a fit with the firm's strategic timing and motivation needs would also appear to be drivers. To-date, research into internationalization stages has principally covered only one of the motivations for FDI - home country market-seeking. Other strategic motivations have yet to be addressed.

Eclectic Paradigm of International Production

The Eclectic Theory of International Production, first put forward by Dunning in 1976, offers a holistic framework for identifying and evaluating the significance of the factors influencing FDI (both initial and subsequent expansions) (Dunning, 1988a).[54] It draws on several strands of economic theory as it seeks to provide a full explanation of the activities of MNCs. The word "holistic" association with this theory seems well chosen as it seeks to explain both inter and intra firm behavior and embraces both structural and transactional market imperfections in the search for the determinants of the ownership advantages sought by MNCs. In fact, by 1988, Dunning himself had commenced to use the term "paradigm" in lieu of the term "theory", as he had come to the conclusion that : "precisely because of its generality, the eclectic paradigm has only limited power to explain or predict particular kinds of international production, and even less, the behavior of individual enterprises." (Dunning, 1988b). The theory postulates that firms will engage in FDI when three conditions are satisfied (1) possession of net "ownership" advantages when compared to others serving the market, and (2) ability to internalize the advantage(s) and (3) be in the firm's best interest to utilize some non-home country factor endowments. (Dunning, 1988b).[55] Casson (1987:33)[56] put forth the view that the assumption of ownership advantages, such as superior technology, was unnecessary, as the benefits of internalization could "in principle" be sufficient to outweigh the costs. When republishing the theory as a paradigm in 1988, Dunning may have responded to the critique by including a distinction between the asset (Oa) and transaction (Ot) advantages of multinational enterprises.   The theory draws heavily on Factor Endowment Theory, Internalization Theory and Transaction Cost Theory but also includes in its locational parameters some acknowledgment of the role played by government. (Brewer, 1993)[57] . Although the theory discusses mostly the structural market imperfections introduced by governments, it at least has gotten government "on the board" so to speak. The Foreword to Grosse's 1980 "Foreign Investment Codes and Location of Direct Investment", enters a strong plea for what appears as obvious but what has been singularly lacking in classical and neoclassical FDI theory to-date: in addition to the behavior patterns of firms, explanations must take into account the constraints imposed by governments.[58] The Eclectic Paradigm of International Production is very wide ranging. In its drive to surmount the shackles of unrealistic assumptions surrounding the classical and neoclassical approaches to FDI it has sacrificed some of the precision characteristically accompanying theories and some theorists have criticized the theory for its insufficiency of predictive power.

Strategic Trade Theory and Beyond

During the 1980s, as dissatisfaction increased with explanations of international trade, newer theories were advanced, such as Michael Porter's advocacy that nations themselves possess competitive advantages.[59] This revised the factor endowment approach to include factors of production, domestic demand, domestic rivalry and supporting industries, i.e., firms responding to the natural incentives of their home base (or if they don't, someone else - domestic or foreign - will.). Porter contends that for companies to successfully compete they must have access to people with appropriate skills , access to related supporting industries and have home-demand conditions that give the right signals including domestic rivals that can create the pressure to innovate. Essentially, this is a national environment explanation, whom its critics say can only be applied ex post facto and, thus, risks becoming a rationalization. So-called "Strategic" trade theories have been developed which base their case on the observations that some industries are strategic, generate high profits, have desirable "spill over" effects for other sectors of the economy. These theories conceived of trade as the outcome of strategic rivalry conducted by a limited number of firms and governments with each taking into account the reactions of their competitors. (Yoffie. 1993).[60] Strategic trade theories have given rise to "managed trade" advocates who have focused on trade conflict in the high technology industries because of their substantial and growing importance in trade between advanced industrial nations and the "knock on" effects that high technology industries have on the productivity, technological development and high wage job creation for the nation. The advocates contend that trade in these products tend to be influenced or manipulated by promotional and protectionist policies and that apropriate country-counter measures are required. (Tyson 1992)[61]. Others recommend more structural approaches to balance the effects of international trade without direct government intervention into the mechanisms of international trade. (Bergsten 1993)[62]. Like many of the forerunners, the strategic theories have been criticized on the reality of the assumptions made. At minimum, they deserve credit for advancing the prominence of attention being given to governments and their ability to "distort" trade. The attempts to understand the role of firms and governments in international trade and investment are on-going. Much of the more recent efforts focus heavily on the large, high-tech firm, and the advanced countries offering very large domestic markets.

SUMMARY

International trade commenced with imports and exports and these provided the framework of the theories and policy debates which so concerned the governments of the day - free trade - relative (world) competitiveness - domestic competitiveness - factor mobility (and identification of factors) - job security - national protective barriers, etc. Governments legislate in their perceived national interest - encourage "desirable" activity and discourage "undesirable" activity. In so doing, structural imperfections to the "free" flow of trade are knowingly or unknowingly introduced. Given adequate incentive, self-interest will find a way to convert imperfections into competitive advantage. After some interval has passed to allow for various innovative approaches for converting imperfections to be recognized, attempted, modified and retried, a body of experience is accumulated that permits analysis and explanation.

Factor Endowment Theory, expanding Ricardo's concentration on labour and embracing the then current economic thought which recognized the required production factors of land, labour, and capital, looked at the current experience and postulated the "export-the-abundant" theory. International Product Life Cycle Theory recognized that it was the individual firm that made the investments into foreign lands and expanded international business theory to include the search for the "why" of these FDI decisions by firms. IPLC theory concentrated on the product market and the investment sequence necessary to sustain profitability as a product moved from a non-standardized item to a standardized commodity. IPLC, in the instance of firms investing for non-raw material, non-national market reasons, married the concepts of product life cycle with the concepts of factor endowment where least-cost manufacture was the goal of the foreign investment.

As other theorists commenced investigation of the firm and its connections with FDI, the scope of the connections under investigation continued to enlarge. Focus on the market imperfections took two directions - the imperfections of the market itself (including the structural imperfections introduced by government) and the imperfections of the external market. Transaction costs theory examined the governance structure. If the market (via contract purchasing) provided the least cost arrangement for obtaining the good/service (including both ex ante and ex post costs), then there would be no economic need for FDI. The theory postulates those conditions that predict when contract or FDI might be the favored method of transaction governance.

Internalization theory looked at the firm itself for an explanation of FDI. In intermediate products, the marginal cost of incremental additions to the governance structure is low and therefore, "firms internalize imperfect markets until the cost of further internalization outweighs the benefits". (Buckley, 1989) Further, although the degree of internalization may vary with the motive for the FDI (market, raw material or cost reduction), internalization occurs in all three instances. Transaction costs theory (with its markets versus hierarchies orientation) and internalization theory seem to lend support to each other. The eclectic approach also embraces both the transaction cost and the internalization approach, although it makes a separate point of "ownership advantages" which some view as being already included in the substance of internalization theory. Eclectic theory expands the thought process to include both intra and inter firm transactions and seeks explanations for FDI in both structural and transactional imperfections. It recognizes some of the structural imperfections are initiated by government (host and home) and thus recognizes that government plays some role in FDI. However, recognition of the central role of government (its scope, purpose, pervasiveness and co-equality) and its impact on and involvement in the FDI process is lacking. The recognition of the role government plays in international trade is continuing to increase and several new theories, such as the strategic trade theories, have been recently advanced. Some of the more recent studies, however, tend to focus on international trade and the appropriate government response for improving national position. Trade theory can, and does, affect the total attraction or opportunity package presented by a country to an MNC and the MNC, in turn, is affected by the host country's reaction to advocates of the various trade theories. It is premature to speculate whether the newer trade theories and their offspring, like those advanced by Yoffie et al (1993) in "Beyond Free Trade"[63] , are explanations of fundamental economic forces underlying international trade - and perhaps investment - or are reactions to transitory distortions attempted by governments seeking to utilize national sovereignty to tilt the balance of international trade in their "favor". What is known, however, is that FDI is made by individual firms interacting with the total attraction package offered by host countries.

No general economic theory currently exists that applies exclusively to international business and/or seeks to predict any claimed unique economic behavior of international business. Though much interest and an increasing volume of writings center on international business, theories propounded to-date - including those discussed above - apply equally well to domestic business. (Grosse and Behrman, 1992).[64] Although the theories provide valuable insight into the decision parameters and the workings of firms in general - both domestic and international - they provide no insights into the international side of the equation., i.e., the interaction between the firms and the national host governments. (Boddewyn, 1988).[65] MNCs must operate within the parameters set by the sovereign host governments that permit them to exist and to conduct business within their territorial borders. The host governments are not necessarily interested in MNCs per se or even in maintaining a "market economy" per se. The host governments are interested in the distribution of the benefits these entities bring. Governments can and do "distort" the market (via laws, policies, practices and incentives) in attempts to alter the distribution of the gains. (Brewer, 1993).[66] As

Grosse and Behrman (1992) astutely observe, if government allowed markets to make major economic decisions and allowed business alone to set the rules of market behavior, the result would <u>not</u> be free markets - no firm likes competition for itself and no firm wants to operate in a classical free market. They call attention to the fact that FDI has not always followed the paths indicated by classical theory which positioned production around the globe on comparative advantage bases. While encouraging the trend of seeking explanations of the behavior patterns within horizontally and vertically integrated enterprises, Grosse and Behrman insist that government constraints on investment location - and for FDI - on investment entry must be examined. The task of an international business theory has been mooted by Grosse and Behrman in the following words:

> "The essence of the theory must explain differential barriers and incentives of foreign business imposed by sovereign Governments in an effort to alter the distribution of benefits, and the effect of those policies on TNC(s) decisions and operations. In addition, it must focus on the impact of TNC(s) on government policies."[67]

Boddewyn summarizes crisply: "MNEs may internalize the market but not the government."

---

[1]International Monetary Fund. 1977. *Balance of payments manual*. Wash. D.C.: para.408.
[2]Weekly, J. and Aggarwal, R. 1989. *International business. operating in the global economy*. Orlando, FL.: Dryden Press, p.80.
[3]Robock, S. and Simmonds, K. 1989. *International business and multinational enterprises*. 4th Ed., Homewood, IL.: Irwin, p.523.
[4]Behrman, J. 1974. *Decision criteria for foreign direct investment in latin america*. N.Y., Council of the Americas, p.11.
[5]Rugman, A. 1981. *Inside the multinationals. The economics of internal markets*. N.Y.: Columbia University Press, p.156.
[6]Ball, D. and McCulloch, W. 1993. *International business. Introduction and essentials*. 5th Ed., Homewood, IL.: Irwin, p.8.
[7]Vernon, R. 1971. *Sovereignty at bay: The multinational spread of U.S. enterprises*. N.Y.: Basic Books, Ch.2.
[8]Sturdivant, F. 1981. *Business and society. A managerial approach*. Rev. Ed., Homewood, IL.: Irwin, p. 396.
[9]Martyn, H. 1970. *Multinational business management*. Lexington, MA.: D.C. Heath and Co., p.1.
[10]Weekly and Aggarwal. 1989. *op cit*, p. 9.
[11]Buckley, P. and Casson, M. 1976. *The future of the multinational eterprise*. London: MacMillan Press Ltd, p.1.
[12]Buckley, P. 1985. "A critical review of the theories of the multinational enterprise" in Buckley, P. and Casson, M. 1985. *The economic theory of the multinational enterprise. Selected papers*. Hong Kong: Macmillan, p. 1-2.

[13]Sturdivant. 1981. *op cit*, p. 396.

[14]Robock and Simmonds. 1989. *op cit*. p. 6.

[15]Teece, D. 1980. "Economics of scope and scope of enterprise". *Journal of Economic Behavior and Organization*. Vol 1, pp. 223-47

[16]Schnitzer, M. 1991. *Comparative economic systems*. Cincinnati, OH.:South-West Publishing, p. 16

[17]Fusfeld, D. 1990. *The age of the economist*. 6th Ed., London: Scott, Foresman, and Company, p. 41.

[18]Johnson, C. 1982. *MITI and the Japanese miracle*. Stanford, CA.: Stanford University Press.

[19]Sakaibara, E. 1992. "Japan: capitalism without capitalists", *International Economic Insights* 3, No.4 (July-August): 45-47.

[20]Nakatani, I. 1992. "The asymmetry of the Japanese-style vs. American-style capitalism as the fundamental swource of Japan-U.S. imbalance problems". National Bureau of Economic Research and Japan Center for Exconomic Research. Background paper for the U.S.-Japan Economic Forum (February).

[21]Okita, S. 1992. "Transition to market economy". Mimeographed.

[22]Ball and McCulloch. 1993. *op cit*, p. 81.

[23]Fusefeld. 1990. *op cit*. p.83.

[24]Flam, H. and Flanders, M., (Ed.). 1991. " Introduction", in: Heckscher, E. and Ohlin, B. *Heckscher-Ohlin trade theory*. Cambridge, MA.: M.I.T. Press, p.25.

[25]Kreinin, M. 1991. *International economics. A policy approach*, 6th Ed., N.Y.: Harcourt, Brace, Jovanovich, p.291.

[26]Leontief, W. 1954. "Domestic production and foreign trade: The American capital position re-examined", *Economica Internazionale*. 7 (Feb, 1954) pp.3-32.

[27]Harris, Phillip R. and Moran, R. 1991. *Managing cultural differences*. 3rd Ed., Houston, TX.: Gulf Publishing, p. 15.

[28]Grosse, R. and Behrman, J. 1992. "Theory in international business". *Transnational Corporations*, Vol 1, No.1.

[29]Vernon, R. 1966. "International investment and international trade in the product life cycle", *The Quarterly Journal of Economics*. No.2, Vol 1. p. 190-207.

[30]Weekly and Aggarwal. 1989. *op cit*, p.181..

[31]Lane, H. and DiStafano, J. 1992. *International management behavior*. 2nd Ed., Boston, MA.: PWS-Kent Publishing, p. 233.

[32]Buckley, P. 1992. *Studies in International Business*l. N.Y.: St Martin Press, p.18.

[33]Coase, R. 1960. "The problem of social cost". *Journal of Law and Economics*, Oct.,1960, p. 15.

[34]Teece, D. 1981. "The multinational enterprise: Market failure and market power considerations., *Sloan Management Review*, Spring, 1981, Vol. 22, p.4.

[35]Rugman. 1981. *op cit*, p. 41.

[36]Hymer, S. 1976. *The international operations of national firms: A study of direct foreign investment*. Cambridge, MA.: MIT Press, pp.91-96.

[37]Weekly and Aggarwal. 1989. *op cit*, p. 182.

[38]Buckley and Casson. 1976. *op cit*, p. 32.

[39]*Ibid*, p. 32.

[40]Buckley, P. 1989. *The multinational enterprise*. London: MacMillan Press, p.13.

[41]*loc cit*

[42]Commons, J. 1934. *Institutional economics*. Madison: University of Wisconsin Press, p. 6.

[43]Williamson, O. 1986. *Economic organization. firms, markets and policy control*, N.Y.: University Press, p. 176.

[44]Arrow, K. 1969. "The organization of economic activity". *The Analysis and Evaluation of Public Expenditure: the PPB System*. Joint Economic Committee, 91st Congess, 1st Session, p. 48.

[45]Williamson. 1986. *op cit*, p. 3.

[46]Coase, Ronald (1952). "The Nature of the Firm". *Economica NS*. 1937, Vol.4, pp.386-405; reprinted in Stigler, G. and Bouldings, E. (Eds), *Readings in price theory*, Homewood, IL.: Irwin.

[47]Simmon, H. 1982. *Models of bounded rationality*. Campbridge, MA.: M.I.T. Press.

[48]Knight, F. 1965. *Risk, uncertainty and profit*, N.Y.: Row, p. 270.

[49]Hennart, J. 1989. "Can the 'new forms of investment' substitute for the 'old forms'?. A transaction cost perspective". *Journal of International Business Studies*, Vol. XX, No.2 (Summer), p. 217.

[50]Welsh, L. and Luostarinen, R. 1993. "Internationalization: evolution of a concept", *Journal of General Management*, 1988, Vol 14, No 2; reprinted in Buckley, P. and Ghauri, P. (Eds), *The internationalization of the firm. A reader*. London: Academic Press, p.156.

[51]Johanson, J. and Wiedersheim-Paul, F. 1993. "The internationalization of the firm: Four Swedish cases", *Journal of Management Studies*, 1975, pp 305-322; reprinted in Buckley, P. and Ghauri, P. (Eds), *The Internationalization of the Firm. A Reader*. London: Academic Press, p.17.

[52]Buckley, P.; Newbould, G. and Thurwell, J. 1988. *Foreign direct investment by smaller U.K. firms: The success and failure of first-time investors abroad*. Hong Kong: Macmillan Press, pp 45-46.

[53]Turnbull, P. 1993. "A challenge to the stages theory of the internationalization process". *Management export entry and expansion*, Rosson P. and Reed, R. (Eds) Greenwood Publishing, Inc., Westport. 1987, reprinted in Buckley, P. and Ghauri, P. (Eds), *The internationalization of the firm. A reader*. London: Academic Press, pp172-173.

[54]Dunning, J. 1988a. "The eclectic paradigm of international production: A restatement and some possible extensions". *Journal of International Business Studies*, Vol.XIX, No.1, p. 1.

[55]Dunning, J. 1988b. *Explaining international production*. London: Unwin Hyman Ltd., p. 26.

[56]Casson, M. 1979. *Alternatives to the multinational enterprise*, N.Y.: Holmes & Meier, p 33.

[57]Brewer, T. 1993. "Government policies, market imperfections, and foreign direct investment". *Journal of International Business*, Vol 24, No 1, p. 104.

[58]Grosse, R. 1980. *Foreign investment codes and the location of direct investment*. N.Y.: Praeger, p. iii.

[59]Porter, M. 1990. *The Competitive Advantage of Nations*. N.Y.: Free Press.

[60]Yoffie, D. 1993. *Beyond Free Trade. Firms, Governments and Global Competition*. (David Yoffie, Ed.) Boston, MA.: Harvard Business School Press, p. 8.

[61]Tyson, L. 1992. *Who's Bashing Whom. Trade Conflict in High-Technology Industries*. Washington, D.C.: Institute for International Economics, p.2.

[62]Bergsten, C. Fred, Noland, Marcus. 1993. *Reconcilable Differences? United States - Japan Economic Conflict*. Washington, D.C.: Institute for International Economics, p.206.228.

[63]*Ibid*. p.8.

[64]Grosse and Behrman (1992). *op cit*, p. 91.

[65]Boddewyn, J. 1988. "Political aspects of MNE theory". *Journal of International Business Studies*, (Fall), pp. 341-363.

[66]Brewer. 1993. *op cit*, p. 105.

[67]Grosse and Behrman. 1992. *op cit*, p.96.

CHAPTER III

WHO SEES WHAT ?

Protagonists and Their Perceptions of FDI

"Oh wad some power the giftie gie us
To see ourselves as ithers see us!"

Robert Burns
The Twa Dogs

From the time of Marco Polo, to the Dutch East India Company and the U.K.'s Hudson Bay Company, to the first U.S multinational (Singer Sewing Machine Company), through two World Wars, and into the fifties, history was rich with recognition that the apparently benign MNC had played a positive role in the consolidation of sprawling countries and in assisting economic growth. Generally, MNCs were deemed to be of no particular threat to the established order. Transportation was slow. Communications - especially in developing countries - was primitive. Tariff barriers insured that markets were national. Operating necessity required "home offices" to delegate wide discretionary powers to their expatriate managers, who stayed in their adopted countries for lengthy periods of time. Little real attention was paid by governments to MNCs. For all intents and purposes, MNCs acted like national companies and were treated much like the same as no threats to government or governing were perceived. As the world recovered from World War II, this benign posture toward MNCs began to be re-accessed and to recede.

The Organization for Economic Cooperation and Development (OECD) has estimated that the total value of FDI in 1967 was $105 billion but 20 years later (1987) total value was estimated at $650 billion! The growth rate of 10% per annum in the 1960s escalated to 12% in the 1970s. World economic conditions slowed the rate in the early 1980s but by the late 1980s the trend had again heated up. The UN estimates that there are now about 37,000 TNCs with about 174,000 foreign affiliates. (Gold,1993).[1] Host nation governments became alarmed by this explosive growth. The growth was coupled with the closer headquarters control which had been made possible by communication and transportation breakthroughs and had been necessitated , among other things, by new market opportunities that followed the crashing of tariff barriers and the search for cost competitiveness. The host nation governments began to realize that the establishment of an increasing number of businesses controlled by management outside of their jurisdiction was resulting in "local" firms (the MNC subsidiaries) that could pursue objectives in conflict with their own. Perhaps no one captured the tenor of the times better than did Raymond Vernon in his seminal 1971 work, "Sovereignty At Bay". [2]

Ostry (1992) argues for " accelerating interdependence" as the more accurate terminology for the popular word "globalization". [3] She pinpoints the MNC as the primary agent of globalization but affixes the primary driving force as the revolution in information and communications technologies. Drawing parallels with the international linkage commenced by the expansion of trade and furthered by the internationalization of the financial markets, Ostry predicts that this third phase of globalization - dominated by flows of investment and technology and by increased corporate and research networking - will enhance opportunities for growth but will also increase the risks and vulnerabilities. She points out that globalization creates growing pressure for convergence of policies which increases the risk because pressure for convergence raises the issue of sovereignty. Ostry notes that the globalizing world has a low tolerance for system-divergence.

Weekly and Aggarwal (1987) declare that the essence of MNC activity is the transmission of resources from country to country and that the ways in which countries responds to MNCs is likely to be determined by whether the nation is a net contributor or net receiver of the resources being reallocated by the MNCs. [4] This "win/lose", zero sum game outlook adopted by some - while explaining why there is conflict occurring - may itself be at the heart of the conflict. Reuber et al. (1973) have maintained that FDI is not a zero sum game. [5] Others add vehemence by stating that if it were zero sum, the correct LDC response would be to nationalize and be done with it. However, neither position has effectively supported its conclusion with empirical data.   More research is needed to clarify for all the participants whether FDI is, in truth, a zero-sum game or a positive-sum pie-enlarger. Research enabling consensus to be achieved on result of FDI does not require consensus to be achieved on means or development philosophy but could be of assistance in defusing the debate about value which, in turn, could permit focusing on the core issues emanating from both dichotomy and similarity of interests.

DEBATE: FDI / MNC VALUE
Proponent View of FDI

Walters and Blake (1992)[6] maintain that most host countries hold fears of MNCs yet almost all not only accept MNCs but actively recruit their FDI via a large array of incentives. Frequently cited key benefits received by host countries from MNC/FDI presence are:

1. Mobilization and productive use of investment capital.

2. Employment generated by FDI.

3. Import substitution and export promotion.

4. Facility establishment in depressed areas of the country.

5. Aid in improving balance-of-payments via exports.

6. Technology and managerial skills transfer.

7. Generation of taxable income.

Brewer (1986) and others elaborate on the importance of FDI to developing countries as contributing - in one package - scarce capital, technology, entrepreneurship, and managerial, professional and technical expertise.[7]

Investment by MNCs provides a means for continuing to access international capital. In a period when little public capital is available to the LDCs, and when such brings with it the unwelcome addition to host country debt service, the potential for private capital inflow addresses the growth requirements of LDCs without increasing the obligations of the government to the international financial community. Reuber et al.(1973)[8] point out that direct investment carries no fixed-debt obligations. In the late 1980s, World Bank, IMF and other international creditors imposed "conditionality requirements" on many developing countries as the price for continued access to international debt capital. Such conditionality "surpassed (the developing countries) worst nightmares about loss of control due to MNE investment and operation "(Lecraw, 1992)[9]

U.S. proponents of claims that the home (U.S.) country benefits from MNCs investing externally generally fall into three broad categories: MNCs contribute generally to a U.S. balance-of-payments surplus (Senate Finance Committee, 1970)[10]; international involvement keeps U.S. enterprises competitive in both domestic and foreign markets (Department of Commerce, 1977)[11]; fosters rather than decreases employment in the U.S.

For the MNC the ferocity of the debate can be puzzling. MNCs take for granted that all the world knows that the business firm is an enterprise grounded in the concept of private property rights, owned by private property holders and dedicated to pursuing profit for private interests. Its search for profit is global. It brings capital, managerial skills and technology to exploit opportunities (imperfections) that are not currently (in the MNC' eyes) being served. To the MNC, serving the opportunity fulfills some real or perceived need of host country or else an opportunity would not exist or their presence not be permitted. In bringing its capital, skills and technology to a country, the MNC sees the country being enriched both directly and indirectly. It acknowledges the sovereignty of both home and host governments, knows that the MNC itself is not government and wishes others would not ascribe "government-type" duty and obligations to it. It hopes that it will continued to be allowed to pursue its private interests. The MNC is aware that should its activities be an abuse, or be perceived as being an abuse, of its legally permissible activities, then its right to continue the activity will be curtailed.

Opponent View of FDI

Brewer et al (1986) summarize the ambivalent - sometimes, hostile - attitude of developing countries toward FDI by citing the oft-reported claims: short term capital inflow generates long-term outflow for profit remittance, interest, licensing, "know how" and capital repatriation; heavy dependence upon imported materials and equipment; costly and often inappropriate technology; potential for foreign entrepreneurship to stifle indigenous enterprise.[12] Claims are made that frequently the government incentives, subsidies, and infrastructural provisions are unfair and extravagant as they increase the foreigner's profit. MNCs are accused of evading taxes and of exploiting the work force via wages and conditions that are below the standards of the home country (but usually above local standards). In a "Catch-22", paying above local standards also attracts the criticism of drawing scarce talent away from local industry. Frequently, the strongest opposition to FDI comes from the local business class who feel particularly disadvantaged by the competition. (Brewer, et al. 1986).[13]In the political and ideological arena, nationalists desiring economic independence and self-sufficiency resent what they view as neo-colonial domination by foreigners and the perpetuation of dependency. (See Grant L. Ruber's Private Foreign Investment in Development, OECD, 1993, pages 20-21 for a catelogue of allegations of the adverse external effects of foreign direct investment that have been mentioned by various writers.)

The host developing country knows its own history, its culture and its internal politics as well as its economic situation. For much of the developing world in general, and for the Caribbean and Barbados, Jamaica, and Trinidad-Tobago in particular, that history's pivotal heritage includes slavery and colonialism - with actual emancipation substantially lagging legal emancipation. Searing memories of dependency and the mercantilist policies of the former "mother-countries" initially engendered the reaction of "never again" in the newly Independent. When economic independence did not accompany political independence (1960s for the subject countries), a number of developing countries began to question the economic, political and social impact of foreign technology and investment. Coinciding with this time period was the first oil shock, which hit non-oil producing developing countries particularly hard. This shot up the borrowing requirements of the countries as they attempted to keep afloat.

Perhaps nowhere has the cry, the anguish and the case of the developing countries been better or more succinctly phrased than in the 1972 election slogan of the People's National Party of Jamaica: "Better Must Come". Others have stated the case and proposed solutions with far more scholarly impact but none with more simple honesty. At the international level, Mahbub ul Haq (1976) spoke of the "trade union of the poor" and observed: "the so-called market mechanism mocks poverty, or simply ignores it, since the poor hardly have any purchasing power to influence market decision". [14]

By the early 1970s , many saw the central agent of their discomfort as the MNC and its handmaiden - FDI. Studies were made by regional, international and academic bodies of real and purported abuses emanating from decisions made in far away board rooms that adversely effected the economic development and sovereignty of the third world. [15] It is a truism that laws are made to correct real or perceived abuse. It is in the area of perceived abuse that virtually unlimited scope exists for the injection of other agendas into an already inflamed atmosphere.

The debates generally covered ideology (neo-imperialist view and the dependencia school of thought that flourished in Latin America) (Bergsten, 1978)[16]; (Hope, 1986);[17] impact on national sovereignty; the political challenge (both internally from the foreign subsidiaries within the host country and externally from home countries either pushing the MNC's interest or pushing cases involving extra-territoriality); reduction in economic independence (and economic domination - concerns not limited to the developing countries but especially sensitive for those countries); resource transfer effects (capital, skills, technology - appropriateness, costs, benefits); balance of payments effects; and employment effects.[18]

For some, the words have not changed much in recent times. Alex Rubner (1990) reports the words of Paul Harrison "The poor nations.....are exploited by the great multinational corporations which dominate a growing proportion of economic and social life of the Third World. They are the gunboats and the soldiers of the new economic style of imperialism".[19]

Current Position of FDI Debate

Much of the heat has gone out of the storm over MNCs. Streeten (1992) proclaims that all developing countries now welcome FDI, even those possessing the least economic linkage to other countries, such as Albania and Myanmar. He proclaims that relations between governments of host countries and MNCs have moved from ideological heat to pragmatic light. "Transnational corporations are considered by many observers and by host countries as wholly benign agents".[20] Expropriation acts have dropped from a peak of 83 in 1975 to 1 in 1985 (World Investment Report 1991).[21] Only one (1) act of expropriation was recorded for the period 1986-1992. (Minor, 1994).[22] Forty three countries adopted 79 new legislative measures affecting FDI in 1992. All 79 were intended to liberalize the rules. In 1991, 80 of 82 legislative measures promulgated by reporting governments were more liberal (Gold, 1993).[23] Kline (1993) summarises the regulatory trends of the 1990s as including less restrictive national laws, proliferating bilateral investment treaties (BITs) and expanding regional and multilateral negotiations on FDI issues.[24]

Contractor (1991) summarized the current trend toward global liberalization of FDI policies as being driven by seven possible causes: recession of the '80s; relative decline in the position of developing countries; loan finance shrinkage occasioning greater reliance on FDI; host nation competition to attract FDI; NICs generating their own MNCs; increased confidence and competence of regulators negotiating with MNCs; and decline in perceived value of centrally-planned economies and their ideology.[25]

Still, the emerging consensus retains its critics. There is no gainsaying the fact that MNCs are agents of change in developing countries. Such change encompasses political, cultural and social change as well as economic change. The direction of the change is toward more openness and pluralism - both economic and political.(Lecraw, 1990).[26] As such, countries valuing stability, continuity and maintenance of social and economic "relativity" within their society find MNCs can have negative effects. Some of the concern has shifted away from the direct ills alleged to be caused by MNCs and has shifted to the host countries themselves and their "eagerness" for FDI. Korten (1991) warns: "(intense competition today) is between governments that find themselves competing with one another for investors by offering the cheapest and most compliant labour; the weakest environmental, health, and safety standards; the lowest taxes and the most fully developed infrastructure. Often governments must borrow to finance the social and physical infrastructure needed to attract private investors. Having pushed almost all of the social and environmental costs of production onto the community, many firms are able to turn a handsome profit."[27]

Perhaps Robert Cornell (1989) had his finger on the pulse when he observed at the OECD Tokyo Conference that there was a clear trend in a number of developing countries toward relaxing controls but that motives on liberalization differed. Cornell detected some disenchantment with policy rationales that were provided during the 1970s and early 1980s for the more restrictive regimes but he cautioned that in some cases, countries which bear severe debt burden may have felt more pushed rather than led into relaxation of policies which discouraged FDI.[28]

"Transnational corporations have become central organizers of economic activities in an increasingly integrated world economy." (World Investment Report 1992).[29] Stopford and Strange (1991) point out that there is a growing interdependence between states and firms as the quest by each for security becomes ever more competitive with their counterparts. The fierce competitive rivalry between states has brought governments to the recognition of their increased dependence on the scarce resources controlled by the firms.[30] It is equally clear that MNCs no longer question the fundamental rights of government sovereignty. In all likelihood, the themes of economic nationalism will continue to be heard throughout every nation of the globe for many years to come, especially during domestic "hard times" of either an economic or political origin. Nationalism's time tested appeal to the domestic constituencies is simply too great to be ignored by the vigorous political process. But away from the spotlights - in the corridors of national power - the reality of interdependence, like the voice of the turtle, will be heard in the land... and is likely to be increasingly served.

ALTERNATIVES TO FDI

Difficulty in aligning the objectives of the MNC and the host country have particularly arisen when the host is a developing country and the FDI becomes a significant proportion of the total manufacturing investment in the host country.(Casson, 1979).[31] Host countries have sought techniques for obtaining technology that did not involve ceding control of key-sector investment and employment decisions to the MNCs. Arrangements such as licensing, subcontracting, turnkey contracting, etc., seek to separate the control of the development of the technology from the control of the operating processes that incorporate within them the use of the technology. The arrangements seek to use the market, via negotiated contractual arrangements, for obtaining the technology (including managerial skills technology) in lieu of permitting the transfer of the technology via MNC internalization. The process is frequently referred to as "unbundling" the investment package. The capital transfer portion of the avoided FDI is provided by domestic investment of either locally owned firms or by the host country itself (usually via state borrowings from international lending agencies). In the state borrowing sector, Kahler (1986) notes that a range of "new" forms may require initial public support if they are to develop and he encourages careful thinking about new forms of financial intermediation that will better serve the interests of the lenders and the borrowers.[32] However, Cable and Persaud (1987) warn that alternative arrangements, such as management contracts in the mining and tourism sector and subcontracting for manufacturing exports, have some disadvantages in that they do little to reduce external control while removing risk from the private investor.[33]

Half-way house arrangements, such as joint-ventures or cost partnerships, contain elements of both FDI and "alternative" arrangements. When required by government mandate, their host country purpose is to seek the desired capital inflow while limiting the amount of foreign control to be ceded. Most of the early debate (1980s) on this "new form" of FDI centered upon the question of whose interest it served - the LDC's quest for extracting a greater share of the economic rent generated by FDI or the MNCs obtaining the same returns as previously enjoyed at reduced capital risk.(UNCTC 1983).[34]

Hennart (1989) has called attention to the fact that while most of the attention on the "new forms" have focused upon the distribution of the economic rents, little attention has been paid to the question of the form's impact upon the size of the rents to be divided.[35] Hennart points out the appropriateness of using a transaction cost approach to the analysis of the three forms of governance organizations involved - contracts, hierarchies (FDI) and joint ventures - and makes analysis of each. Gerlinger and Hebert (1989) have commented upon the control aspects of international joint ventures and the criticalness of the control concept to international joint-venture (IJV) performance.[36] Reuber et al.(1973) warns that the unbundling or unscrambled approach would seem likely to prove difficult in the context of the vertically integrated, export-oriented investment while allowing that the approach may sometimes be practical in other situations.[37]

The research reported in this study is concerned with FDI and the attraction of same into developing countries, with Barbados, Jamaica, and Trinidad-Tobago representing the focal point. The citing of alternative approaches to FDI is for the purpose of conceptual completeness and further investigation is beyond the scope of the research. The words of Buckley (1989), however, seem particularly appropriate: "Firms internalize imperfect markets until the cost of further internalization outweigh the benefits."[38] The "new forms" are an alternative. As usual, the critical questions to be answered - whether contracting, FDI, or "new forms" - involves costs, benefits and risks.

SUMMARY

Approximately one quarter of FDI is located in the less developed countries. (Robock and Simmonds. 1989).[39] The 20 largest developing countries received almost 90% of this total in the early 1980s as compared to 70% in the early 1970s.(UNCTC. 1985).[40] The investment funds went for three specific purposes: develop oil resources and other minerals; take advantage of relatively large domestic markets; utilize disciplined, low-wage labour force for export manufacture. (Robock and Simmons. 1989).[41] Only a small amount of investment remained for the other 100 or so Third World countries.

The countries forming the focal point for this study (Barbados, Jamaica, and Trinidad-Tobago) are members of the Commonwealth of Nations. The Secretary General of the Commonwealth made these observations in 1987: "Few subjects have been more controversial in the past than foreign investment and the role of transnationals in development. Yet within recent years there has been a broad-based recognition that foreign investors do have a positive role to play in development within the general context of a stronger private sector."[42] Williams (1988) found that there was a statistically significant relationship between FDI and the economic growth patterns of four Pacific Basin countries.[43] "The Economist" (March 27th, 1993), predicts that the new openness will only last as long as governments believe it is bringing them benefits and it warns that the greatest danger to the openness is not the multinationals (although they are an inviting target to use as an excuse) but the high expectations of the liberalizing governments. "Multinationals do bring assets to the developing countries, such as capital, skills and technology, but they cannot, by themselves, make up for domestic shortcomings. They are no short-cut to prosperity."[44]

MNCs possess great economic power. Political and legal power resides in the nations and their governments. (Weekly and Aggarwal, 1987). Boddewyn (1988) analysed the political behavior of MNCs and maintained that they are better understood as political actors who actively try to influence their political environment.[45] The way in which nations and governments exercise legal and political power effecting the MNC determines the MNCs exercise of its economic power. This interaction, in turn, determines the residual benefits the individual country receives from the exercise by the MNC of its permitted economic activities.

A review of the FDI debate , the alternatives, and the perceptions of value appears to make some statement of basics worth repeating: Government cannot compel investment by a firm domiciled in and subject to the powers of another government. MNCs incorporated in one country cannot conduct business activities in another country without the permission of government (prospective host country, always; home government, sometimes). The MNCs primary motivation is to serve the interests of its owners. The governments primary motivation is to serve the interest of its citizens. That the interests of foreign owners and host country can, at times, diverge is self evident.

Thus, whether or not acknowledged, sought, or desired, interdependency exists between the two independent powers whenever, in the exercise of their respective independent "sovereign" rights, they determine to make common cause. Walters and Blake (1992) observe: "....much evidence indicates that these firms (MNCs) are willing to operate under regulated conditions as long as it is profitable for them to do so."[46] Those who have much to offer (country or MNC) can demand much. Those with less to offer must restrain their demands if they choose to participate.

The question for determination is which better serves the balanced best-interest of their respective constituencies - autarky or voluntary interdependence. Case by case judgment is obviously required but the thrust of recent FDI history is running strongly in the direction of interdependence. If autarchy is rejected, the question becomes one of entry price. Perhaps it might be helpful if all parties to FDI stepped back, took a deep breath, and recalled that the definition of market price is built around the concept of willing buyer - willing seller.

The reasoning of Proponents and Opposition to FDI is extensive, complex, sometimes based on hidden agenda, etc., and a full presentation of it would exceed the intended scope of this study. The above illustrates the point, however, that government can and does take effective action to encourage or discourage FDI as it deems appropriate. As such, the points of Grosse and Behrman are reinforced: any theory of international business behavior that purports to explain and predict such behavior must take into account the potential for decision-altering actions of government.

---

[1]Gold, D. 1993. "World investment report 1993:Transnational corporations and integrated international production. An executive summary". *Transnational Corporations*, Vol.2, No.2, Aug., 1993, p.99.

[2]Vernon, Raymond (1971). *Sovereignty at Bay: The Multinational Spread of U.S. Enterprises.* N.Y.: Basic Books, pp.190-207.

[3]Ostry, S. 1992. "The domestic domain: The new international policy arena". *Transnational Corporations*, Vol.1, No. 1, p. 7.

[4]Weekly and Aggarwal 1989. *op cit*, p. 316.

[5]Reuber, G., Crookell, H.,Emerson, M., and Gallais-Hamonno, G. 1973. *Private foreign investment in development.* Oxford: Clarendon Press, p.22.

[6]Walters, R. and Blake, D. 1992. *The politics of global economic relations.* 4th Ed, Englewood, N.J.: Prentice Hall, p.124

[7]Brewer, T.; David, K.; Lim, L. 1987. *Investing in developing countries. A guide for executives.* Lexington, MA.: Lexington Books, D.C. Heath & Company, p.82.

[8]Reuber, et al. 1973. *op cit*, p.19.

[9]Lecraw, D. 1992. "Multinational enterprises and developing countries" in *New directions in international business.Research priorities for the 1990s.* Peter J. Buckley (Ed.), Hants: Edward Elgar, p.41.

[10]U.S. Congress, Senate Committee on Finance. 1970. *Implications of multinational firm,* Wash., D.C.: U.S. Printing Office, p.173

[11]U.S. Department of Commerce 1977. *U.S. direct foreign investment abroad, 1977.* Wash., D.C.: Government Printing Office, p. 340.

[12]Brewer et al. 1987, *op cit*, p. 81.

[13]*Ibid*, p.81.

[14]Haq, Mahbub Ul. 1976. "The third world and international economic order". *Development paper no. 22,* Overseas Development Council. N.Y.: Random House, pp.1-11.

[15]Folsom, R.; Gordon, M.; and Spanogle, J. 1988. *International business transactions in a nutshell.* 3rd Ed., St. Paul, MN.: West Publishing Co., p. 218.

[16]Bergsten, C.; Horst, T.; Moran, T. 1978. *American multinationals and American interests.* Wash., D.C.: Brookings Institute, pp. 309-353.

[17]Hope, K. 1986. *Economic development in the Caribbean.* N.Y.: Prager, Greenwood Press, pp.4-6.

[18]Robock, S. and Simmonds, K. 1989. *International business and multinational enterprises* 4th Ed., Homewood, IL.: Irwin, pp.310-24.

[19]Rubner, A. 1990. *The might of the multinationals. The rise and fall of the corporate legend.* Westport, CN: Praeger, p.1.

[20]Streeten, P. 1992. "Interdependence and integration of the world economy: The role of states and firms". *Transnational Corporations*, Vol 1, No 3, Dec. 1992, p.133

[21]United Nations Commission on Transnational Corporations. 1991. *World investment report, 1991: The triad in foreign direct investment.* N.Y.: p.287.

[22]Minor, Michael S. (1994). "The demise of expropriation as an instrument of LDC policy, 1980-1992". *Journal of International Business Studies.* Vol.25, No.1, 1st Qt 1994. p. 182.

[23]Gold, D. 1993. *op cit* p.113.

[24]Kline, J. 1993. "Research note: International regulation of transnational business: Providing the misssing Leg of global Iivestment standards". *Transnational Corporations*, Vol.2, No.1, Feb.1993, p.155.

[25]Contractor, F. 1991. "Government policies and foreign Direct investment". *UNCTC Studies, Series no. 17,* N.Y.: United Nations, p.19.

[26]Lecraw, D. 1992. *op cit*, pp. 34-35.

[27]Korten, D. 1991. "Sustainable development: A review essay." *World Policy Journal,* 9, 1 (Winter 1991-92), pp. 157-190.

[28]Cornell, R. 1989. *International direct investment and the new economic environment: Tokyo round table.* Paris: OECD, p. 10-11.

[29]United Nations. 1992. *World investment report 1992: Transnational corporations as engines of growth.* N.Y.: Transnational Corporations and Management Division, Department of Economic and Social Development, p.1.

[30]Stopford, J. and Strange, S. 1991. *Rival states, rival firms: Competition for world market shares.* Cambridge: University Press, p. 1.

[31]Casson, M. 1979. *op cit*, p.xi.

[32]Kahler, M. 1986. *The politics of international debt.* Ithaca, N.Y.: Cornell University Press, p.1.

[33]Cable, V. and Persaud, B. 1987. "New Trends and Policy Problems in Foreign Investment: The Experience of Commonwealth Developing Countries", in *Developing With Foreign Investment*, The Commonwealth Secretariat, Kent: Croom Helm Ltd, p.8.

[34]United Nations Centre for Transnational Corporations. 1983. *Transnational Corporations in World Development: Third Survey*, N.Y., p.12.

[35]Hennart, J. 1989. "Can the 'new forms of investment' substitute for the old forms?'. A transaction costs perspective". *Journal of International Business Studies*, Vol.XX, No. 2, Summer 1989. p. 211.

[36]Geringer, J. and Hebert, L. 1989. "Control and performance of international joint ventures. *Journal of International Business Studies,* Vol.XX, No.2, p.236.

[37]Reuber et al. (1973). *op cit*, p.250.

[38]Buckley, P. 1989. *The multinaional enterprise: Theory and applications.* London: MacMillan Press, p.12.

[39]Robock and Simmonds. 1989. *op cit*, p.30.

[40]United Nations Centre on Transnational Corporations. 1985. *Trends and issues in foreign direct investment and related flows.* N.Y.: p.28

[41]Robock and Simmonds. 1989. *op cit*, p. 31.

[42]Commonwealth Secretary-General. 1974. *New trends in foreign investment: The experience of Commonwealth Countries*, Eds. Cable & Bishnodat, London: Croom Helm, Foreword.

[43]Williams, J. 1988. "'The Attractiveness Index'. An investigation of direct investment economic policies of four newly industrialized countries: Hong Kong, South Korea, Singapore, Taiwan". D.B.A. Dissertation. United States International University. *Journal of International Business Studies*, Vol.XX, No.2, Summer 1989, p.406.

[44]"A Survey of Multinationals". *The Economist,* March 27th, 1993. p.19.

[45]Boddewyn, J. 1988. *op cit*, pp.341-363.

[46]Walters and Blake. 1992. *op cit*, p. 150.

CHAPTER IV

WHO WANTS WHAT ?

MNC Strategic Motivation & FDI Attraction Research

"Theirs not to make reply,
Theirs not to reason why,
Theirs but to do and die."

Alfred,
Lord Tennyson
The Charge of the Light
Brigade

Although the quote from Tennyson's immortal poem may also give effect to the inner thoughts of more than a few expatriate subsidiary managers, the quote is used here to butress the obvious: investments are not made without reason. In particular, FDI is not made without strategic objective.

MNC MOTIVATION FOR INITIATING FDI

Buckley (1989) has compressed MNCs strategic objectives for conducting FDI into three motivations (reasons): (a) market (b) raw materials and (c) cost reduction.[1] Weekly and Aggarwal state virtually identical motivations.[2] Market motivated FDI is usually directed towards those countries that possess large, or potentially large, home markets. The largest number of FDIs (though not necessarily the largest in terms of individual capital investment) is provided by this category. Even where the home market is not large, corporate strategy of market penetration, market presence, competitor containment, regional market base, etc., can still attract FDI for market based reasons. Raw material, or the extractive type investment, is the "traditional" source of FDI and the source that has attracted much of the contention between MNCs, host countries and home countries. The motive of cost reduction has two major sub groupings: cost reduction related to labour cost differentials and cost reduction germane to tax reduction (emanating from either host or home country benefits). Clegg (1992)[3] concludes that the generation of entrepreneurial activity is the most significant determinant underlying FDI and that the hall marks of such activity are technological change and the growth of markets.

Grosse (1980) and many others agree that the majority of foreign manufacturing is market seeking rather than cost minimizing.[4] Some authors (Dunning and Brewer among others) have lumped raw materials into the cost reduction category and compressed MNC motivation down to two categories. While the theoretical correctness of such an amalgamation has merit, the practical problems associated with such a lumping together are not beneficial to research efforts - the quantum invested, the time horizon, the risk, the host country attractions, the available of viable alternatives - are all distinctly different for the two categories. MNC cost reduction motivation is frequently paralleled by host country desires for attracting "export only" type industry. Host country incentives to accomplish their export-only goals are generally not available to the raw material exporting category. Accordingly, lumping together obscures the benefits of differentiation that is fundamental to certain types of research.

Guisinger (1985) equated host countries with "sellers" and firms seeking locations for FDI with "buyers", which enabled him to draw the analogy between product markets and the producer competition for market share on the one hand, and investment markets with host country competition for FDI share on the other. Guisinger segmented his "market" for FDI into three separate markets: domestic market of the host country, common market of the region housing host country, and worldwide export market.

Woodward and Rolfe (1993) note that since the early 1980s, the attitudes of developing countries towards FDI have changed and that export-oriented FDI has been a special target of attraction efforts by developing countries. They remind that the emphasis on export-oriented FDI is in sharp contrast to the prior favorites of promoting home domestic market or import substitution and that the current promotion is being undertaken in spite of the criticisms leveled at export processing "enclaves" for their weak linkage to local inter-industry. Woodward and Rolfe see the developing countries drive for export-oriented FDI as being fueled by the promise of increased capital, employment and foreign exchange with the foreign investor bearing the investment risk in lieu of the state. Looking to the future, they see export assembly platforms reflecting an underlying trend toward global sourcing in intermediate products and that firms will seek the low-wage, LDC location where the intermediate manufacturing task can be divided into highly routine operations.[5]

A comparison of the views of Buckley and Guisinger germane to MNC motivation for FDI could look something like the following:

Buckley	Guisinger
market	domestic market
	regional market
raw materials	
cost reduction	worldwide export market
	regional market

Others (Woodward and Rolfe) segment MNC reasoning into domestic and export-oriented investment, while granting that raw materials are something of a special and declining case. Such segmentation fits easily within the above framework as it appears clear that export-only platforms are cost reduction vehicles. What is not clear or capable of neat "pigeonholing" is the vertically integrated firm - some will be export-only while others utilize the domestic market as a base for establishing the economies of scale required for competitive exporting to either regional or worldwide markets. There are even further breakdowns of the latter - some are required by government to supply the local market and others are limited by government as to extent of permitted local sales. Horizontally integrated firms appear to fit comfortably within the domestic market, yet the regional export capability raises the question of "domestic vs. regional export" when searching for the primary motivation for the location decision.

Given the motivation for the FDI, a number of factors influence the individual firm's choice of location. Larimo (1993)[6] lists six (6) main factors which explain the choice of locations of the foreign unit: 1) the nature of the technological edge and its life-cycle stage. 2) the demand stage of the product in its life cycle and the location of the main markets. 3) the competitive situation vis-a-vis attempts to safeguard market shares and position in main market. 4) the factor endowments between countries. 5) the institutional factors, such as government incentives for investments and restrictions on imports. 6) physical, cultural and economic distance from the investing firm. While acknowledging that these factors influence the individual firm's choice, factors #1-3 are internal to the firm and #4 and #6 are recognition of reality relatively uncontrollable by the host country - at least in the short and medium term. Therefore, the concentration of this study is on the area of #5 where the interests of firms and government can effectively interact - the firms motivation for investing and the institutional reaction of host government

This study adopts the Buckley configuration on MNC strategic motivation for conducting FDI - host country market-seeking, raw material-seeking, and cost reduction-seeking. There is much to recommend the addition of technology to any listing of basic strategic motivations. Much of the current literature on international trade and international competitiveness makes a convincing case. Porter (1990) has summed up: "Classical theory has been overshadowed in advanced industries and economies by the globalization of competition and the power of technology."[7] Dunning (1994) has called attention to the progress of alliance capitalism, the decline of hierarchical capitalism, and the implications for FDI.[8] However, it is clear - at least for the present and foreseeable future - that the potential inclusion of technology as a separate strategic motivation for MNCs seeking FDI locations would be confined to advanced industries and countries where "The catalyst is a new wave of multi-purpose generic technological advances and innovation driven production demands." (Dunning 1994)[9].

Any eventual amending of the more classical configuration of strategic motivation is likely to pertain to the developed or near-developed countries only. It is an unfortunate fact that one of the defining features of the poorer developing countries is the lack of capital available for innovation. This study focuses on the investment-attraction keys to developing countries. Therefore, the adoption of the more classical configuration of strategic motivations appears appropriate. It is recognized that the keys to developed country FDI are likely to be quite different and may require an expansion of the strategic motivation configuration.

HOST COUNTRY FDI ATTRACTION POLICIES

The research published to-date concerning the value of FDI for developing countries is oftimes contradictory and not infrequently partisan. No less contradictory is the research published on the value of investment-attraction conditions, policies and practices required or expected of those developing countries that choose to participate in the FDI process. There seems to be little of accepted wisdom or consensus surrounding the key issue of the priorities utilized by investors when accessing potential locations for FDI nor is there agreement as to which policies and incentives, if any, are the more helpful.

Effectiveness of Attraction Policies and Incentives

Shaw and Toye (1978) concluded that the effectiveness of fiscal incentives in increasing the level of FDI in LDCs was either slight to unknown.[10] Lim (1983) performed a cross sectional study of 27 LDCs (including Barbados, Jamaica, and Trinidad-Tobago) and confirmed the view that there was no support for the belief by LDC governments that it is necessary to provide fiscal incentives in order to attract FDI. Lim did find that the presence of natural resources is an important factor in persuading foreign investors to invest in LDCs, and that foreign investors are more concerned with proven economic performance over a long period of time (rather than recent economic performance).[11] Kumar (1994) suggests that, except for export processing zones, government regulations and incentives do not significantly affect the pattern of export-oriented production by MNCs.[12]

Reuber et al. (1973)[13] and Root and Ahmed (1978)[14] and the Group of Thirty (1984)[15] suggest that market size may be much more important than government incentives in attracting FDI.

Guisinger (1985), in a study of 74 cases involving over 30 MNCs and government officials of 10 countries (both developed and developing), found that in two-thirds of the cases, incentives of one sort or another were the decisive factor in determining whether an FDI would have been made or would have been located in another country. In the study, a broad definition of incentives was used (incorporating both explicit and implicit incentives).[16] Reuber et al. (1973) using a narrower definition, concluded that the effect of incentives on stimulating FDI into developing countries, while of some consequence, were relatively ineffective.[17] Wint (1989)[18] researching during a latter period, found that promotion programs, properly done, are both effective in attracting investment and are cost-effective, but only in attracting export-oriented investment.

Contractor (1990) concludes that FDI policy changes appear to have a weak and scattered influence on FDI flows (exception - Performance Requirements) but speculates that the extent of the liberalizations carried out by many nations between 1977-1987 may have canceled each other's policy change effect.[19] However, Contractor (1991) highlights the difficulty and cautions against the inadvisability of making general statements about the effectiveness of FDI policies, "since each policy instrument has a different effect on a different aspect of operations".[20] Contractor pointed out that most of the literature that seeks to access the effectiveness of FDI policies concentrates on the issue of incentives being offered and do not necessarily distinguish between the different impacts of the various types of incentives nor is the issue of potential nullification of the incentives by disincentives and performance mandates addressed.

Cable and Persaud (1987) segment their conclusions - depending upon the country's domestic market size and the nature of the investment. While noting that tax holidays do not offset the lack of markets or high production costs, their survey suggested that the right kind of tax regimes and incentives might be important - especially in the export-oriented investment. They also noted the apparent need for incentives for large-scale investments in developing countries, even those with large domestic markets. They comment that investors are conscious of the absence of incentives and conclude that it might be unwise for a country not to offer them.

Cable and Persaud recognized that their conclusions were "contrary to some conventional academic wisdom" but insisted that fiscal incentives may be important in attracting FDI. They cautioned that such incentives should be reviewed in the context of corporate tax levels as a whole and the needs of particular types of investors. [21] Root and Ahmed, (1978) state that of the policy variables studied by them, only corporate taxation emerged as being a significant determinant of FDI in manufacturing.[22]

While inconclusive over the efficiency of incentives, most of the international location literature examined is in harmony over the positive direction that Per Capita GNP plays in location decisions of market-oriented investment. For many observers (Root and Ahmed, Lim, and Contractor, among others) per capita GNP is Priority #1 for market-oriented investment, yet Evans and Doupnik (1986)[23] stated the #1 concern of U.S. MNCs in making foreign direct investments was profit repatriation. Export-oriented investment, perhaps because of its more recent emergence, is far less reported and, accordingly, a consensus on the incentives and/or country conditions that positively or negatively affect FDI has not yet arrived.

Guisinger's observation (1985) appears to have a certain "ring of truth" when he speculates that investors, faced with similar incentives from various countries, can quite correctly state that the presence of an incentive in a country does not influence their location decision. "This statement does not mean, however, that the absence of incentives would not affect investment location decisions."[24] Root and Ahmed (1978) join in this cautious approach by pointing out that competitive tax incentices appear to be necessary but are not sufficient, in and of themselves, to attract foreign investment.[25]

Pending some change (such as a rationalization or harmonization of competitor incentives), the consensus seems to be that, while effectiveness may be in some doubt, small countries cannot afford to take the risk of being perceived as uncompetitive.

Investor Priorities

Guisinger (1985) provides a portfolio of available incentives and disincentives that a country can employ in attracting and controlling FDI. He has categorized the list into three groups composed of those (1) affecting FDI revenue (2) affecting FDI Inputs and (3) Affecting components of FDI value added.[26] In total, the Guisinger list of incentives/disincentives being utilized by host countries is most comprehensive and appears to cover the presently known basic approaches, given that the details of each incentive/disincentive are limited only by the imagination.

Robock and Simmonds (1989) provide a list of complications an MNC encounters during capital budget analysis of foreign projects as compared to domestic projects:

"1. Cash flows to a project and to a parent must be differentiated.

2. National differences in tax systems, financial institutions, and financial normsand constraints on financial flows must be recognized.

3. Different inflation rates can effect profitability and the competitive position of the affiliate.

4. Foreign exchange rates can alter the competitive position of a foreign affiliate and the value of the cash flows between the affiliate and the parent,

5. Segmented capital markets create opportunities for financial gains or they may cause additional costs.

Political risks can significantly change the value of a foreign investment."[27]

Since the area of capital budgeting usually falls within the financial manager's responsibilities and since the financial manager is likely to be a key player in the MNC location decision-making process, the above capital budgeting complications may offer some insights into the priorities expected by the investor to be addressed by a host country seeking to attract FDI.

Shaw and Toye (1978)[28] divided incentives into three groups: (1) pure tax holiday - exempts firm from corporate tax for certain designated period of time. (2) modified tax holiday - duration and value of exemption depends upon investment level. (3) cost lowering incentives, such as, accelerated depreciation, investment allowances, grants, subsidies, etc. Pure holiday is questioned on effectiveness grounds - no help when needed/help provided when not needed. Modified holiday has similar deficiencies. Cost lowering incentives appear more attractive, usually extend over longer periods and lower costs of production in the often difficult early years plus gives incentive for risky investment programmes. However, many of the cost lowering incentives constitute immediate cash flow drain for the host countries.

Differing Effects of the Host Country Incentives

Guisinger (1985) has extensively detailed the effect on after-tax return on owner's equity of a full range of typical host country incentives/disincentives. Further, he has categorized "protection" (defined in its broadest sense as providing relative advantage via government intervention) into "factor protection" ,which usually depends upon positive profitability for effectiveness, and "commodity protection" which generates profitability independently. Guisinger emphases that the choice between factor and commodity instruments has significant implications for the distribution of the costs and benefits among the different groups within the society.[29]   Guisinger notes that commodity protection is the host country's instrument of choice for attracting investors interested in the domestic market, whereas factor protection is the choice of the export-oriented investor.[30] When commodity protection is provided by tariff, consumers pay the cost and existing as well as new investors get the benefits (plus government). Though not efficient as an incentive, it is more easily sold to the electorate than its more efficient cousin, factor protection, which typically transfers income from tax payers to the new investors, eliminating the windfall for existing producers. However, the taxpayers are not necessarily the consumers of the product being subsidized, and revenue for the incentive must be obtained from taxation.

Cable and Persaud (1987) state that for those seeking access to a large host country market (or regional market), the key factor is a country's overall attractiveness and that low labour costs and tax/financial incentives are relatively unimportant. For export-oriented industries labour costs and tax incentives matter more than they do with import substituting or resource processing industries, which are location specific. Large scale projects in developing countries do require incentives which are alleged to be looked upon as an offset to the costs of overregulation. "Free Trade Zones" are useful in those situations where the developing country seeks to attract export-oriented investment yet desires to maintain a high level of protection which raises domestic costs. (FTZ are criticized on the grounds of poor backward linkage to local development and alleged wasting of resources).[31]

Contractor (1991) notes that a reduction in taxes is equal to a subsidy and vice-versa. Specifically, Contractor suggests that cost sensitive export-platform location seekers may react better to factor incentives (such as tax holidays, accelerated depreciation). He cautions, however, that some firms, especially those domociled in the U.S. where the tax system nullifies much of the host country tax incentives, may prefer lump-sum subsidy or capital grant. Contractor found that investors more interested in local markets are more likely to place greater emphasis on the viability of the country's market and the protection enjoyed than on tax holidays. Distinguishing between capital subsidies and tax holidays under circumstance of a poor or competitive market or a risky political environment, Contractor believes that a cash grant might draw investors better than a future tax holiday of equal present value, inasmuch as the cash grant lowers the assets at stake.[32] (It is of reverse preference to the host country - immediate outlay versus "self liquidating" future benefit.)

"Rifle Shot" versus "Shot Gun" Approach to Incentives

Rueber et al. (1973) points out that lack of available negotiating expertise is manifested in government attempts to lay down "rules of thumb" or statutory regulations and to apply these across the board irrespective of the highly heterogeneous nature of investment projects and the widely different circumstances applicable in each case. They note that, as a consequence, exceptions to the rule can be more common than the rule's observance.[33]

Behrman (1974) notes as follows:

"For host governments (or the U.S. government) to adopt a single policy toward all direct investment is to make it more difficult to gain the desired advantages while avoiding the disadvantages.... For governments not to recognize distinctions in the various types of investment arrangements and apply different treatments as appropriate will mean that they relinquish the advantages that they could gain, at little cost, in an effort to reject those elements considered most undesirable." (Behrman. 1974)[34]

The concept of variable attraction packages is at difference with a number of distinguished authors. Lecraw (1992) states that the host country has limited ability to "price discriminate" among MNEs and that, within one class of investment project, the government must offer the same package of price cuts to all comers.[35] Lecraw illustrates his one class-of-investment contention by referencing an export-oriented, labour-intensive manufacturing project.

Rolfe, et al (1993), declare that the FDI incentive preferences of MNCs indicate that the country should determine the type of industry they want to attract and match the incentives to the needs of their target industry. They amplify this as follows: "Countries seeking large companies should focus their efforts on incentives that are a function of the amount of investment."[36] The implication is that a country can have only one incentive law or, at best, broad banding as per Lecraw above.

Guisinger (1985) states that all of the ten (10) countries in his survey (including both developed and developing) had the <u>administrative</u> capacity to vary the levels of incentives not only between industries but also between firms of the same industry. He noted that some countries preferred automatic and uniform incentive packages among firms while others actively discriminated among firms. Those interested in discriminating gave four reasons: minimizes redundancy and reduces fiscal cost of achieving a given level of investment; incentive level can be altered to compensate the firm for burdens of performance requirements; discrimination helps make the country's incentive system more opaque to its competitors; and positive benefits to the host when firm thinks its getting a special deal. [37]

The U.N.'s Transnational Coprporations and Management Division (1992) points out that the effectiveness of an incentive system is measured by its flexibility, objectivity, simplicity, and administrative speed, ease, and certainty. While recognizing that there was a dichotomy between the uniform and the case-by-case incentive systems, it summarized that the more simple, clear, objective, and the less discretionary a policy and its incentives (promotional and regulatory), the better were its chances of being administered effectively .[38]

The assumption that there can or should be only one investment incentive law per country - or at least, only one law covering a general class of investors - appears elsewhere in the literature of FDI. In addition to its marketing appeal, the apparent transparency benefits are powerful. "Treat 'em all alike" theoretically eliminates investor concerns of "is someone getting a better deal" and reduces the scope for corruption implicit in individual deal making. However, not all of the transparency is real. Differences in the value to host countries of individual FDI proposals has led many to hedge equal-treatment with phrases like, "subject to the approval of the appropriate Minister". Such flexibility is needed and reflects the reality that not all investments are equal. However, there is the downside:

> Transparency suffers and investor concerns of equity and corruption are resurrected.

> Minister's flexibility appears unidirectionally skewed as publicly announced incentives tend to become minimums.

The former discourages FDI and the latter implies that a higher "price" than required may be being paid to some entrants. Further, internal constraints on Minister flexibility - out of fear of setting undesirable precedent - may restrain exceptional offers causing loss of FDI offering exceptional benefits.

Changing Scene, Changing Knowledge Needs

Helleiner (1987) observes: "if exports - and export-oriented investments - are to be expanded, government policies must be directed at the provision of the required incentives."[39] This begs the question: What is the identity of those "required" incentives? What are the needs of the targeted investor?

Guisinger (1985) reports that poor countries lack tax revenues to finance factor protection policies, such as cash grants, or to undertake aggressive price incentives. The scope for commodity protection is necessarily limited to those sectors for which a large internal market is available, such as consumer goods. Guisinger reflects that high effective rates of protection are self defeating when domestic prices are pushed above affordable levels."[40] He concludes that small countries - with an internal market insufficient to provide scale-of-efficiency for many industrial goods -   must give priority to industries that offer export opportunities or efficient import substitution. Where is the research data upon which the   "poor countries that lack tax revenues" can base a cost effective investment attraction plan?

Woodward and Rolfe (1993) point out that the location of export processing plants has rarely been investigated as a separate phenomenon with the result that important questions remain unanswered, such as the response of export-oriented investors to the factors that normally govern the location of MNCs facilities in lesser developed countries (LDCs).[41] They argued that the determinants of export-oriented investment might be different from those factors which govern the location decisions of market-oriented FDI. It is becoming clear that a difference in investor preferences does exist between the market-oriented and the export-oriented FDI. Knowledge of the specifics of the differences is required.

Wells (1987)[42] argues that export-oriented investment requires inexpensive labour and reasonable infrastructure, transport and communications facilities. Austin (1990)[43] states that wage cost is the primary reason for MNCs to integrate developing countries into their global plans. Kumar (1994)[44] agrees. Woodward and Rolfe (1993)[45] note that most developing countries have low wage costs and, hence, the actual wage cost of a particular country is not significant unless that wage cost is relatively high. The Rolfe and White (1992)[46] judgmental model of export-oriented Caribbean manufacturers evaluated the attractiveness of hypothetical Caribbean Basin countries and confirmed that a country's infrastructure and wages effected its attractiveness for export-oriented FDI. Empirical data from actual investors is needed to confirm investor preferences.

Rolfe et al (1993)[47] tested the investment incentive preferences of 103 U.S. corporate respondees with interest in 18 of the 35 Caribbean Basin countries (including Mexico and Central America). Utilizing 20 host country incentives on seven proposition, the data indicated the existence of investment incentive preference differences as between exporting firms and local market firms; startup, expansion and acquisition firms; the Caribbean Basin countries themselves; products; large and small investors; and year investment was made. No difference was detected as between firms with large or small labour forces.

The United Nation's Division of Transnational Corporations and Management (1992) noted the danger inherent in uniform systems potentially leading to sub-optimal results stemming from the application of equal rules to unequal entities. On the other hand, the report highlighted the case-by case drawbacks which lead to lack of clarity and simplicity for TNCs in making their initial assessment of a host country and to the potential for abuse inherent in a system granting wide discretionary powers for administrators. The Division report observed that striking a balance between simplicity and objectivity on the one hand, and the discretionary authority over how the criteria of an incentive system are to be applied on the other, might prove difficult to accomplish. The implication of need for research into potential alternative systems for achieving the better parts of both systems while limiting the drawbacks of each was evident.[48]

SUMMARY

The actions of at least one of the major forces involved in FDI - Government (both host and home) - demonstrably respond to multiple forces, including, but not limited to, economic forces. Correspondingly, at least one investigator (Davies, 1987)[49] has identified that management (another major force in FDI) may also react to forces other than those of "economic man". Davies observations appear to confirm Schollhammer's (1974)[50] observation re: the subjective considerations of decision makers playing a major role in location decisions. Since FDI behavior is subject to many forces outside the ambit of economic theory it would seem that a search should be made for identifying potential building blocks for use in evolving an overall theory of international business.

One aspect of FDI location criteria that would appear to be essential in building an international theory is the investment attraction process - both government action and MNC reaction. Since governments seek to "appropriately" distort markets in order to alter the distribution of gains, host governments have initiated a wide variety of laws, policies and investment incentives to attract MNCs to their territory on terms deemed acceptable by the governments. To what effect? Further, the "Investment Attraction Package" of each country can be defined as including conditions (real or perceived) concerning the country itself as well as the more obviously included incentives and restrictions.

It is potentially useful to the construction of an overall international business theory if it can be determined whether existing business theories (Transaction cost and investor motivation) have predictive value in determining what elements of a developing country's investment attraction package are favored or disfavored by MNCs. Such information could be useful not only in formulating policies for attracting MNCs but also in determining avenues potentially available for altering the distribution of gains.

The growth needs (and, hence, capital, skills, and technology needs) of small countries with small markets, low growth, little scope for new raw material investment, and possessing abundant, low cost, potentially trainable labour have long been recognized but little researched in the specifics of investment-attraction. Over the years, the great bulk of FDI research tended to focus on the countries (developed and developing) that provided larger markets and growing GNP. The debate centered on the reasons why, the value of, and incentives for FDI. Pride of place went to analysis of host markets - the major motivator for FDI - with raw material relegated to the sidelines and cost reduction receiving only an occasional nod of acquaintance. The relatively recent rise of MNC global product strategy and global sourcing, especially of intermediate products, has led to the rediscovery of cost reduction as a motivation for FDI - clearly recognizable in its new wrapper of "export-oriented market". Outsourcing is based primarily upon the cost advatages offered by a particular host country for a particular component. The maker of the component (affiliate or sub-contractor) does not "stand alone" but depends upon the parent firm for key activities and the parent firm depends upon the outsource for part of its overall value chain.(Gold, 1993).[51] Rediscovered too, are the potential locations for cost reduction FDI - the developing countries.

In this emerging environment, the surveyed literature reflects little attempt to discover discrete units of investors possessing homogeneous attributes and investment attraction preferences. A need exists for identifying the FDI micro-groups existing within the host country framework for the purpose of determining if the package of attraction preferences change with the established profile of the various micro-groups constituting the host country's foreign investor population. Should the package of preferences change with individual micro-group profile, then a series of opportunities will potentially be opened for both host country and MNC, i.e., the potential will exist that host country funds for some incentives are being "wasted" on some FDI entrants and that FDI is not attracted in other cases because the "standard" package was inappropriate to the MNC's needs. The need is to identify micro-groups exhibiting similar investor profile and preferences. Given identification, the prospects for improving both FDI cost efficiency for the host country and FDI benefit efficiency for the MNC may be enhanced.

---

[1]Buckley, P. 1989. *The multinaional enterprise: Theory and applications*. London: MacMillan Press, p. 115.
[2]Weekly, J. and Aggarwal, R. 1989. *International business. Operating in the global economy*. Orlando, FL.: Dryden Press, p.86.

[3]Clegg, J. 1992. "Explaining foreign direct investment flows" in *Multinational enterprises in the world economy*. Peter Buckley and Marc Casson, Hants: Edward Elgar, p.72.

[4]Grosse, Robert. 1980. *Foreign investment codes and the location of direct investment*. N.Y.: Praeger, p.12.

[5]Woodward, D. and Rolfe, R. 1993. "The location of export oriented foreign direct investment in the Caribbean basin". *Journal of International Business Studies*, Vol.24, No.1, p. 121.

[6]Larimo, Jorma. 1993. *Foreign direct investment behavior and performance*. Finland: Acta Wasaensia, University of Vaasa, p.33.

[7]Porter, M. 1990. *The Competitive Advantage of Nations*. N.Y.; Free Press.

[8]Dunning, J. 1994. "Reappraising the eclectic paradigm, in an age of alliance capitalism". Newark, New Jersey: Rutgers University. Mimeograph.

[9]*Ibid*. p.29.

[10]Shah, S. and Toye, J. 1978. "Fiscal incentives for firms in some developing countries: Survey and critique" in *Taxation and Economic Development*. J.F.T.Toye (Ed.), London: Frank Cass, p.209.

[11]Lim, D. 1983. "Fiscal incentives and direct foreign investment in less developed countries". *Journal of Development Studies*. Jan. pp. 207-12.

[12]Kumar, N. 1994. "Determinants of export orientation of Foreign production by U.S. multinationals: An inter-country analysis". *Journal of International Biusiness Studies*. Vol.25, No.1, Fall, 1st Qt., 1994., p. 150.

[13]Reuber, G.,Crookell,H.,Emerson,M., and Gallais-Hamonno, G. 1973. *Private foreign investment in development*. Oxford: Clarendon Press, p.22.

[14]Root, F.R and Ahmed, A. 1978. "The influence of policy instruments on Mmnufacturing foreign direct investment in developing countries". *Journal of International Business Studies*, Vol 9, No.3, pp. 81-94.

[15]Group of Thirty. 1984, *Foreign direct investment 1973-87*. N.Y.: Group of Thirty, p.31.

[16]Guisinger, S. 1985. *Investment incentives and performance requirements: patterns of international trade, production and investment*. Westport, CN.: Praeger, Greenwood Press, p.48.

[17]Reuber et al. 1973. *op cit*, p.131

[18]Wint, A. 1988. *Investment promotion: How governments compete for foreign direct investment*. PhD Dissertation Abstract, Boston: Harvard University.

[19]Contractor, F. 1990. "Government policies towards foreign investment. An empirical investigation of the link between national policies and FDI flows". A paper presented to Annual Conference, Academy of International Business. Miami: p. 21.

[20]Contractor, F. 1991. "Government policies and foreign direct investment". *UNCTC Studies, Series No. 17*, N.Y.: United Nations, p.23.

[21]Cable, V. and Persaud, B. 1987. "New trends and policy problems in foreign investment: The experience of Commonwealth developing countries" in *Developing With Foreign Investment*. The Commonwealth Secretariat, Kent : Croom Helm Ltd, p. 11.

[22]Root and Ahmed. 1978. *op cit*, p.87.

[23]Evans, T., and Doupnik, T. 1986. "Foreign exchange risk management under Standard 53.83". Stamford, CN.: *Financial Accounting Standards Board*.

[24]Guisinger. 1985. *op cit*, p. 41.

[25]Root and Ahmed. 1978. *op cit*, p. 87.

[26]Guisinger. 1985. *op cit*, pp.26.

[27]Robock, S.H. and Simmonds, K. 1989. *International business and multinational enterprises*. 4th Ed., Homewood, IL.: Irwin, p. 543.

[28]Shaw and Toye. 1978. *op cit*, p. 209.

[29]Guisinger. 1985. *op cit*, p. 7.

[30]*Ibid.* p. 24.

[31]Cable and Persaud. 1978. *op cit*, p. 11.

[32]Contractor. 1990. *op. cit*, p. 26

[33]Rueber et al. 1973. *op cit*, p. 14.

[34]Behrman, J. 1974. *Decision criteria for foreign investment in Latin America.* N.Y.: Council of the Americas, p. 2.

[35]Lecraw, D. 1992. "Multinational enterprises and developing countries" in *New Directions in International Business,: Research for the 1990s*, Peter Buckley (Ed.), Hants: Elgar, p.46.

[36]Rolfe, R.; Ricks, D.; Pointer, M.; and McCarthy, M. 1993. "Determinants of FDI preferences of MNEs". *Journal of International Business Studies*, Vol 24, No. 2 (Spring, 1993), p.352.

[37]Guisinger. 1985. *op cit*, p.29.

[38]United Nations. 1992. *Formulation and implementation of foreign investment policies. Selected key issues.* N.Y.: Transnational and Management Division, Department of Economic and Social Development, p. 64.

[39]Helleiner, G. 1987. "Direct foreign investment and manufacturing for export: A review of the issues", in *Developing With Foreign Investment*. The Commonwealth Secretariat, Kent: Croom Helm, Ltd, p. 76.

[40]Gusinger. 1985. *op cit*, p. 34.

[41]Woodward, D. and Rolfe, R. 1993. "The location of export oriented foreign direct investment in the Caribbean basin". *Journal of International Business Studies*, Vol.24, No.1, p. 121.

[42]Wells, L. 1986. "Investment incentives: An unnecessary debate." *CTC Reporter*, Autumn, pp. 58-60.

[43]Austin, J. 1990. *Managing in developing countries.* N.Y.: Free Press.

[44]Kumar, N. 1994. *op cit*, p.148.

[45]Woodward and Rolfe. 1993. *op cit*, p.128.

[46]Rolfe, R., and White, R. 1992. "The influence of tax incentives in determining the location of foreign direct investment in developing countries." *Journal of American Taxation Association*, Vol.13, No. 2, pp. 39-57.

[47]Rolfe et al. 1993. op cit, p.342.

[48]United Nations 1992. *World investment report 1992: Transnational corporations as engines of growth.* N.Y.: Transnational Corporations and Management Division, Department of Economic and Social Development, p.65.

[49]Davies, L. 1987. *Senior managerial perceptions of the foreign direct investment decision.* PhD Thesis, University of Bradford, Management Centre.

[50]Schollhammer, H. 1974. *Location strategies of multinational firms.* Los Angles, CA.: Center for Business, Pepperdine University.

[51]Gold, D. 1993. "World investment report 1993:Transnational corporations and integrated international production. An executive summary". *Transnational Corporations*, Vol.2, No.2, Aug., 1993. p.113.

CHAPTER V

WHERE TO TEST?

Barbados, Jamaica, and Trinidad-Tobago

> *"The Caribbean was borne like an elliptical basin*
> *in the hands of acolytes, and a people were absolved*
> *of a history which they did not commit"*
>
> Derek Walcott
> *The Star-Apple Kingdom*

Situated between the land masses of North and South America, bordered to the West by Central America and to the East by the Atlantic ocean, rests the Caribbean Sea. (See Figure 5.1) The Caribbean washes many islands which have been arranged by the forces of history into 16 nation states and 13 dependencies, possessions, and territories. (Deere, et al, 1990).[1] The Caribbean Economic Community (CARICOM), a common market made up of the English-speaking nations of the region, represents the region's only operating trade arrangement. The membership of CARICOM consists of Antigua and Barbuda, the Bahamas, Barbados, Belize, Dominica, Grenada, Guyana, Jamaica, Montserrat, St. Kitts-Nevis, St. Lucia, St. Vincent, and Trinidad-Tobago.(Worrell, 1987).[2] Total population served by CARICOM countries is approximately 5.8 million (1990). Administered as colonies of Great Britain until the 1950s, the islands traded primarily with the U.K. Coinciding with the ending of colonial rule came the development of new economic activity, such as bauxite mining and tourism, which led to a shift in the orientation of economic relations towards the U.S. The CARICOM countries continue to export the traditional agricultural products to the U.K., such as bananas and sugar, but their principal market for the dominant foreign exchange earning sectors - mining, tourism and manufacturing - is the U.S. As a group, CARICOM countries tend to produce a narrow range of commodities for export and import a wide diversity of goods - both finished and intermediate.

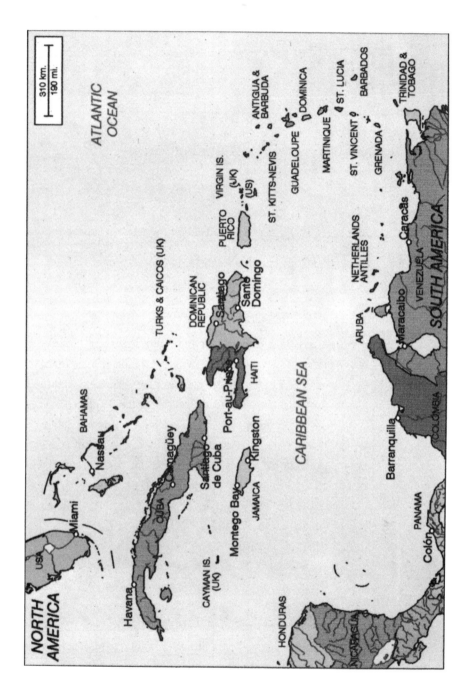

FIGURE 5.1   THE CARIBBEAN SEA
Map reproduced from P.C. Globe, Maps N Facts. Copyright 1993. Broderbund
Software, Inc.

Their economies depend heavily on exports to generate foreign exchange to support the import spending. (Worrell, 1987)[3].

The island nations of Barbados, Jamaica, and Trinidad-Tobago are the focus, or "trial horses", of this study of MNC preferences for the investment attraction packages offered by developing countries. These nation-states represent a small, large and medium size economy in the English-speaking Caribbean, a sub-region of the hemisphere that is composed entirely of "developing" countries. All three subject countries have historical, political and economic ties to the U.K. and historical, proximity and economic ties to the U.S. The Caribbean itself is regarded as a sub-region of Latin America by The World Bank. Latin America as a whole experienced Gross Domestic Product growth of -0.1%, 3.7% and 2.9% for the years 1990, 1991, and 1992 ,respectively, whereas the growth experienced by the sub-region of the Caribbean over the same period was -0.9%, -0.2% and 0.3%. The Caribbean accounts for less than 3% of the total GDP of the Latin America group. (Inter-American Development Bank, 1993).[4]

INTRODUCTION TO HOST COUNTRIES

The economies of Barbados and Trinidad-Tobago are classified by the World Bank as upper middle-income countries. Jamaica is classified as a lower middle-income country. The per capita income groups are defined by the World Bank (1992) as: low-income, $610 or less per annum in 1990 ; lower-middle income, $611-$2,465; upper-middle-income, $2,466-$7,619; and high-income, $7,620 or more. .(World Development Report, 1992).[5] The following is a brief "thumb-nail" sketch of the three countries:

Barbados

Geography

Barbados is regarded as being a Caribbean territory although it is actually in the Atlantic. As such, it is the most easterly island of the Caribbean being located some 1200 miles southeast of Miami, Florida. Its land mass covers an area of 166 square miles and is generally flat with a slight rise in the center. Located 13 degrees north of the equator, its climate is typically tropical with steady trade winds moderating the extremes of heat.[6]

Demographics

Population in 1992 was estimated as 264,000[7], predominantly of African descent, with a small minority descended from Britain, India and Middle East countries. English is the common language. Education is based on the British model and is compulsory from ages 5 -16. (Price Waterhouse, 1989)[8]. Per capita income in 1992 was approximately U.S. $5,586 (IDB, 1993)[9].

Political Development

Arawak Indians of South America were the first known inhabitants. They departed prior to British arrival in 1627. Barbados remained a British colony until it became an independent nation within the British Commonwealth in 1966. It is a member of the United Nations; the Organization of American States; The African, Caribbean and Pacific group of countries; the Commonwealth; and the Caribbean Common Market (CARICOM).

The Barbadian political system is modeled on the Westminster Parliament, i.e., bicameral, with the Prime Minister as Head of Government and the Governor-General as Head of State. The legal system is derived from the English common law and statutes.

Economic Development

Barbados presents a small economy utilizing a market-oriented economic system grounded in private ownership and international trade. The economy is based on four key industries: tourism, agriculture, manufacturing and off-shore financial services. Mining and quarrying are limited but sufficient petroleum and natural gas is produced to meet approximately 50% of domestic needs. (USDOC, 1993).[10] The tourist industry is the principal source of foreign exchange earnings with the second major source being offshore business services. Sugar is the major agricultural export and manufacturing is composed of relatively small, closely held manufacturing and import substitution enterprises. Barbados imports most products including inputs for the manufacturing industry as well as for domestic consumption. (USDOC, 1993)[11]

In addition to CARICOM membership, Barbados is a beneficiary of the Lome Convention with the European Community, the Generalized System of Preferences (GSP), the Caribbean Basin Initiative (CBI) legislation of the U.S., and CARIBCAN, a Canadian incentive program. (Price Waterhouse, 1989)[12]

Jamaica

Geography

Jamaica is located 18 degrees north of the equator in the Caribbean Sea, some 588 miles southwest of Miami, Florida. Its land mass covers an area of 4,411 square miles, with a mountainous central spine and broad coastal plains. Its climate is typically tropical with little seasonal variation in temperature and virtually no extremes of heat. (Price Waterhouse, 1993)[13].

Demographics

Population in 1992 was estimated as 2,469,000[14], predominantly of African descent, with a small minority descended from Britain, India and Middle East countries. English is the common language. Education is based on the British model and is compulsory from ages 5 -16. 1992 per capita income was approximately U.S.$1,457 (IDB, 1993).[15] Jamaica is the largest English-speaking country in the Caribbean.(Price Waterhouse, 1993).[16]

Political Development

Arawak Indians of South America were the first known inhabitants. Initially colonized by the Spanish, the island was conquered by the British in 1655. Jamaica remained a British colony until it became an independent nation within the British Commonwealth in 1962. It is a member of the United Nations; the Organization of American States; The African, Caribbean and Pacific group of countries; the Commonwealth; and the Caribbean Common Market (CARICOM).

The Jamaican political system is modeled on the Westminster Parliament, i.e., bicameral, with the Prime Minister as Head of Government and the Governor-General as Head of State. Although the legal system is derived from the English common law and statutes, Jamaica has its own Constitution.

Economic Development

Jamaica presents a relatively small economy essentially utilizing a market-oriented economic system grounded in private ownership and international trade. The economy is based on four key industries: tourism, bauxite/alumina, agriculture, and manufacturing. Jamaica has no petroleum or natural gas production. (USDOC, 1993).[17] The tourist industry is the principal source of foreign exchange earnings with the second major source being bauxite/alumina. Sugar is the major agricultural export and manufacturing is composed of relatively small, closely held manufacturing and import substitution enterprises. Jamaica is highly dependent upon imports for both production and consumption.(USDOC, 1993)[18]

In addition to CARICOM membership, Jamaica is a beneficiary of the Lome Convention with the European Community, the Generalized System of Preferences (GSP), the Caribbean Basin Initiative (CBI) legislation of the U.S., and CARIBICAN, a Canadian incentive program. (Price Waterhouse).[19]

Trinidad-Tobago

Geography

Trinidad and Tobago is located 10 and 12 degrees north of the equator in the Caribbean Sea, some 1300 miles southeast of Miami, Florida. Trinidad's land mass covers an area of 1864 square miles, while Tobago (20 miles northeast of Trinidad) has a land mass of 116 square miles. The two islands form one political and administrative entity. Trinidadian terrain is approximately one-half covered by tropical forests, with low lying mountain ranges crossing east to west and with coast partly swampy. Tobago features a main ridge along the center descending to flat coastal lands. The climate is typically tropical with steady trade winds moderating the extremes of heat.(Price Waterhouse, 1991)[20]

Demographics

Population in 1992 was estimated as 1,265,000[21], with ethnic division evenly proportioned between those of African and those of East Indian descent, plus a small minority having British or Chinese ancestry. English is the common language, although some French, Spanish, Chinese, Hindi and Urdu are also spoken. Education is based on the British model and is compulsory from ages 6 - 16.(Price Waterhouse,1991)[22] . Per capita income in 1992 was approximately U.S.$4,188. (IDB, 1993).[23]

Political Development

Arawak Indians of South America were the first known inhabitants. Trinidad was initially colonized by the Spanish in 1592, the French were given immigration facilities in the late 18th century and the island was captured without resistance by the British in 1797. Tobago was settled by the Dutch, followed by the English and then the French. The island changed hands frequently and final British sovereignty was established in 1803. Trinidad and Tobago were joined politically in 1899 and remained a British colony until it became an independent nation within the British Commonwealth in 1962 and a Republic within the Commonwealth in 1976. It is a member of the United Nations; the Organization of American States; The African, Caribbean and Pacific group of countries; the Commonwealth; and the Caribbean Common Market (CARICOM).

The Trinidad-Tobago political system is modeled on the Westminster Parliament, i.e., bicameral, with the Prime Minister as Head of Government and the President as Head of State. Although the legal system is derived from the English common law and statutes, Trinidad-Tobago has its own Constitution.

Economic Development

Following the oil boom of the early 1970s, Trinidad-Tobago embarked on a capital expenditure programme designed to create a "mixed economy", via increasing state participation in the productive sector. The economy is based primarily on oil, gas and downstream petrochemical industries, (30% of GDP).(USDOC, 1993)[24] Agriculture accounts for 2+% of GDP while employing

12% of the labour force. Tourism is minimal though growing. Trinidad-Tobago has a highly import dependent economy in spite of an emphasis on import substitution. Its imports, however, are concentrated primarily into a few areas, i.e., petroleum and steel industry supplies. (USDOC, 1993)[25]

In addition to CARICOM membership, Trinidad-Tobago is a beneficiary of the Lome Convention with the European Community, the Generalized System of Preferences (GSP), the Caribbean Basin Initiative (CBI) legislation of the U.S., and CARIBICAN, a Canadian incentive program. (Price Waterhouse, 1991)[26]

Summary Comparison

All three host countries present small economies with a limited range of export alternatives and a large diversity of import requirements. As members of the British colonial system, the three countries possess similar historical and political backgrounds . The ethnic distribution of Trinidad-Tobago differs due to plantation owner reaction to the 1834 abolition of slavery whence the plantation owners turned to contract-indentured labourers from India. With the exception of the common export industry of agriculture (a dwindling base for export earnings), the three share few export similarities: Trinidad-Tobago exports petroleum products; Jamaica exports bauxite/alumina; Barbados has no natural resources for export. Barbados and Jamaica have capitalized on their natural endowments and possess well developed tourist industries. Trinidad-Tobago has more recently shown interest in developing this endowment. Host country market size is small to very small (Jamaica, Trinidad-Tobago, and Barbados, in population size order). Tariff and non-tariff barriers were erected by each of the counties to protect domestic producers. The extent of protection varied by country, and the protection is currently in varying stages of dismantlement. However, the legacy of protection - an uncompetitive manufacturing base - lives on, in varying degrees, in each of the countries. All three countries have substantial unemployment and the reduction of same is a priority with each of the governments.

See Table 5.1, "Summary of Selected Indicator: - Barbados, Jamaica, Trinidad-Tobago".

FDI AND THE HOST COUNTRIES
Host Country Perceptions of FDI
From Pre-Independence to the 1970s

Prior to Independence, the subject host countries generally followed the British approach to foreign direct investment, which might best be described as neutral/positive. Motivation for FDI was primarily to circumvent prohibitive tariff and non-tariff barriers designed to protect domestic producers or to obtain access to

Table 5.1
Summary of Selected Indicators

RF		Barbados	Jamaica	Trinidad-Tobago
RF	Size:			
1	Sq. Miles	166	4411	1980
2	Population (000) ('92)	264	2469	1265
1	Location	13N/	18N/	10N/
1	Political System	Westminster Model	Westminster Model	Westminster Model
1	Independence	1966	1962	1962
1	Legal System	Derived-Engl. C.L.	Derived-Engl. C.L.	Derived-Engl. C.L.
1	Language	English	English	English
1	Education System	English Model	English Model	English Model
2	GDP per Capita ('92)	U.S.$5586	U.S.$1457	US$4188
	GDP Growth Rate/Cap.			
2	'70-'80	1.7%	-2.9%	4.4%
2	'80-'90	1.1%	0.9%	-4.2%
2	'90-'92	-3.6%	-1.1%	0.6%
	Unemployment			
3	89	15.5%	17.2%	22.4%
3	90	15.0%	15.3%	20.1%
3	91	18.0%	15.0%	18.0%
			(37% self employed	
			of total employed)	
	Consumer Price Increase			
4	'80-'90	5.4%	18.3%	7.5%
2	'90	3.1%	22.0%	11.0%
2	'91	6.2%	51.1%	3.8%
2	'92	6.0%	77.3%	6.5%
	Avg. Annual Growth Rate-Gross Domestic Investment			
2	'70-'80	1.3%	-9.4%	16.6%
2	'80-'90	-0.2%	6.2%	-12.4%
2	'90-'92	-35.6%	0.4%	7.6%
	Foreign Direct Investment Inflows- Net (Millions U.S.$)			
5	'87	$4.6	$53.5	$33.1
5	'88	$10.6	($12.0)	$62.9
5	'89	$5.4	$57.1	$148.9
5	'90	$9.9	$137.9	$109.4
5	'91	$21.0	$68.4	$144.1
5	'92	$17.2	$101.0	$155.1
	1992 ($MM)			
2	GDP	$1,444	$3,599	$5,296
3	External Public Debt	$540	$3,874	$2,507

RF:
1. Doing Business in Barbados (1989), Jamaica (1993), Trinidad (1991), Price Waterhouse.
2. Economic and Social Progress in Latin America, 1993 Report, Inter-American Development Bank, Wash. D.C.. Tables A-1, B-2, pp. 35,121,167, Table B-5.
3. Economic and Trade Policy - Barbados, Jamaica, Trinidad-Tobago, USDOC, International Trade Administration, Wash. D.C. ETP920300, Apr 24, 1993.
4. World Development Report 1992, Development and the Environment. The World Bank, Oxford University Press, pp.284,306.
5. "Direct Foreign Investment to Caribbean Countries, 1980-92", IMF Balance of Payments Statistics. Source: National Governments and IBRD. Courtesy of Badrul Haque, LA3 Caribbean Division, The World Bank, via fax dated May 20, 1994.

natural resource and agricultural inputs for further processing in another country. The motivation of cost reduction for its own sake was relatively rare and the cost reduction features of export-oriented investments had not yet evolved. FDI was generally welcomed as being a "good" thing for the country but little in the way of special treatment, incentives, or restrictions were thought to be necessary or prudent for attracting or controlling FDI. All three countries had experienced economic growth during the 1960s and the 1970s were expected to continue or increase the growth trend.

During the waning days of the 1960s and early 1970s a number of events occurred that had global economic impact. Two of the more catalytic events were the 1971 U.S. dollar devaluation and the 1973 OPEC led oil price increase. (Worrell, 1987).[27] The twin catalysts were accompanied by a rising level of world inflation. For import-dependent small nations, the global effects of the former heightened economic instability and created a drain on reserves. The effect of the latter depended upon the energy sufficiency of the nation. These events and their many tenacled effects, together with the growing recognition of the activities and goals of MNCs, helped set the framework for the host countries perceptions of FDI in the 1970s and 1980s. Chapter 3 reviews the debate on these differing perceptions of MNCs and FDI. The debate reached its zenith in the mid-70s, at the time the developing nations were struggling to adjust to the effects of the changing times. As the perception of FDI and its value evolved over the period, so too did legislation that reflected the perceptions formed by the individual countries.

The 1970s-'80s

Barbados

With the advent of CARICOM's call for harmonization of fiscal incentives, Barbados incorporated their previous investment incentive measures into the Fiscal Incentives Act of 1974 (FIA). The Act provided for tax benefits which lowered the operating costs and increased the investment return of "approved enterprises" that produced "approved products". Export incentives were made available to companies which did not receive benefits under the FIA. These benefits depended upon the percentage of non-CARICOM exports to total sales and provided for percentage rebate of taxes up to 50%. (Worrell, et al, 1987)[28]

Jamaica

Until mid-1974, government reacted to the impact of the unfavorable changes in external circumstances by tightening expenditure controls and the prior FDI posture remained in tact.

"This policy was abruptly abandoned in 1974 and replaced by an attempt at counter cyclical expansion, largely via government activity. Funding was secured by unilaterally imposing an increased bauxite production levy. Receipts from the levy....were diverted to a crash program of expanded government employment.....The situation was made worse by experiments with socialized production in agriculture which depressed output.". (Worrell, 1987).[29]

Legislation to recover patrimony and control over the "commanding heights" of the economy was directed at the raw materials motivated MNCs. Tourism, ever sensitive to social and political factors, declined by 33% between 1975-77 and leading hotel chains sold their equity interests - primarily to government (who had guaranteed the loans for the hotel operators). The state became the major investor in the economy. Government corporations were set up to deal with a number of the foreign export markets. From the early 1980s, divestment of state ownership was attempted in the tourist industry and by the mid-1980s substantial FDI incentive legislation had been passed.

Trinidad-Tobago

In a 1972 White Paper (Third Five Year Plan), the government announced that certain sectors of the economy (i.e. utilities) would be closed to wholly- or majority-owned foreign investment. Soon thereafter, oil revenues increased and the perceived need for FDI decreased. The state became the major investor in the economy and relationships with foreign corporations were sought as contractors, consultants and, occasionally, as joint venture partners. With the slackening of the oil revenues in the early 1980s, a renewed interest in FDI was aroused. However, the government remained wary of foreign ownership of land, and sought speedier technology transfer and protection of employment opportunities for nationals via an aggressive application of "work permit" policies. (Trevor and Farrell, 1987)[30]

Summary of the Era's FDI Perceptions.

The 1965-90 average growth rate of the GNP of Barbados, Jamaica, and Trinidad-Tobago was 2.3%, (1.3%), and 0.0% respectively. (World Development Report 1992).[31] Revenue from oil and refining made Trinidad-Tobago the only country in the region to make economic gains in the 1970s. Maintenance in output growth slowed in 1978 and ceased in 1983. (Worrell, 1987).[32] Other Caribbean economies suffered bouts of economic instability in the 1970s, but none so prolonged or severe as for Jamaica and Guyana. (Worrell, 1987)[33]

In previous studies of investment in the Caribbean, social and political climate have been placed high on the list of considerations used by MNCs in determining FDI location. Those countries which have experienced political or social unrest have experienced FDI decline. In reference to the 1970s and 1980s, Worrell (1987) makes the following conclusions:

"The deterioration of the political and social climate in Jamaica is partly to blame for the decline in foreign investment there... In Trinidad and Tobago private investment was not viewed with much enthusiasm, particularly when oil revenues were high. Only Barbados actively continued to solicit foreign investment with some success." [34]

As the oil revenue continued its nine year decline for Trinidad-Tobago and as Jamaica struggled to find more effective policies for the relief of its many problems, both countries began to realign their policies with respect to FDI.

FDI Stock and the Host Countries.

World-wide, the accumulated total stock of FDI reached the $2 trillion mark in 1992. However, for the first time since 1982, the annual world-wide outflows of FDI declined in 1991 and declined further in 1992. Most of the decline was attributed to the economic downturn in Japan and Western Europe, with the outflow from the two home countries involved in this study - the U.S. and the U.K. - remaining unchanged. From the developing country perspective, their share of FDI received exceeded 25% in 1991 and further increased to an estimated $40 billion in 1992. All parts of the developing world received some increase, including the Latin America - Caribbean region. It is felt that MNCs have been attracted to the region by its economic recovery, liberalization of FDI policies and, in many countries, privatization opportunities. (UNCTAD, 1993)[35]. Preliminary reports of UNCTAD place developing country share of world FDI outflow for the years 1992 and 1993 as having grown to 33% and 37% respectively. (Financial Times, 1994).[36] Although the percentage increase may have more to do with the lowered base than an absolute increase, absolute increase there has been and the subject host countries of Barbados, Jamaica, and Trinidad-Tobago appear to have participated in varying degrees. (See Table 5.1, "Summary of Selected Indicators: Barbados, Jamaica, Trinidad-Tobago" for the Net FDI Inflow trend of the three countries for the six year period 1987- 1992). Although the accuracy of current inflow/outflow data on FDI in the subject countries is most encouraging, historical data for affixing the total stock of FDI in each of the countries is less encouraging. Recapture of unregistered information from bygone years is problematic at best. The unpublished manuscript of UNCTAD for the Latin American/Caribbean region section of the "World Investment Directory" is reported to contain data that is quite dated and its reliability apparently suffers from unavailability of appropriate historical records. (Brandwayn, 1994).[37]

FDI Receptivity of the Host Countries In the 1990s
Current Perceptions of FDI

Until recently, the extent of government influence in the economy was roughly similar in Trinidad-Tobago and Jamaica, where government owned all public utilities and a number of large businesses. Government direct influence on the economy was somewhat less in Barbados. (Worrell, 1987). In the early 1990s privatization of some government held public-enterprise assets commenced in Jamaica and in Barbados. By 1993, 90% of Jamaica's state-owned enterprises had been subject to privatization. This percentage of privatized state-owned firms, of which almost 25% involved FDI, constitutes the largest proportion of any developing country and may account for as much as 40% of the FDI inflows into Jamaica in recent years. (UNCTAD, 1993).[38]

Barbados, Jamaica, and Trinidad-Tobago are members of the Caribbean Common Market (CARICOM), the region's only operating trade arrangement. Agreement was reached in 1991 on a new common external tariff structure, which has been generally accepted by most members, but the new tariffs have a range of 0% to 45%, with high duties being placed on goods that compete with domestic producers within the CARICOM. Further, many members have added surcharges, stamp duties, etc., to the basic external tariff, thereby further raising protection for certain industries, encouraging costly import-substitution regimes and discouraging the efficiencies required for extra-regional exports. (World Bank, 1992).[39]

Current Host Country FDI Legislation.

The rapidly changing socio-economic and political atmosphere of the late 1980s - early 1990s have led to a general liberalization of host country laws, regulations and incentives affecting FDI locational decision-making. In addition, for the Caribbean, there is a fear that multilateral trade liberalization will narrow or eliminate their preferential trade margins, leading to a reduction of their exports. (World Bank, 1992).[40] The foreboding is particularly strong with reference to the North American Free Trade Agreement - NAFTA - which links the economies of the U.S., Canada and Mexico. The subject host countries of Barbados, Jamaica, and Trinidad-Tobago have each reacted to the global and regional economic influences by liberalizing their respective Investment Attraction Packages, in varying degrees.

The Caribbean countries utilized for testing the initial investment/transaction costs/strategic motivation research model for examining the MNC preferences each have their own laws, regulations, incentives and economic environment. It is beyond the scope of this study to attempt an evaluation of the efficiency or effectiveness of their specific investment attraction packages. They are what they are. Their effectiveness is a matter of concern to the individual country's government and to the MNCs they attempt to attract. Without regard for what they currently are, and with acknowledgment that much effort has gone into the work of improving them, the inward bound annual FDI being recorded by each of the focus countries would indicate that more remains to be done. However, with apologies to the Great Bard, what's done is done but can be undone if present results are not to the liking of those involved. To this end, the summaries in Figures 10.1 and 10.2 may be of some assistance.

---

[1]Deere, C.; Antrobus, P.; Bolles, L.; Melendez, E.; Phillips, P.; Rivera, M.; Safa, H. 1990. *In the shadows. Caribbean development alternatives and U.S. policy.* Bolder, CO.: Pecca, Westview Press, p.6.

[2]Worrell, D. 1987. *Small island economies. Structure and performance in the English-speaking Caribbean since 1970.* Westport, CN.: Praeger, Greenwood Press, p. 1.

[3]Ibid, p.1.

[4]Inter-American Development Bank. 1993. *Economic and social progress in Latin America, 1993 report.* Special Section: Human Resources, Wash. D.C.: p.7.

[5]The World Bank. 1992. *World development report 1992. Development and the environment.* Oxford: University Press, p.306.

[6]Price Waterhouse. 1989. *Doing business in Barbados.* p.1.

[7]Inter-American Development Bank. 1993. *op cit*, Table A-1.

[8]Price Waterhouse. 1989. *op cit*, p. 3.

[9]Inter-American Development Bank. 1993. *op cit*, p.263.

[10]U.S. Department of Commerce. 1993. *Barbados - economic and trade policy - ETP920300.* Wash., D.C.: International Trade Administration, Market Research Reports, Apr. 24, 1993.,

[11]Ibid.

[12]Price Waterhouse. 1989. *op cit*, p.10.

[13]Price Waterhouse. 1993. *Doing business in Jamaica.* p.1.

[14]Inter-American Development Bank. 1993. *op cit*, Table A-1.

[15]Inter-American Development Bank. 1993, *op cit*, p. 263.

[16]Price Waterhouse. 1993. *op cit*, p. 3.

[17]U.S. Department of Commerce. 1993. *Jamaica - foreign economic trends - FET9211.* Wash., D.C.: International Trade Administration, Market Research Reports, Apr. 24, 1993.

[18]U.S. Department of Commerce. 1993. *Jamaica - economic and trade policy - ETP920300.* Wash, D.C.: International Trade Administration, Market Research Reports, Apr. 24, 1993.

[19]Price Waterhouse. 1993. *op cit*, p.10.

[20]Price Waterhouse. 1991. *Doing business in Trinidad and Tobago.* p.1.

[21]Inter-American Development Bank. 1993. *op cit*, Table A-1.

[22]Price Waterhouse. 1991. *op cit*, p. 3.

[23]Inter-American Development Bank. 1993. *op cit*, p.263.

[24]U.S. Department of Commerce. 1993. *Trinidad - economic and trade policies - ETP920300.* USDOC, Wash., D.C.: International Trade Administration, Market Research Reports, Apr. 24, 1993.

[25]Ibid.

[26]Price Waterhouse. 1991. *op cit*, p.10.

[27]Worrell. 1987. *op cit,* p. 115.

[28]Worrell, D.; Coderington, H.; Khan, Z.; Lawson, M. 1987. "Private foreign investment in Barbados". *Developing With Foreign Investment.* London: Croom Helm, p. 122-142.

[29]Worrell. 1987. *op cit*, p.116.

[30]Trevor, M.A. and Farrell. 1987. "Direct foreign investment, The transnational corporation and the prospects for LDC transformation in today's world: Lessons from the Trinidad-Tobago experience" in *Developing With Foreign Investment.* London: Croom Helm, p.221-44.

[31]The World Bank. 1992. *op cit*, pp.284,218.

[32]Worrell. 1987. *op cit*, p.42.

[33]Worrell. 1987. *op cit*, p.8.

[34]Worrell. 1987. *op cit*, p. 42.

[35]UNCTAD. 1993. *World investment report, 1993. Transnational corporations and integrated international production.* N.Y.: pp.13-15.

[36]Williams, F. 1994. "Poorer countries grab more investment". London: *Financial Times,* May, 4, 1994.

[37]Brandwayn, Susan. 1994. Advisory Service for International Business, Transnational Corporations and Investment Division, N.Y.: UNCTAD, Private telephone conversation with Edward Coyne, May 20, 1994.

[38]UNCTAD. 1993. *World investment report, 1993. op cit* p. 53..

[39]The World Bank. 1992. *The World Bank annual report 1992.* Wash. D.C.: p. 148.

[40]The World Bank. 1992. *op cit,*p. 44.

CHAPTER VI

WHAT'S THE ROUTE ?

Study Methodology

"Nothing is so difficult but that it may be found out by seeking"

Publius Terentius Afer
(190-152 B.C.)

NATURE OF INFORMATION SOUGHT

The study sought information from primary sources (the MNCs themselves) as the nature of the information sought concerned the evaluations and judgments of individual firms and their officials relative to a series of specific items thought to be included in the FDI location-decision process. The information sought from the MNCs enabled segmentation of the MNCs into identifiable smaller groups (micro-groups) for the purpose of determining if the micro-groups had similar or different preferences to the preferences of the FDI group as a whole for the various elements of developing countries' investment attraction packages.

The information requested from the firm was capable of comparative analyses to determine relative and absolute importance accorded by the MNCs to a range of specified incentives, disincentives and conditions. In the examination of the individual firm's response to the range of specified attraction package items, a search was conducted to identify groupings of firms that felt differently from other firms about particular items of the attraction package. Should such groupings exist, variation in the importance attached to individual items by such discrete groups may suggest alterations of the attraction package by the developing countries for the purpose of enhancing the effectiveness of the investment attraction package. In this context, effectiveness is defined as potential for an increase in the present level of FDI received by the developing country, a mutually beneficial increase in the benefits received by the country and MNC from present FDI, an increase in the benefits received from FDI by one party to the transaction without detriment being experienced by the other, or any combination thereof .

Characteristics of Firms Contacted

The firms contacted were those U.S. and U.K. domiciled corporations with FDI in the countries of Barbados, Jamaica and/or Trinidad-Tobago. The number of MNCs with FDI in the focus countries and whose country of origin was other than the U.S. or U.K. was known to be few in 1993 and valid statistical comparison would not have been achievable. The contact was with the parent corporation in the U.S. or U.K. and not the subsidiary in the focus countries. Purpose of contact with the parent was that the initial FDI location-decision is generally a headquarters decision as the host country subsidiary may not yet exist. Further, it was felt that the perspective of the two levels of organization could be different and, to minimize country bias, the headquarters view was favored. Specifically, the perspective of the Chief Executive Officer of the firm or the Division Manager in charge of international operations was sought. This level of organizational influence was pursued on the basis that it most likely represented the firm's final authority on investment location decisions and that the position's endorsement of the decision would be critical in seeking any required Board of Directors approval for the investment.

The characteristics of the firms and their host country investment that were searched for evidence to segment the firms into discrete micro-groupings were principally those capital risk attributes suggested by transaction cost theory (non-trivial investment, redeployability and asset-transaction specificity); the strategic motivations for investing (market of host country, raw materials, cost reduction); dollar size of initial investment; corporate organization (type integration with subsidiary); and corporate and subsidiary location (U.S. or U.K., and Barbados, Jamaica or Trinidad-Tobago, respectively).

Wells (1986)[1], Contractor (1990)[2] and Woodward and Rolfe (1993)[3] point out that the effectiveness of incentives may depend upon the specific investor's situation. This study addresses the "specific" in the foregoing phrase "specific investor's situation" by introducing two (2) distinctions that, while noted by other researchers as "possibly" affecting MNC preferences, have rarely been utilized in reported empirical findings.

The study included only initial FDI into the three focus countries. The rationale is obvious: unless the initial investment is attracted, its expansion cannot exist. Brewer (1993)[4] gives examples of government FDI entry incentives increasing initial investments but not effecting reinvestment of subsequent earnings. Rolfe et al. (1993)[5] compared investor preferences of start-up investments to acquisition and expansion investments and found differences existed in respondees assessment of desirability. Xiaohong (1991)[6] showed theoretically and empirically that FDI consisting of retained earnings responded differently to tax policy than did fresh investment. The literature review for this study found little in the way of empirical research that examined the attractiveness of incentives separately for initial entry FDI and for expansion FDI. It was anticipated that the findings detailed in this study could be different from those of a study focusing only on expansion FDI (including expansion by acquisition) and different again from studies that have amalgamated the two types of investments.

This study segmented the different motivations for FDI and examined the preferences of MNCs for the elements of the Investment Attraction Package for each of the three motivations or strategies. Although a difference in perception based on motivation had been speculated by some, the findings of prior researchers have been reported as being based upon an amalgamation of all motivations (with comment focusing on host country market-seeking but frequently with notation reflecting that the other motivations were included and could respond differently) or upon a single motivation (for instance, cost reduction. Woodward and Rolfe, 1993[7]).

Survey Design

Conceptual Model

The model used in this study to analyze MNCs preferences for host country incentives/disincentives is based primarily on transaction cost theory (Williamson, 1986) and the strategic motivations for FDI (Buckley, 1989). These theories are reviewed in Chapter #2. Williamson assigns the key role in transaction cost theory to the capital risk elements of non-trivial investment, redeployability of assets and transaction-specificity of assets. These quantifiable elements of transaction cost theory may help explain the outward impetus propelling consideration of an FDI by the firm since they represent one branch of the economic foundation for the essential "make or buy" decision. Buckley spells out the firm's strategic motivations for FDI as the search for markets (host), for raw materials or for cost reduction (including export-oriented markets). The model assumes that the governance concerns interact continually with the firm's basic motivation for investment and that the decision tree is actualized by reference to specific location candidates, which, in turn, produce a specific "make or buy" decision. When the "make" decision involves ownership and control of facilities in another country, FDI is born. Search for differentiation in MNCs preferences for elements of the IAP based on industry attachment of the MNCs was not attempted. It was felt that the location-decision portion of the "make or buy" governance decision of MNCs with the same initial-investment motivation to invest would be sufficiently homogeneous and that the inclusion of other potential determinants could potentially and adversely   effect model complexity, replicability, and sample population .

The study hypothesized that the strength of the preferences of U.S. and U.K. MNCs for specific incentives/disincentives contained in the investment attraction packages of Barbados, Jamaica, and Trinidad-Tobago will be revealed by location of the firm on a matrix composed of the elements identified by transaction cost theory and FDI motivation. The specific reference points on the two-dimensional model were formed by the intersections of non-trivial investment (investment dollar size, or quantum) along one axis and the FDI strategic motivation elements of market, raw materials and cost reduction along the other axis.   The single capital risk element of "quantum" was employed in as much as it was believed to have a relatively fixed directional relationship with redeployability of assets and transaction-specificity of assets and therefore could be used as a single surrogate for the three transaction cost capital risk elements. This belief was tested as a hypothesis and found to be supported. Quantum was subdivided to indicate relative degrees of investment. The grid formed by strategic motivation and quantum rests on the single plane composed of initial investment with the result being initial investment segmented into six micro-groups of investors: small host country marketing-seeking, large host country market-seeking, small raw materials-seeking, large raw material-seeking, small cost reduction-seeking, and large cost reduction-seeking. (See Figure 1.1, "Foreign Direct Investment Stages).

Elements of Investment Attraction Package

The Investment Attraction Package of each focus country constitutes that compendium of incentives/disincentives presented by the country to potential foreign direct investors. Some of the elements believed to be included by MNCs in their evaluation of the attraction package are subject to the direct control of the government; for some, government control is indirect; and for a few, government control is virtually non-existent. The survey of the firms was conducted in order to obtain the relative and absolute reactions of firms to items presumed to be of potential importance to the firms in making FDI locational decisions. For purposes of identification, the collective of these items, which includes incentives disincentives and conditions, has been labeled a country's total Investment Attraction Package (IAP).

In preparation for drafting the survey instrument, entitled "Foreign Direct Investment in Barbados, Jamaica, and Trinidad-Tobago - Postal Interview", review of the following work was particularly helpful: draft of a proposed 1992 "The World Bank Direct Investment Survey", which sought investment quantum information as well as investor reaction to host country conditions[8]; Guisinger (1985) provided an extensive listing of incentives/disincentives together with an estimate of effect on after-tax MNC returns[9]; the Contractor (1990) categorization of FDI policy changes in seven principle attributes[10]; Bradberry (1986) listing of incentives/disincentives and motivation for investment [11]; and Wallace (1990) survey of critical elements faced by direct investors in developing countries[12].

The survey instrument for this study sought to examine the incentive/disincentive preferences of U.S. and U.K. MNCs investing in the focus countries in three major areas wherein the government has the capability of exercising direct control and in six general areas wherein government capability for control is either indirect or non-existent. Of the three major areas directly controllable by government, the presence of restrictions (laws or regulations whose application tends to limit FDI) were examined in the Financial and Investment & Ownership areas and the presence of incentives (laws or regulations generally regarded as favorable to FDI) were examined in the Tax & Subsidies area. For those areas wherein government control was indirect or non-existent, the firms were asked to rate the effect on the location-decision should the listed items be deemed to be uncompetitive with other developing countries. The listed items covered Economic, Legal, Political, Labour, Infrastructure, and Administrative conditions in the subject countries. In total, 49 specific elements were covered - 28 in the direct control areas and 21 in the indirect/non-existent control areas. Each firm was asked to evaluate the effect on the firm's location-decision of each of the 49 elements. For purposes of identification and segmentation, the two groups were labeled Direct Control Group and Indirect Control Group. As such, it enabled a closer examination of MNC preferences for the analysis for significant differences.

The nominated items covered some of the more common provisions established by developing countries for the purpose of affecting FDI within their borders or represented some of the more common services or conditions which can exist within developing countries and which may affect FDI within their borders.

Figure 6.1, titled "Investment Attraction Package - Classifications and Elements", presents the classifications and elements that made up the Investment Attraction Package for which respondee evaluation was sought. Chapter 3 highlights the conflicting evidence and claims made in relation to both the primary areas of interest to MNCs when evaluating a country for FDI and the effectiveness of specific incentive actions taken by host countries to attract FDI.

FIGURE 6.1

Investment Attraction Package
CLASSIFICATIONS & ELEMENTS

Government Control - Direct

Financial Restrictions
    Mandated Minimum Exports
    Foreign Exchange Control/Conversion
    Capital Repatriation
    Foreign Personnel & Input Limits
    Profit Repatriation
    Mandated Local R&D Minimums
    Mandated Local Content Minimums
    Dividend Repatriation/Utilization
    Foreign Exchange Balancing Required
    Financing from Abroad Required

Investment & Ownership Restictions
    Equity Ownweship Limitations
    Diversification/Expansion Restricted
    Profit Reinvestment Restricted
    Divestiture of Ownership Required
    Appointments to Board Restricted
    Certain Sectors of Economy Denied
    Intellectual Property Rights Limited
    Right to Own Land/Business Premises

Taxes & Subsidies
    Accelerated Depreciation Schedules
    Subsidies (incl. below market loans)
    Low Corporate Income Tax
    Protection Against Imports
    Low Rent FTZ Facilities
    Government Tender Preferences
    Withholding Tax (non-existant)
    Tax Holidays
    Capital Grants
    Duty Free Importation of Inputs

Government Control - Indirect/None

Economic Conditions
    Exchange Rate Fluxuation
    Inflation Trend
    GDP Growth Rate
    Level of Tariffs or Quotas

Legal Conditions
    Expropriation Guarantees
    Host Co. Dispute Resolution Req'd.
    Clarity/Simplicity of Law/Procedures

Political Considerations
    Political Leadership Turnover
    Political Stability of Country
    Potential for Civil Disturbance

Labour Conditions
    Availability of Skills
    Education Facilities
    Hire/Fire Restrictions
    Local Wage Levels

Infrastructure
    Transportation System Adequacy
    Telecommunications Facilities
    Electricity Reliability

Administration Conditions
    FDI Screening Procedures -
        "Red Tape"
    Public Safety Provisions
    Integrity of Officials - Corruption
    Effectiveness of Host Co. Admin.

The rationale for classification and element inclusion in the Investment Attraction Package considered by this study is as follows:

<u>Financial Restrictions</u>

The importance of the ability to repatriate profits, dividends and capital is assumed to be fundamental to many firms as the justification for investment is generally based on (a) maximizing after-tax profits of the parent corporation and (b) the comparison of the contribution expected from the potential FDI to the next best investment alternative available to the parent corporation. Therefore, the logic supporting repatriation is that the funds so earned must be available to the parent for use in its total system as it deems appropriate. However, what is true in general may or may not be true in all cases. Mandated restrictions,- such as foreign exchange controls, limits on free convertibility of currency, limits on foreign inputs (both personnel and material), local content requirements, local R&D minimums, foreign exchange balancing, foreign source financing and export requirements,- all can adversely effect repatriatability either directly or indirectly (via profit reduction). All MNCs may or may not be equally affected by such government actions.

Investment & Ownership Restrictions.

The literature reflects that some MNCs may feel strongly about what might be termed "traditional" rights of ownership - of subsidiary, of real or intellectual property, of managerial control, of use of profits. Other MNCs may vary in their reactions from less resistive to pleased. Some may see investment and ownership restrictions as risk reduction. Others may see such restrictions as threats to their firm-specific advantages.

Taxes and Subsidies

Part of the differing evidence and claims concerning the effectiveness of tax and subsidy incentives,- such as, holidays, accelerated depreciation schedules, low income taxes, low rent FTZs, grants, subsidies, tender preferences, duty free entries, and market protection, - could be due to the differing motivations that the firms have for making FDI. Studies showing low/no/negative effectiveness have generally (but not always) tended to be studies that concentrated on host country market-seeking investors. Those confirming effectiveness of incentives have tended to focus more strongly on export-oriented investment. There appears to be a scarcity of empirical studies segmenting investor motivation into the two orientations for comparison of preferences and effectiveness of incentives.

Other Conditions Potentially Affecting FDI

The existence of conditions over which the government has only indirect or non-existent control are cited by some as being the real determinants of the FDI locations selected by the MNCs. Most frequently cited are:

Economic Conditions (such as GDP growth rates, inflation trend, exchange rate fluctuations and quotas or levels of tariffs),

Legal conditions (such as, expropriation guarantees, locus of dispute resolution, clarity of laws),

Political Conditions (such as political stability, leadership turnover and potential for civil disturbance),

Labour Conditions (such as availability of skills, education facilities, wage levels, hire/fire restrictions),

Infrastructure Conditions (such as, Transportation adequacy, electricity reliability, telecommunications availability), and

Administrative Conditions (such as FDI screening procedures, corruption, public safety, effective administration).

Others have attached much less significance to these areas. Again, the different investigators appear to have focused on somewhat different targets and some of the difference in reported results may be due to target divergence.

Study Design

In this study, the transaction cost/FDI strategic motivation matrix has been used to develop a set of discrete subgroups of original investments by FDI investors known to have made investment in Barbados, Jamaica, and Trinidad-Tobago. Each sub-grouping is treated as an independent variable. The dependent variables consist of the individual firm's evaluation of its preference for the nominated elements of the investment attraction package. The discrete subgroups were tested to determine if there were significant preference differences between the subgroups.

The respondees were asked to rate each of the 49 specifics items covered by evaluating at two different levels:

1) the relative importance of each element, within the general classification, using forced ranking, with "1" representing the highest importance to the firm and successive higher numbers equaling successively lesser relative importance, and

2) The absolute importance of each element to the firm's decision to locate in the subject country, using a ranking of "A" to indicate the item was fundamental to the investment; "B" to indicate moderately important; and "C" to indicate low priority.

The standard for measurement of the firm's relative and absolute evaluations of the listed elements was "in the eye of the beholder". The survey sought the recipient firm's opinion of each element and requested the evaluation in terms of the nominated relative and absolute values.

Additionally, respondees were asked to give their opinions on additional effective actions the host country could take to increase FDI into the country, the most important things that persuaded the firm to invest and the greatest impediments to attracting FDI into the subject country.

A replica of the Postal Interview Form is included as Appendix A.

Canvassing Procedure

Selection of Survey Recipients

The survey questionnaire focused on determining MNC preferences for elements within the host country investment attraction package for their <u>original</u> investment into the host country. Several writers have pointed out that the factors affecting initial investment and retained profits investment are likely to be different and thus require different incentives. (Brewer, 1993)[13]. The accuracy of the statement is acknowledged and appears particularly pertinent for MNCs domiciled in the U.S, or other countries, wherein retained earnings are subject to favorable home country tax treatment. However, the Contractor (1990) finding that "developing nations exhibited a very low rate of reinvested earnings by TNCs" [14]would appear to lend some support to the efficiency of concentrating on initial investment factors when analyzing the investment attraction packages of small developing countries.

Postal questionnaires were dispatched to all U.S. and U.K domiciled firm known or suspected to have made an FDI in one or more of the countries of Barbados, Jamaica, and/or Trinidad-Tobago. The list of all potential investors was compiled from lists supplied to the researcher by governmental and private sector organizations of each host country, governmental and private sector sources of each home country, from private sources in each host country, and from information published in the Directory of American Business Firms Operating in Foreign Countries (1991)[15], Million Dollar Directory (Dun & Bradstreet), (1992)[16] Wards Business Directory, 1992[17], Standard & Poors, (1993)[18] and Hoover's Handbook, (1993).[19]

In total, a listing of 311 corporations was compiled from the various lists. Although it was obvious from the mismatches contained in the separate lists that some were probably not current investors and others may have registered for business purposes but not necessarily for conducting FDI as defined in this study, questionnaires were dispatched to all.

Solicitation

The questionnaire was sent to the Chief Executive Officer (Chairman, President or Managing Director, as appropriate) of the U.S. or U.K. domiciled parent corporation on the assumption that the occupant of this position would have had the final decision responsibility (or been the key advocate in any required Board of Directors action) in the instance of the firm's initial investment into a "new" country location. Table 6.1 ("Postal Interview Respondee Profile") summarizes the organizational positions of the actual respondees. As can be seen from the table, 81% of the respondees were organizationally positioned to have had probable direct impact on the investment location decisions of the corporation.

	NO.	PCT.	CUML. PCT.
CEO (Chairman, President,) Managing Director) Owner)	28	39%	39%
VP&GM International Div.] VP&GM Product (incl Int'l)]	6	8%	47%
VP&GM - Geographic Area) Non-Line Corporate Officers)	18	25%	72%
Other Corporate VP Personnel (Corp. Dir. / Finance, Stratrgic] Planning, Development or] Controller)]	6	8%	81%
Non-Line Regional Support (Int'l Sales Dir., Portfolio Mgr., Regional Controller, Int'l Business Unit Analyst, Planning Advisor, Acct. / Pers. Mgr.)	14	19%	100%
Total	72		

Table 6.1
POSTAL INTERVIEW RESPONDEE PROFILE

The survey questionnaire consisted of two principal parts: those firm-description queries designed to facilitate subdivision and placement of the firm on the transaction cost / FDI strategic motivation matrix and those preference-seeking queries designed to determine the firm's evaluation of the host country's Investment Attraction Package. To reduce or eliminate respondee bias, the investment attraction package queries were unnumbered and the selection of the order in which each element within a classification appeared on the questionnaire was accomplished by blind drawing of individual element-statement from a basket. Neither mailings nor replies could be randomly selected as the survey was sent to 100% of U.S. or U.K. MNCs with known or alleged FDI in one or more of the focus countries and the useable returns were of number and percentages as indicated in the following pages.

In order to maximize response rates to the survey, a campaign was conducted that included a total of three complete mailings, two follow up reminders, one telephonic secretary-assistance request, one fax campaign directed to "missent" inquiries returned by the post offices, and one "networking" campaign consisting of contacts with intermediaries personally known to the researcher and who potentially had personal acquaintanceship with appropriately placed personnel in the targeted corporations. The survey and study were funded solely by the author. Outside funding was neither solicited nor accepted.

Summary of Survey Response

Of the total 311 U.S. and U.K. firms surveyed, 37 (11.9%) were returned by the respective Postal Services as "Addressee Unknown", "Addressee Moved - No Forwarding Address", etc., i.e., missent. The U.S. postal authorities returned 13.8% of the total dispatched to U.S. firms and 6.9% of the total dispatched to U.K. firms were returned. Since the mailings originated in the U.S., the low U.K. return rate could, among other potential reasons, indicate either reluctance of local authorities to return undeliverable survey requests to an overseas originator, or superior accuracy of information supplied by the U.K. Government agencies concerning U.K. corporations presence in the host countries.

One hundred and fifty-one questionnaires were returned (55.1% of presumed deliveries). 52 questionnaires were returned by respondees who indicated that the request was inappropriately address to the firm. In the great majority of such cases, the firm annotated the return indicating no FDI in any of the subject countries, - some stated operations in subject countries never existed, some stated no FDI but relationship was with a non-owned distributor, a few stated past FDI connection but none currently. "Inappropriate" returns were 19.7% of correctly addressed U.S. mailing and 17.2% of correctly addressed U.K. mailing.

Twenty-seven firms returning the questionnaire declined to participate in the survey. (12.3% of valid U.S mailing.; 11.9% of valid U.K. mailing). "Too busy" was the almost universal reason cited.

Seventy-two usable responses were received representing 32.43% of the valid (apparently delivered and appropriately directed) inquiries. (38.1% U.S.; 19.4% U.K.). Unreturned inquiries totaled 123 or 55.4% of total valid mailing. Tables 6.2 - 6.5 ("Postal Interview Summary - Total"; "Barbados"; "Jamaica"; "Trinidad-Tobago") summarize survey responses in total and by home/host country.

Table 6.2

POSTAL INTERVIEW RESPONSE RATES
Total Survey

	U.S.		U.K.		TOTAL	
	NO.	PCT.	NO.	PCT.	NO.	PCT
Total Mailed	224		87		311	
Misaddressed & Returned	31		6		37	
Total Correctly Addressed	193		81		274	
Returned as Inappropriate	38		14		52	
Valid Mailing	155		67		222	
Unreturned	77	50%	46	69%	123	55%
Returned & Refused to Participate	19	12%	8	12%	27	12%
Returned & Useable	59	38%	13	19%	72	32%
ADJUSTED FOR INAPPROPRIATENESS CONTAINED IN NON-RETURNS:						
Total Responsiveness	116		35		151	
Inappropriate Percentage	33%		40%		34%	
Unreturned Factored for Inappropriateness	52	40%	28	57%	81	45%
Returned & Refused to Participate	19	15%	8	16%	27	15%
Returned & Useable	59	45%	13	27%	72	40%
Total Valid Mailing - Adjusted	130	100%	49	100%	180	100%

Table 6.3

POSTAL INTERVIEW RESPONSE RATES
Barbados

	U.S.		U.K.		TOTAL	
	NO.	PCT.	NO.	PCT.	NO.	PCT
Total Mailed	51		17		68	
Misaddressed & Returned	7		1		8	
Total Correctly Addressed	44		16		60	
Returned as Inappropriate	10		6		16	
Valid Mailing	34		10		44	
Unreturned	15	44%	5	50%	20	45%
Returned & Refused to Partricipate	1	3%	2	20%	3	7%
Returned & Useable	18	53%	3	30%	21	48%
ADJUSTED FOR INAPPROPRIATENESS CONTAINED IN NON-RETURNS:						
Total Responsiveness	29		11		40	
Inappropriate Percentage	34%		55%		40%	
Unreturned Factored for Inappropriateness	10	34%	2	31%	12	33%
Returned & Refused to Participate	1	3%	2	28%	3	8%
Returned & Useable	18	62%	3	41%	21	58%
Total Valid Mailing - Adjusted	29	100%	7	100%	36	100%

Table 6.4

POSTAL INTERVIEW RESPONSE RATES
Jamaica

	U.S. NO.	PCT.	U.K. NO.	PCT.	TOTAL NO.	PCT
Total Mailed	103		35		138	
Misaddressed & Returned	15		2		17	
Total Correctly Addressed	88		33		121	
Returned as Inappropriate	14		5		19	
Valid Mailing	74		28		102	
Unreturned	41	55%	18	64%	59	58%
Returned & Refused to Partricipate	7	9%	3	11%	10	10%
Returned & Useable	26	35%	7	25%	33	32%

ADJUSTED FOR INAPPROPRIATENESS
CONTAINED IN NON-RETURNS:

	U.S. NO.	PCT.	U.K. NO.	PCT.	TOTAL NO.	PCT
Total Responsiveness	47		15		62	
Inappropriate Percentage	30%		33%		31%	
Unreturned Factored for Inappropriateness	29	47%	12	55%	41	49%
Returned & Refused to Participate	7	11%	3	14%	10	12%
Returned & Useable	26	42%	7	32%	33	39%
Total Valid Mailing - Adjusted	62	100%	22	100%	84	100%

Table 6.5

POSTAL INTERVIEW RESPONSE RATES
Trinidad-Tobago

	U.S. NO.	PCT.	U.K. NO.	PCT.	TOTAL NO.	PCT
Total Mailed	70		35		105	
Misaddressed & Returned	9		3		12	
Total Correctly Addressed	61		32		93	
Returned as Inappropriate	14		3		17	
Valid Mailing	47		29		76	
Unreturned	21	45%	23	79%	44	58%
Returned & Refused to Partricipate	11	23%	3	10%	14	18%
Returned & Useable	15	32%	3	10%	18	24%

ADJUSTED FOR INAPPROPRIATENESS
CONTAINED IN NON-RETURNS:

	U.S. NO.	PCT.	U.K. NO.	PCT.	TOTAL NO.	PCT
Total Responsiveness	40		9		49	
Inappropriate Percentage	35%		33%		35%	
Unreturned Factored for Inappropriateness	14	34%	15	72%	29	47%
Returned & Refused to Participate	11	28%	3	14%	14	23%
Returned & Useable	15	38%	3	14%	18	30%
Total Valid Mailing - Adjusted	40	100%	21	100%	61	100%

Non-response by firms leaves hanging the question of "for what reason?" - too busy or inappropriate query. The question is of pertinence when evaluating the relative confidence level to be placed in the survey. The survey was targeted to all firms known or suspected to have FDI in the subject countries. Two other options were considered: randomly drawn sample and targeting all companies appearing on the largest single list. Both unused options were rejected on limited population grounds and the largest list option was additionally faulted for obvious and known incompleteness. The question of determining the "true" list of qualified MNCs remains and would appear to be masked somewhere in the "missent", "Inappropriate" and "unanswered" categories.

The question of "true" response is complicated by the 100% greater returns for "missent" received from the U.S. postal service than from U.K. and further confused by the virtual unanimous reply of "too busy" from those returning but refusing to participate. It would appear likely that some percentage of "unanswered" is more properly described by the classification of "inappropriate" as non-response would be the respondees' least time consuming method of indicating no useful information existed for them to impart and, hence, the query was inappropriately directed to the firm. Such a line of reasoning suggests that the more accurate assessment of the total number of eligible MNC participants (those which actually have FDI in the subject countries) should be estimated by applying the same percentage that "Inappropriate" represents of the total returns to the total inquires assumed to have been delivered. (Total sent minus "missent" minus estimated "inappropriate").

Thus, the 34.44% replies received as "inappropriate" represent 94 inappropriate inquires projected to be contained in the total of the 274 delivered questionnaires. Therefore, the total appropriately qualified recipients of the questionnaire were likely to have been approximately 180. In as much as the number of returned and useful replies is known to be 72, the estimated true response rate is approximately 40% (45.5% U.S.; 26.75% U.K.).

Whether the usable return rate is taken as 32% of questionnaires actually dispatched to listed FDI firms or 40% of questionnaires dispatched to the estimated qualified FDI firms, the response rate is considered quite high for cross-border survey research. However, the potential of sample bias remains. The findings and conclusions of this research are vulnerable to the potential that the views of those firms supplying useful replies to the questionnaire may or may not accurately reflect the views of the entire FDI population in the subject countries.

ANALYTICAL METHODS EMPLOYED

The data base accumulated for this research on the preferences of MNCs for the specific elements of the IAP offered by the focus countries consists primarily of data qualifying as ordinal level of measurement. In gathering data concerning the relative attractiveness within a classification of similar elements and the absolute attractiveness over all items, there is no assurance that the interval between responses ratings is uniform, i.e. the distance between response rating of "1" and

"2" may or may not be the same distance of interval envisioned by the respondee when denoting attractiveness levels of "6" and "7"). Further, as noted above, there can be no assurance that the survey returns are truly representative of the entire population.

Statistical Techniques Commentary.

In the calculation of means, standard deviations and the other parametric tests utilized in this study, the numerical scores have been treated as thought they were real values. Controversy exists over the effect of violations of classical statistical theory assumptions upon which tests like t and F are founded. Some believe that violation of assumptions is serious enough to invalidate the results of parametric statistical tests. Others believe that tests like t and F are so robust that they operate well under assumption violations, provided the violations are not gross. (Kerlinger, 1986)[20]. Babbie (1992) states that the key is utility and that "you should be lenient in the application of statistical techniques to data that do not warrant them" when such statistical calculations are useful in revealing the nature of social affairs. However, Babbie cautions that

> "the danger (is) being lulled into thinking that the results represent something truly precise...for example, you might question the utility and appropriateness of carrying the means and standard deviations out to three decimal points".[21]

Kerlinger (1986) also advocates this view:

> "The best procedure would seem to be to treat ordinal measurement as though they were interval measurements, but to be constantly on the alert to the possibility of gross inequality of intervals."[22]

Gardner (1975)[23] supports the use of parametric statistics in such instances whereas Bradley (1975)[24] and Glass, Peckman and Sanders (1972)[25] disapprove. In Rolfe et al (1993) "Determinants of FDI Incentive Preferences of MNEs", published by the Academy of International Business, the technique of imparting interval significance to ordinal data was used in the construct of mean, t and F tests, Manova, etc.[26] Present day practice in the behavioral science areas appears to adopt the more liberal interpretations for using parametric tests. The present study has followed the advice of Kerlinger (1986)[27]:

> "Use parametric statistics, as well as the analysis of variance, routinely, but keep a sharp eye on data for gross departures from normality, homogeneity of variance, and equality of intervals".

Accordingly, the investor preference data received from the U.S. & U.K. MNCs has been processed utilizing parametric statistical tests. The data for classifying the MNC/FDI investors into micro-groups is nominal data and was processed utilizing non-parametric statistical tests.

Statistical Tests Utilized

Capital Risk Elements of Transaction Cost

The Chi-Square test was utilized to examine the two levels of quantum of investment (<$1.0 million and $1 million & above) for same or different sample population. Two populations were examined: redeployability of assets, subdivided into ranges - more than 67%, 34-67%, less than 34%; and transaction-specific assets, subdivided into ranges - less than 34%, 34-67%, more than 67%. The level of confidence was set as less than .05. The non-parametric chi-square test was utilized as the division of the population into the two levels of investment presented a nominal data base.

A finding via chi square that the population contained in the three ranges of redeployability for investments under $1.0 million were likely to be different from the population contained in the three ranges of redeployability for investments over $1.0 million will not reveal whether the relationship between investment quantum and redeployability is monotonic or nonmonotonic nor is the direction of that relationship indicated in a chi-square test. Simularly, chi square is equally non-committal on the nature and direction of the quantum/transaction-specificity relationship.

The Spearman Rank Correlation test was utilized to examine for the existence of a monotone relationship between the capital risk elements of transaction costs theory. Specifically, the Spearman test was used to examine the relationship of quantum, redeployability and asset specificity for being monotone-increasing, i.e., as one variable increases, the second variable also increases. Three Spearman tests were conducted on each of the populations of redeployability and transaction-specificity: total survey population without regard to the MNC's reason for making the investment; population of those MNCs investing for host country market reasons; and population of those MNCs investing for cost reduction reasons.[28] The critical values were based on one-tail (right), with the confidence level set at .01. The higher level of confidence was selected based on the criticalness that the relationship between quantum invested and the "sunk" nature of the investment bears to the use made of quantum in the preference analysis portion of this study. Granted, substance of the finding is not effected by the higher level of confidence demanded, but confidence is increased that sampling error has not tainted the findings.

MNC Investment Attraction Preferences

Tests of significance were conducted to test the null hypotheses:

The t-distribution was performed on each set of paired data for each segment of each hypothesis. This test was used to determine whether the difference in the means of the paired groups was statistically significant, i.e., exhibited greater variability than would be expected by virtue of sampling error or chance. The level of significance was tested at the .01, .05 and .10 confidence levels.

Since t-distribution tests are limited to two groups of data and is a test of means only, the ANOVA (Analysis of Variance) procedure was performed on those segmentations of data that permitted simultaneous comparison of three groups, i.e., host country market, raw materials, and cost reduction motivation and those segmentations that permitted comparisons of the IPA's of Barbados, Jamaica, and Trinidad-Tobago. For the three-group comparisons, the Anova procedure permits the inclusion of the variable's "spread" (within-group variance) in addition to the comparison of variances between the groups. Accordingly, another dimension is added in determining the significance of differences. As with the t-distribution, the level of significance was tested, at the .01, .05 and .10 confidence levels.

For the three-group cases tested via the Anova procedure, Duncan's Multiple Range Test was also employed for the purpose of assisting in denoting which pair(s) in the three pair relationship evidenced statistically significant differences at the .05 level of confidence. Although the Duncan test is similar to the t-distribution test in that the groups are analyzed for significance of differences in their means, the Duncan test injects the Anova element of spread within a population (i.e., within-group variance). As such, the test is more rigorous than the t-test as it compares both means among and spread within the groups and reflects a more representative significance of variance.

All of the above tests of significance were performed on the "relative ranking" of each IAP element within a specified inquiry classification. (Recall that each MNC was asked to indicate the relative importance of each element, within a specific classification, to the corporation's decision to locate within the given country). In order to obtain a "feel" for the degree of importance attached to the individual element - in comparison to all elements queried - the MNC was requested to categorize each element on a three-choice, "absolute" scale: highest importance (a "go/no go item", deal killer); moderately important (could be a deal killer but mutually satisfactory solution anticipated); low importance ("preferred item" but no deal killer if not present). The median evaluation of each element was employed as a visual cross-check for confirming and/or interpreting the order of relative rankings within each classification and for broad, directional support in affixing substantive importance of the findings.

The basic standard used throughout this portion of the study is to test for sampling error at the .05 level of confidence. The existence of evidence at the .10 level of confidence and the existence of differences detected in MNC level-rankings of the absolute importance of the IAP elements as determined by the medians of the responses is also noted, where appropriate. The inclusion of this supplemental evidence is for the purpose of attempting to gain a more complete understanding of the potential interrelationships involved with the subject matter. None of the statistical procedures attest to the actual veracity of the findings. Their function is to address the creditability of the findings. Accordingly, when evidence is considered that does not enjoy the .05 creditability level for being free of sampling error, it is so noted in the text.

The procedure used for analysis of the investment attraction preferences of the MNC consisted of subdividing the 49 elements chosen to be included in the Investment Attraction Package into 9 classifications. (See Figure 6.1). The first three (3) classifications (Financial Restrictions, Investment & Ownership Restrictions, and Taxes and Incentives) are within the direct control of the focus Caribbean countries. The governments can decide unilaterally whether or not to legislate in these areas and can decide unilaterally the extent, type and form of any such legislation enacted. Further, the included elements all impact MNC financial performance to a greater or lesser extent. These three classifications contain 28 of the IAP elements. The remaining 21 elements are contained in six (6) classifications - Economic Conditions, Legal Conditions, Political Considerations, Labour Conditions, Infrastructure, and Administrative Conditions. The government's ability to control these elements vary from indirect to non-existent. As such, the included elements tend to have a general rather than a specifically identifiable impact upon MNC financial performance. For the purposes of reporting and interpreting the significance of the findings, the first three classifications collectively have been given the label "Direct Control Group" and the latter six classifications have been labeled the "Indirect Control Group". In view of the conflicting evidence concerning the effectiveness of incentives, financial performance and country conditions on the location decisions of MNCs as presented by previous researchers (Root and Ahmed, Lim, et al, on the one hand, and Guisinger, Contractor, Cable and Persaud, et al, on the other) it was anticipated that dividing the IAP into Direct and Indirect Control Groups could be of assistance in sorting out the conflicts apparent in the evidence. To facilitate the literary flow of the Findings Section, to enhance the visual grasp of data, and to reduce tedious recital of the statistical results of the tests of significance for each of the individual hypotheses and sub-hypotheses, two (2) tables accompany the Findings for each of the hypotheses - a presentation of the statistical data pertinent to the hypothesis, and a ranking of the IAP elements for the Direct Control Group and for the Indirect Control Group.

The responses of the MNCs to the elements of the IAP are analyzed as a whole, as a group, as a classification and as individual element. Since the objective of analysis is to determine whether significant difference exists between or among compared segmented-groups of data and since the IAP itself is a collection of a large number of elements, the finding of significant difference or non-difference is more a matter of judgment than of science. A finding of a statistically significant difference in one element of the IAP might technically suffice to make a finding that the IAP preferences of one segmented-group is significantly different from that of the compared segmented-group. However, the substantive value of such a finding is likely to be questionable unless that element containing the difference could be reasonably assumed to be of overarching value to the total IAP. In the evaluation of the evidence for support or non-support of each proposition, effort has been made to present findings that have a substantive as well as a statistical foundation. This approach requires the exercise of judgment and, by definition, judgment is scientifically imprecise. It is accepted that others looking at the same set of individual statistics could reach dissimilar conclusions as to how those individual statistics impact the evaluation of the subject as a whole.

Where three (3) group comparison was possible, major weight was accorded to the Anova procedure analysis, especially when it was corroborated by Duncan's Multiple Range test. Although *t*-distribution was utilized in each of these cases, in general the heavier weight was given to Duncan's since it represented the more rigorous of the two tests. Where two (2) group comparison was occasioned, only the *t*-test could be performed on the paired data. As the rigor of Anova and Duncan were not available to add their strength to the finding, corroboration was sought in the medians of the levels of the absolute rankings accorded the IAP elements by the MNCs. Such rankings help shed light on both the perceived importance of the individual elements and the extent of the differences, if any, that may exists between the compared groups.

---

[1]Wells, Louis. 1986. "Investment incentives: An unnecessary debate." *CTC Reporter*, Autumn, pp. 58-60.

[2]Contractor, F. 1990. "Government policies towards foreign investment. An empirical investigation of the link between national policies and FDI flows". A paper presented to Annual Conference, Academy of International Business, Miami: p. 21.

[3]Woodward, D. and Rolfe, R. 1993. "The location of export oriented foreign direct investment in the Caribbean basin". *Journal of International Business Studies*, Vol.24, No.1, p. 121.

[4]Brewer, T. 1993. "Government policies, market imperfections, and foreign direct investment". *Journal of International Business Studies,* Vol 24, No. 1, p.113.

[5]Rolfe, R.; Ricks, D.; Pointer, M.; and McCarthy, M. 1993. "Determinants of FDI preferences of MNEs". *Journal of International Business Studies*, Vol 24, No. 2 (Spring, 1993), p.338.

[6]Xiaohong, H. 1991. *International tax trends and competition: Tax sensativity of U.S. foreign investment abroad.* PhD Dissertation Abstract, The University of Texas at Dallas.

[7]Woodward, D. and Rolfe, R. 1993. *op cit, p.*121.

[8]The World Bank. 1992. "The World Bank foreign investment survey". Survey Form - Draft, Wash., D.C.: CECTM (CECSE).

[9]Guisinger, S. 1985. *Investment incentives and performance requirements: Patterns of international trade, production and investment.* Westport, CN.:Praeger, Greenwood Press, p.2-8.

[10]Contractor. 1990. *op cit,* p. 2.

[11]Bradberry, W. 1986. *U.S. multinational corporate managers' response to investment incentives and performance requirements.* Dissertation, University of Texas at Dallas. p. 203.

[12]Wallace, C. 1990. *Foreign direct investment in the 1990S. A new climate in the 3rd world.* Dordrecht, Netherlands: Martinus Nijhoff Publishers, p.177.

[13]Brewer, T. 1993. *op cit,* p. 104.

[14]Contractor. 1990. *op cit, p.*21.

[15]*Directory of American business firms operating in foreign countries.* 1991. 12th Ed. Vol. 3. N.Y.: Unipub.

[16]*Million dollar directory. America's leading public and private companies series. 1992.* N.Y.: Dun & Bradstreet Inc, USA.

[17]*Ward's business directory of U.S. private and public companies, 1992.* Detroit MI.: Gale Reaseach Co., Book Tower.

[18]*Standard & Poors registrar of corporations, directors and executives, 1993.* N.Y.: Standard & Poors.

[19]Hoover, G.; Campbell, A.; Spain, P. 1993. *Hoover's handbook of American business 1993.* Austin, TX.: The Reference Press, Inc.

[20]Kerlinger, F. 1986. *Foundations of behavioral research.* 3rd Ed. Orlando, FL.: Holt, Rinehart and Winston, Inc., p. 266.

[21]Babbie, E. 1992. *The practice of social research.* 6th Ed. Belmont, CA.: Wadsworth Publishing Co, p.393-4.

[22]Kerlinger, F. 1986. *op cit, p.*403.

[23]Gardner, P. 1975. "Scales and statistics". *Review of Educational Research*, Vol. 45 (1975), pp.43-57.

[24]Bradley, J. 1968. *Distribution-free statistical tests.* Englewood, N.J.: Prentice-Hall, Chap. 2.

[25]Glass, G.; Peckham, P.; Sanders, J. 1972. "Consequences of failure to meet assumptions underlying the fixed effects analysis of variance and covariance". *Review of Educational Research,* Vol. 42 (1972), pp. 237-288.

[26]Rolfe, et al. 1993.*op cit,* p.342.

[27]Kerlinger. 1986. *op cit,* p. 268.

[28]Brace, C., Brace, C. P. 1991. *Understandable statistics, concepts and methods.* 4th Ed. Lexington, MA.: D.C. Heath & Co., p.601.

CHAPTER VII

WHAT TO EXPECT

THE HYPOTHESES

"To be or not to be: that is the question:"

William Shakespeare
Hamlet, Act III

In the absence of autarchy, what price does the host country attach to its "permission to enter"? The "willing seller - willing buyer" concept will determine the actual price in a freely negotiated transaction. The regular determinants, - such as product attributes, quality, quantity, availability, competitor offering - all enter the price equation on the part of the seller. Among other things, the buyer must assess his motivation and product-offering fit in determining value to be received. In essence, the postal survey upon which this research study is founded, is a "Customer Survey". It was designed to elicit information concerning customer differentiation, motivation and needs. Via use of transaction cost theory and motivation segmentation, the hypotheses are designed to test customer ranking of the product attributes of the investment attraction packages offered by the focus countries under conditions of varying buyer differentiation and motivation.

THE RESEARCH HYPOTHESES

This section describes the specific hypotheses examined in this study. The general thrust of these hypotheses is that U.S and U.K domiciled multinational corporations (MNCs) making their initial investment in Barbados, Jamaica, and/or Trinidad-Tobago respond differently to elements of the investment attraction packages (laws, regulations, incentives) depending upon their investment motivation and their investment size. Further, the differences in response becomes more evident when the MNCs are positioned on a matrix formed by the three principle reasons or strategic motivations for FDI (market, raw materials and cost reduction)(Buckley, 1989)[1] in juxtaposition with the investment characteristics specified in transaction costs theory (non-trivial investment, redeployability and asset transaction-specificity - convertibility). (Williamson, 1986)[2] .

Investment Size (Quantum) -The Asset Specificity Surrogate.

According to transaction costs theory, FDI occurs when the governance cost of a transaction is deemed to be less via owning and controlling the production structure than via contract purchasing of the transaction at market price. Transaction costs economics relies on the conjunction of the human behavior traits (bounded rationality and opportunism) with the capital risk elements of non-trivial assets, redeployability and transaction specificity of assets (convertibility to alternate use).(Willamson, 1986).

It is proposed that as non-trivial investment increases, transaction-specificity tends to increase and redeployability tends to decrease. Stated more simply, it is proposed that as investment quantum increases, assets tend to become more "sunk" - less redeployable to another location and less convertible to another use. Should the evidence support this proposition, then non-triviality will be shown to be in a fixed directional relationship with asset specificity and redeployability in the focus countries. Hence, non-triviality of investment (quantum) can become the single surrogate for the capital risk elements of transaction cost theory when using this theory to examine investment attraction package preferences. The specific hypotheses for this section of the study are:

H1A. It is proposed that the redeployability of assets of an FDI in the focus countries varies inversely with the quantum (non-triviality) of the investment.

H1B. It is proposed that the transaction-specificity of assets in an FDI in the focus countries varies directly with the quantum of investment.

There is the potential that the direction of the fixed nature of the relationship of capital risk elements, if it exists, may not be constant for all FDI in the subject countries. It could vary with investor motivation. The "sunk" elements of capital risk (redeployability and convertibility) may respond differently to investments made for host country market-seeking, raw material-seeking, and cost reduction-seeking reasons. Raw materials investments have a general reputation for being both large and sunk. Host country market-seeking investment conceptually appear to fit the directional pattern of the greater the investment the less redeployable and the less convertible. Cost reduction-seeking investment, however, has a "footloose" reputation which would describe high redeployability. Since the purpose of such an investment is cost reduction, the designation includes productivity as well as labour rates in the search for the efficiency component of cost reduction. High productivity can denote specialized asset investment. Accordingly, while increase quantum of investment in a cost reduction environment may be accompanied by an expected increase in transaction-specificity of the assets (decrease in convertibility), the expected decrease in redeployability could be more problematical. In as much as the thrust of this study is anchored by the matrix formed by transaction costs and FDI motivation, the hypothesis of a fixed, directional relationship existing among the capital risk elements of transaction cost must be tested against each of the three principle motivations for FDI as well as being tested in toto in order to gain a fuller grasp of the relationships.

H1C. It is proposed that, in the case of FDI conducted for host country market-seeking reasons, the redeployability of assets of an FDI in the focus countries varies inversely with the quantum of the investment.

H1D. It is proposed that, in the case of FDI conducted for host country market-seeking reasons, the transaction-specificity of assets in an FDI in the focus countries varies directly with the quantum of investment.

H1E. It is proposed that, in the case of FDI conducted for cost reduction-seeking reasons, the redeployability of assets of an FDI in the focus countries varies inversely with the quantum of the investment.

H1F. It is proposed that, in the case of FDI conducted for cost reduction-seeking reasons, the transaction-specificity of assets in an FDI in the focus countries varies directly with the quantum of investment.

Although the capital risk elements in raw material-seeking investments are generally hypothesized as being in the same directional relationship as they are hypothesized to exist with market-seeking and cost reduction-seeking investments, the relationship will not be formally hypothesized as the data base is insufficient to permit rigorous statistical analyses.

Acceptance of the proposition that quantum of investment, redeployability of assets and transaction specificity of assets tend to move in a fixed, directional relationship with each other would not only facilitate this, and other investigations that seek to utilize transaction costs theory but also has potential significance in other areas. For instance, the concept of alternate-use rigidity increasing as amount of investment increases could be of interest to the accounting profession- both those using lower of cost-or-market valuations and those using versions of current market valuations. Since FDI internalization is a reaction to market undervaluation of company-specific assets, the potential for overvaluation of MNC fixed assets may be present should FDI asset valuations depend upon an unrealistic assumed level of flexibility to redeploy to another location or convert to another use in order to obtain the claimed market valuation. Further, acceptance of the proposition that investment tends to become more "sunk" as the quantum increases may be of some comfort to developing countries as they struggle with MNC demands for liberalization of ownership restrictions. There is antidotal evidence that exit costs can be significant and, as such, could constitute an exit barrier. Although respondees were requested to estimate the percentage of redeployability and convertibility of the original assets, they were not asked whether such "sunk" costs were included in the firms' original-investment return calculations. Acceptance of the proposition that sunk costs vary directly with the quantum of investment could encourage the inclusion of such costs in the original "make or buy" governance decision.

A finding that a specific investor motivation (market, raw material, or cost reduction) may have different directionality in the relationship among the capital risk elements of transaction cost than the other two strategic motivations leaves in tact the hypothesis that a fixed, directional relationship does exist, provided that the directionality within each of the three principle investor motivations is constant (though not in the same direction for each strategic motivation). However, such a variable finding would put the researcher on notice that additional care must be taken in interpreting study results that are impacted by such a non-uniform relationship.

FDI Motivation & MNC Preferences

FDI is undertaken for three principal reasons - markets, raw materials and cost reduction.(Buckley, 1989)[3]. Many studies have acknowledged the domestic market of the host country as the prime influence on FDI location. The inclusion of raw materials-seeking as a basic motivation for FDI is based upon its long tradition of being recognized as a pioneer in this field and the belief that its IAP preferences are sufficiently unique from those of host country and cost reduction motivations. The influence of cost reduction has been given recent prominence via recognition being accorded to "export-oriented" market investment emanating from the relatively recent upsurge in corporate global sourcing strategy and government incentive policies for "export only" investment. A categorization question arises when assigning primary strategic motivation for FDI to investments made to take advantage of the existence of regionalized common markets. Investment motivated by regional common market considerations could be considered as falling within the domestic market if the domestic market is considered as required for base load economy of scale operation. If the regional market is the primary objective and the specific host country location was selected for its relative position on the cost curve of the region, the primary FDI motivation could be categorized as cost reduction. For the purposes of this study, given the relatively weak commitments made by the English-speaking Caribbean nations to CARICOM (Worrel,)[4], the horizontally integrated MNCs responding to the postal questionnaire who cited CARICOM as their prime motivation for FDI have been included in the host country market motivated grouping. Vertically integrated companies who cited export or internal use as their primary motivation have been included in the cost reduction/export-oriented group even though some local sales may be permitted.

It is proposed that investment attraction packages preferred by MNCs operating in the specified countries differ depending upon the MNC strategic motivation for undertaking the investment. Should the evidence support this hypothesis, the identification of motivation-based preferences could permit more precise targeting of those portions of the investment attraction package that are under the direct control of government. This could potentially net more cost effective investment incentives for both government and/or MNCs. Further, the effectiveness of individual host country "one upmanship" would specifically be called into question unless the specific benefit being offered constitutes a clear and sustainable competitive advantage for the offering country. In the absence of being able to offer a sustainable advantage, the potential would then exist for funds to be redirected toward improving the FDI return for either host country, MNCs, or both. The specific hypotheses for this section of the study are:

H2A. It is proposed that investors motivated by host country market seeking reasons prefer a differently configured investment attraction package than those investors motivated by raw material seeking reasons.

H2B. It is proposed that investors motivated by host country market seeking reasons prefer a differently configured investment attraction package than those investors motivated by cost reduction/export-oriented market reasons.

H2C. it is proposed that investors motivated by raw material seeking reasons prefer a differently configured investment attraction package than those motivated by cost reduction/export-oriented market reasons.

Quantum and FDI Motivation

Rolfe et al. (1993) found that difference in investment size (quantum) made more differences on incentive preferences than any other factor in their study of the

Caribbean Basin region.[5] Other investigators to-date have paid little attention to this element. Since non-triviality (quantum) is expected to be the key feature of capital risk in transaction cost theory, investigation of the simultaneous influence of strategic motivation and quantum and the applicability to the IAPs of the subject countries is indicated.

It is proposed that investment attraction packages preferred by MNCs operating in the specified countries differ depending upon the quantum-level of MNC investment and the motivation for MNC investment.

Obtaining some feel for the scope of the impact that investment quantum exerts on the Investment Attraction Package enlarges the investigation beyond the evaluations of simply large scale investment versus small scale investment in toto. Within the classification of host country market-seeking motivation for FDI and within the classification of cost reduction (export-oriented market) motivation for FDI, the IAP preferred by MNCs may differ depending upon the quantum of investment being made. Further, as between investors motivated by host country market-seeking reasons and those motivated by cost reduction-seeking reasons, the IAP preferred may differ as between the larger investors and may differ as between the smaller investors. (There were no small investors responding to the questionnaire who listed motivation for investment as "raw materials". Therefore, a comparison of preferences for large and small investors within and between this category will not be performed).

Should the evidence support these hypotheses, identification of quantum-based preferences and any motivation-based impact on such quantum preferences could permit more precise targeting of those portions of the IAP that are under the direct control of government. This could potentially net more cost effective investment incentives for both government and/or MNCs.

H3A. It is proposed that MNC investors making large investments into the focus countries respond to a differently configured attraction package than those investors making smaller investments.

H3B. It is proposed that investors making large investments and who are motivated by host country market-seeking reasons respond to a differently configured investment attraction package than those smaller investors who are motivated by host country market-seeking reasons.

H3C. It is proposed that investors making large investments and who are motivated by cost reduction (export-oriented) seeking reasons respond to a differently configured investment attraction package than those smaller investors who are motivated by cost reduction-seeking reasons.

H3D. It is proposed that investors making investments of any size and who are motivated by host country market-seeking reasons respond to a differently configured investment attraction package than those investors making investments of any size and who are motivated by cost reduction-seeking reasons.

H3E. It is proposed that investors making large investments and who are motivated by host country market-seeking reasons respond to a differently configured investment attraction package than those large investors who are motivated by cost reduction-seeking reasons.

H3F. It is proposed that investors making smaller investments and who are motivated host country market seeking reasons respond to a differently configured investment attraction package than those smaller investors who are motivated by cost reduction-seeking reasons.

KEY ASSUMPTIONS UNDERLYING THE STUDY

Vital to the confidence level to be placed in the various statistical techniques utilized in this study is the appropriateness of the study's population. Prudence suggests that an investigation into the reasonableness of the key assumptions surrounding the chosen populations be attempted. A key to this survey is that segmentation can reveal homogeneous micro-groups whose needs may be different from those of the larger group. Investigation for reasonableness of those key assumptions were designed to act as a type of watch-dog against the dissemination of inappropriate conclusions, i.e., to provide some assurance that the different needs of micro-groups were not present within the basic assumptions of the study or, if present, that the exceptions to the assumptions were identified and could provide both guidelines and confidence for applying conclusions based on the sum responses of MNCs. Each of the following assumptions were tested for internal consistence by applying the same tests for statistical significance as described for the research hypotheses. The resulting evidence was examined for the presence of substantive exceptions to the reasonableness of the assumption.

This section describes assumptions implied in Hypothesis #2 - FDI Motivation & MNC Preferences- and Hypothesis #3 - Quantum & MNC Preferences. In general the assumptions cover three broad areas: (1) MNCs review potential FDI locations against a set of corporate desires in a reasonably consistent fashion , i.e., the assumption is that, in the main, MNCs measure potential host countries against the same set of desired parameters. 2) the investment attraction preferences of MNCs domiciled in the U.S. and the U.K. are essentially similar. Since the survey consists of responses from MNCs from both the U.S. and the U.K., it is necessary to further investigate this assumption in order to confirm the assumption's reasonableness. 3) the response of U.S. MNCs investing in one of the individual focus countries is not significantly different from the response of the U.S. MNCs to the other two countries.

Assumption #1 -Individual Host Countries and MNC Preferences.

It is assumed that no significant differences should be expected in MNCs preferences for elements of the Investment Attraction Package based on the individual host countries themselves. Contractor (1991)[6], Guisinger (1985)[7], Cable and Persaud (1987)[8] and Shaw et al (1978)[9] have all identified various key factors and incentives in host country investment attraction packages that they believe to be of influence in MNC location decisions. Implicit in their statements is the belief that MNCs look for those elements that the MNCs perceive as aiding and abetting financial success. The logical extension of such thinking is that the MNCs look for financially beneficial elements across the spectrum of the countries they are examining as potential locations and, accordingly, do not change these basic expectations or have significantly different basic expectations for each country they are examining.

Physical and population size-range aside, the countries of Barbados, Jamaica, and Trinidad-Tobago are generally thought of as being similar Caribbean countries. Although there are large percentage differences in the absolute size of their respective domestic markets, the relative size of each is small on a global host country marketing-seeking scale. The distance from the major market of the region varies as between the three host countries: Jamaica is less than one-half the distance from the U.S. than are the other two countries. Given the economic and political differences in the development of the three countries, there may be differences in the perceptions of the receptivity of each of the host countries to FDI. The effect of real or perceived differences, where they exist, could be reflected in MNC evaluations of differing IAP preferences for the different host countries.

This assumption of expecting no difference in preferences based on the individual host country itself was tested for the survey as a whole, for the host country market-seeking investment, for the cost reduction-seeking investment (Barbados and Jamaica only), for large quantum investment ($1,000,000 and above), and for small quantum investments (less than $1,000,000). While some differences are detected among the responses to the IAP elements of the MNCs investing in the three countries in some of the investigated segmentations, such differences are relatively minor, especially in their substantive effects, and do not do violence to the assumption that no significant differences should be expected in MNCs preferences for elements of the IAP based on the individual host countries themselves.

Note : Large raw materials investments were reported by respondees in Jamaica and Trinidad-Tobago, but investment activity (mining, tourism and oil exploration) is not deemed to be sufficiently comparable. As previously stated, small investments were not reported for raw materials motivation. As such, tests comparing IAP preferences of MNCs for raw material investments in Barbados, Jamaica, and Trinidad-Tobago were not performed. Further, tests comparing IAP preferences of MNCs for cost reduction investments in Trinidad-Tobago with Barbados and Jamaica were not performed due to insufficient response of Trinidad-Tobago investing MNCs.

Assumption #2. U.S. & U.K Preference Differences

Excluding the possible effects of differing home country tax laws, there would appear to be little in the way of business reasons for the reactions of U.S. and U.K. respondees to differ in their preferences for host country incentives / disincentives. There is a substantial age-of-investment difference between the two home countries - U.K. investments, in general, were predictably of an older vintage, especially in the host country market-seeking area where a sufficient number of respondees from both countries provides the opportunity for testing the assumption. The number of responses of U.K. MNCs who indicated cost reduction as their motivation for investment was insufficient to permit comparative testing of preferences between the two home countries and no substantive exceptions to the assumption were discerned during visual inspection of the raw data. Only one of the respondees from the U.K. had invested for raw materials reasons. Therefore, comparative testing for raw material-seeking motivation differences is not feasible nor is visual inspection of the raw data meaningful.

The few differences detected in those elements wherein government exercises direct control over the element and wherein the effects of the element directly impinge upon the financial performance of the MNCs (Direct Control Group) show essentially no substantive differences in the perceptions for the elements by the MNCs of the two countries and, hence, do not violate to the assumption. In the Indirect Control Group (those conditions within the country wherein government control is indirect or non-existent and which have a more indirect financial impact upon the MNCs), the assumption of reasonably similar perceptions being held by the MNCs of the two countries is not as evident. U.K. MNCs place the greater importance on the elements of Foreign Exchange Fluctuation, Inflation Trend, Law Clarity, Education Facilities, Transport System and Integrity of officials than do their U.S. counterparts, who place somewhat higher interest in Wage levels, and Public Safety. Such a substantive difference being reflected in 8 of the 21 Indirect Control Group places a type of codicil to the findings in Hypothesis #2., specifically H2B - Host Country Market-seeking MNCs. The codicil must be attached to these finding which reflects that, while the assumption that U.S. and U.K. MNCs have similar preferences for those government legislated actions that effect financial performance can be expected, the preferences U.S. and U.K. MNCs hold for specified conditions within the subject host countries are significantly different. Such a qualification or notation can be useful to Host Countries as they target their investment attraction promotional efforts to the two countries.

Assumption #3. U.S. MNCs Preferences

The distance from the major market of the region; the increasing familiarity of U.S. domiciled management personnel with the region; the favorable U.S. tax and incentive legislation applicable to the Caribbean Basin; and the relative ease of accessing investment-location alternatives within the region, along with other forces, may collectively impact U.S. domiciled FDI location-deciders differently from that represented by the collective home country evaluations for the combined U.S. & U.K. Further, the proximity to the U.S.- coupled with the ever increasing two-way flow of human traffic - can spawn greater awareness of the cultural, political and economic diversity that exists within apparently "similar" host countries. The increase in knowledge flowing from increasing familiarity can breed differing U.S. MNC expectations for the IAP's of the separate nations which, until recently, may have been historically regarded as the "homogeneous" English-speaking Caribbean. Running counter to these "soft" advantages of "proximity begetting greater understanding" is the experience of prior researchers, including Contractor, that the location decision is driven by financial considerations. U.S. investment was not specifically targeted for evaluation in the prior studies.

It is assumed that MNC investors domiciled in the U.S. do not significantly differentiate among or between the three focus Caribbean countries in their investment attraction package preferences. Assumption #1 tested for differences of MNC perceptions among the three host countries. Assumption #2 tested for differences of MNC perceptions between the two home countries. In view of the great bulk of the survey respondees being U.S. domiciled and in view of the larger relative potential for future FDI to emanate from this country, it was deemed prudent to further examine the U.S. sub-set of responses for the reasonableness of the assumption of preference similarity between host countries.

Assumption #3 was tested for the host country market-seeking investment, and for the cost reduction-seeking investment (Barbados and Jamaica only). While some differences are detected among the responses to the IAP elements of the U.S. MNCs investing in the three countries in the investigated segmentations, such differences are relatively minor, especially in their substantive effects, and do no violence to the assumption that no significant differences should be expected in U.S. MNCs preferences for elements of the Investment Attraction Package based on the individual host countries themselves.

NULL HYPOTHESES

Statement of the research hypotheses to be tested in each of the three major areas are described in the foregoing sections. Statement of the null hypotheses to the above cited research hypotheses follows:

H1A: The redeployability of assets of an FDI in the focus countries does not vary with the quantum of investment.

H1B: The transaction-specificity of assets in an FDI in the focus countries does not vary with the quantum of investment.

H1C: In the case of FDI conducted for host country market-seeking reasons, the redeployability of assets of an FDI in the focus countries does not vary with the quantum of investment.

H1D: In the case of FDI conducted for host country market-seeking reasons, the transaction-specificity of assets in an FDI in the focus countries does not vary with the quantum of investment.

H1E: In the case of FDI conducted for cost reduction-seeking reasons, the redeployability of assets of an FDI in the focus countries does not vary with the quantum of investment.

H1F: In the case of FDI conducted for cost reduction-seeking reasons, the transaction-specificity of assets in an FDI in the focus countries does not vary with the quantum of investment.

H2A: Investors motivated by host country market-seeking reasons respond to the same configuration of investment attraction package as do those motivated by raw material seeking reasons.

H2B: Investors motivated by host country market-seeking reasons respond to the same configuration of investment attraction package as do those motivated by cost reduction-seeking/export-oriented market reasons.

H2C: Investors motivated by raw material-seeking reasons respond to the same configuration of investment attraction package as do those motivated by cost reduction-seeking/export-oriented market reasons.

H3A: MNCs making large investments in the focus countries respond to the same configuration of investment attraction package as do those making smaller investments.

H3B: MNCs making large investments in the focus countries for host country market-seeking reasons respond to the same configuration of investment attraction package as do those making small investments for host country market-seeking reasons.

H3C: MNCs making large investments in the focus countries for cost reduction-seeking reasons respond to the same configuration of investment attraction package as do those making small investments for cost reduction-seeking reasons.

H3D. MNCs making investments of any size in the focus countries for host market-seeking reasons respond to the same configuration of investment attraction package as do those MNCs making investments of any size in the focus countries for cost reduction reasons.

H3E: MNCs making large investments in the focus countries for host market-seeking reasons respond to the same configuration of investment attraction package as do those making large investments in the focus countries for cost reduction reasons.

H3F: MNCs making small investments in the focus countries for host market-seeking reasons respond to the same configuration of investment attraction package as do those making small investments in the focus countries for cost reduction reasons.

---

[1]Buckley, P. 1989. *The multinational enterprise*. London: MacMillan Press, p.114.

[2]Williamson, O. 1986. *Economic organization. Firms, markets and policy control.* N.Y.: University Press, p.177.

[3]Buckley. 1989. *op cit*, p. 114.

[4]Worrell, D. 1987. *Small island economies. Structure and performance in the English-speaking Caribbean since 1970.* Westport, CN.: Praeger, Greenwood Press, p.8.

[5]Rolfe, R.; Ricks, D.; Pointer, M.; and McCarthy, M. 1993. "Determinants of FDI preferences of MNEs", *Journal of International Business Studies*, Vol 24, No. 2 (Spring, 1993), p.349.

[6]Contractor, F. 1990. "Government policies towards foreign investment. An empirical investigation of the link between national policies and FDI flows". A paper presented to Annual Conference, Academy of International Business, Miami: p. 21.

[7]Guisinger, S. 1985. *Investment incentives and performance requirements: Patterns of international trade, production and investment.* Westport, CN.:Praeger, Greenwood Press, p.2-8.

[8]Cable, V. and Persaud, B. 1987. "New trends and policy problems in foreign investment: The experience of Commonwealth developing countries" in *Developing With Foreign Investment.* The Commonwealth Secretariat, Kent: Croom Helm Ltd., p.11.

[9]Shah, S. and Toye, J. 1978. "Fiscal incentives for firms in some developing countries: Survey and critique" in *Taxation and Economic Development.* J.F.T.Toye,(Ed.). London: Frank Cass. p.209.

Chapter VIII

WHAT WORKS FOR WHOM ?

STUDY FINDINGS & INTERPRETATIONS

> *"Ride, boldly ride*
> *The shape replied -*
> *'If you seek for Eldorado'"*
>
> Edgar Allen Poe
> *Eldorado*

The findings of the study as presented in this work have been summarized from the the PhD thesis on which this work is based for the purpose of increasing its readability. However, all key tables are included so that interested readers might make their own examination of the data should more detail be desired.

FINDINGS

Hypothesis #1 - Quantum / Asset Specificity Surrogate

The capital risk elements of transaction costs theory were tested to determined if there was a fixed directional relationship between them, i.e., as the amount of the dollar investment (quantum) increases, does rigidity of investment (represented by decreasing redeployability of assets and increasing transaction-specificity of assets) also tend to increase.

Chi-Square Tests

The Chi Square (X^2) test was utilized to evaluate whether the two levels of quantum of investment - <\$1.0 million and \$1.0 million and above - exhibit different degrees of asset rigidity. The null hypothesis tested was that no difference existed between the two levels of investment. Tests were run on the total survey results segmented for three sets of conditions: total population without regard to MNC motivation for investment; total population of those MNCs motivated to invest by the host country market; and total population of those MNCs motivated to invest by cost reduction opportunity. For each set of conditions, three ranges of redeployability of assets (>2/3; 1/3-2/3; <1/3) and three ranges of transaction-specificity of assets (<1/3; 1/3-2/3; >2/3) functioned as the dependent variables for the purpose of testing for differences in the independent variable - represented by the two levels of quantum of investment. The significance level of the chi-square test was set at p<.05, i.e., the probability of rejecting the null hypothesis when the null was actually true was set at 5%.

Under all three sets of conditions, for both redeployability and transaction-specificity, the observed value exceeded the chi-square critical value required for an .05 level of confidence. (See Tables 8.1, 8.2, 8.3 for chi square results - "Investment Quantum and Asset Specificity" - "Total Survey", "Host Country Market", "Cost Reduction"). As such, the null hypothesis is rejected as it is likely that the two samples (<$1.0 million and >$1.0 million of quantum) represent populations (levels of redeployability and specificity) with different variances. The alternative (research) hypothesis that the two levels of quantum of investment - <$1.0 million and $1.0 million and above - exhibit differences in asset rigidity is accepted.

Spearman Rank Correlation

The Spearman Rank Correlation test results are set forth in Table 8.4, "Investment Quantum and Asset Rigidity - Spearman Rank Correlation Test Results". For all three tested conditions (total survey, host country market respondees, and cost reduction respondees), the Spearman Rank Coefficient for both redeployability of assets and transaction-specificity of assets exceeded the appropriate critical values at the .01 confidence level. The coefficient approached the value of 1 (from a low of 0.973 to 0.999). Inasmuch as the "rs" values are in the reject region for all three conditions tested, the null hypothesis is rejected. The Spearman Rank Correlation test results support the finding that the relationship between decreasing redeployability (increasing asset rigidity) and increasing quantum tends to be monotonic-increasing, as is the relationship between transaction-specificity of assets (increasing rigidity) and increasing investment quantum.

Empirical Evidence

Data from the MNC respondees for the survey contained information on the size of the corporation's original investment and on the investment's redeployability and transaction-specificity. Ranges were specified for the quantum of investment as: 1 - less than $1.0 million; 2 - $1.0 - 20 million; and 3 - over $20 million. The redeployability ranges were: 1 - more than two-thirds; 2. - one-third to two-thirds; and 3 - less than one-third. Transaction-specific asset ranges were: 1 - less than one-third; 2 - one-third to two-thirds; and 3 - over two-thirds. The ranges were assigned a relative value equal to their numerical designation (1-2-3) for the

TABLE 8.1

INVESTMENT QUANTUM & ASSET RIGIDITY
TOTAL SURVEY
CHI SQ (X2)

THE NULL HYPOTHESIS IS THAT THE TWO LEVELS OF QUANTUM OF INVESTMENT - <$1.0 AND >$1.0 - EXHIBIT NO DIFFERENCE IN THE DEGREE OF REDEPLOYABILITY OF ASSETS.

REDEPLOYABILITY				ROW
	>2/3	1/3-2/3	<1/3	SUM
<$1.0	O 19	1	16	36
	E 11.50	4.00	20.50	36
>$1.0	O 4	7	25	36
	E 11.50	4.00	20.50	36
COLUMN SUM	O 23	8	41	72
	E 23	8	41	72

		----- <$1. -------			----- >$1. -----	
O - E	7.50	-3.50	-4.50	-8.00	3.00 4.50
SQUARED	56.25	12.25	20.25	64.00	9.00 20.25
SQ/EXPECTED	4.89	3.06	0.99	5.57	2.25 0.99

SUM = X2 = 17.745
df = (3-1) = 2
p <.05 = 5.991
OBSERVED X2 VALUE IS GREATER.
NULL HYPOTHESIS IS REJECTED.

THE NULL HYPOTHESIS IS THAT THE TWO LEVELS OF QUANTUM OF INVESTMENT - <$1.0 AND >$1.0 - EXHIBIT NO DIFFERENCE IN THE DEGREE OF TRANSACTION-SPECIFICITY OF ASSETS.

TRANSACTION-SPECIFIC ASSET				ROW
	<1/3	1/3-2/3	>2/3	SUM
<$1.0	O 13	1	22	36
	E 7.50	2.00	26.50	36
>$1.0	O 2	3	31	36
	E 7.50	2.00	26.50	36
COLUMN SUM	O 15	4	53	72
	E 15	4	53	72

		----- <$1. -------			----- >$1. -----	
O - E	5.50	-1.50	-4.50	-6.00	0.50 4.50
SQUARED	30.25	2.25	20.25	36.00	0.25 20.25
SQ/EXPECTED	4.03	1.13	0.76	4.80	0.13 0.76

SUM = X2 = 11.612
df = (3-1) = 2
p <.05 = 5.991
OBSERVED X2 VALUE IS GREATER.
NULL HYPOTHESIS IS REJECTED.

TABLE 8.2

INVESTMENT QUANTUM & ASSET RIGIDITY
HOST COUNTRY MARKET
CHI SQ (X2)

THE NULL HYPOTHESIS IS THAT THE TWO LEVELS OF QUANTUM OF INVESTMENT - <$1.0 AND >$1.0 - EXHIBIT NO DIFFERENCE IN THE DEGREE OF REDEPLOYABILITY OF ASSETS.

REDEPLOYABILITY				ROW
	>2/3	1/3-2/3	<1/3	SUM
<$1.0	O 12	0	12	24
	E 8.00	2.00	12.00	22
>$1.0	O 4	4	12	20
	E 8.00	2.00	12.00	22
COLUMN SUM	O 16	4	24	44
	E 16	4	24	44

		----- <$1. -------			----- >$1. -----	
O - E	4.00	-2.50	0.00	-4.50	1.50 0.00
SQUARED	16.00	6.25	0.00	20.25	2.25 0.00
SQ/EXPECTED	2.00	3.13	0.00	2.53	1.13 0.00

SUM = X2 = 8.781
df = (3-1) = 2
p <.05 = 5.991
OBSERVED X2 VALUE IS GREATER.
NULL HYPOTHESIS IS REJECTED.

THE NULL HYPOTHESIS IS THAT THE TWO LEVELS OF QUANTUM OF INVESTMENT - <$1.0 AND >$1.0 - EXHIBIT NO DIFFERENCE IN THE DEGREE OF TRANSACTION-SPECIFICITY OF ASSETS.

TRANSACTION-SPECIFIC ASSET				ROW
	<1/3	1/3-2/3	>2/3	SUM
<$1.0	O 9	1	14	24
	E 5.50	0.50	16.00	22
>$1.0	O 2	0	18	20
	E 5.50	0.50	16.00	22
COLUMN SUM	O 11	1	32	44
	E 11	1	32	44

		----- <$1. -------			----- >$1. -----	
O - E	3.50	0.00	-2.00	-4.00	-1.00 2.00
SQUARED	12.25	0.00	4.00	16.00	1.00 4.00
SQ/EXPECTED	2.23	0.00	0.25	2.91	2.00 0.25

SUM = X2 = 7.636
df = (3-1) = 2
p <.05 = 5.991
OBSERVED X2 VALUE IS GREATER.
NULL HYPOTHESIS IS REJECTED

TABLE 8.3

INVESTMENT QUANTUM & ASSET RIGIDITY
COST REDUCTION
CHI SQ (X2)

THE NULL HYPOTHESIS IS THAT THE TWO LEVELS OF QUANTUM OF INVESTMENT - <$1.0 AND >$1.0 - EXHIBIT NO DIFFERENCE IN THE DEGREE OF REDEPLOYABILITY OF ASSETS.

REDEPLOYABILITY				ROW
	>2/3	1/3-2/3	<1/3	SUM
<$1.0	O 7	1	3	11
	E 3.50	2.00	4.00	9.5
>$1.0	O 0	3	5	8
	E 3.50	2.00	4.00	9.5
COLUMN SUM	O 7	4	8	19
	E 7	4	8	19

		----- <$1. -------			----- >$1. -----	
O - E	3.50	-1.50	-1.50	-4.00	0.50 1.00
SQUARED	12.25	2.25	2.25	16.00	0.25 1.00
SQ/EXPECTED	3.50	1.13	0.56	4.57	0.13 0.25

SUM = X2 = 10.134
df = (3-1) = 2
p <.05 = 5.991
OBSERVED X2 VALUE IS GREATER.
NULL HYPOTHESIS IS REJECTED.

THE NULL HYPOTHESIS IS THAT THE TWO LEVELS OF QUANTUM OF INVESTMENT - <$1.0 AND >$1.0 - EXHIBIT NO DIFFERENCE IN THE DEGREE OF TRANSACTION-SPECIFICITY OF ASSETS.

TRANSACTION-SPECIFIC ASSET				ROW
	<1/3	1/3-2/3	>2/3	SUM
<$1.0	O 4	0	7	11
	E 2.00	1.00	6.50	9.5
>$1.0	O 0	2	6	8
	E 2.00	1.00	6.50	9.5
COLUMN SUM	O 4	2	13	19
	E 4	2	13	19

		----- <$1. -------			----- >$1. -----	
O - E	1.50	-1.50	0.50	-2.50	0.50 -0.50
SQUARED	2.25	2.25	0.25	6.25	0.25 0.25
SQ/EXPECTED	1.13	2.25	0.04	3.13	0.25 0.04

SUM = X2 = 6.827
df = (3-1) = 2
p <.05 = 5.991
OBSERVED X2 VALUE IS GREATER.
NULL HYPOTHESIS IS REJECTED.

	Table 8.4

INVESTMENT QUANTUM & ASSET RIGIDITY
Spearman Rank Correlation Test Results

Hypothesis #1: As quantum of investment increases, asset
rigidity tends to increase, i.e.,
Redeployability of assets tend to decrease.
Transaction-specificity of assets tend to increase.

	Relationship Quantum &	
	Redeploy-ability	Transaction Specificity
Total Survey		
rs value	0.999	0.998
Critical value *	0.467	0.467
Null hypothesis	Reject	Reject
Host Country Market		
rs value	0.996	0.995
Critical value *	0.467	0.467
Null hypothesis	Reject	Reject
Cost Reduction		
rs value	0.987	0.973
Critical value *	0.585	0.585
Null hypothesis	Reject	Reject

FINDING: : THE RELATIONSHIP BETWEEN THE TESTED
VARIABLES IS MONOTONIC-INCREASING, i.e., as Quantum
increases, asset rigidity tends to increase.
*Critical value based on one-tail, .01 confidence level.

purpose of obtaining an average relative range valuation of the three capital risk elements under the conditions of total survey population, host country market population, raw material-seeking population and cost reduction-seeking population. Although the procedure bears some similarity to averaging the averages, and thus is reproachable from a technical viewpoint, it would appear to have some use as a directional tool when its use is restricted to a confirmation role only. The results of this "relative range" averaging are shown in Table 8.5 titled "Directional Correlation: Capital Risk Elements - Transaction Cost Theory - Empirical Evidence". The results tend to confirm the directional correlation indicated by the Spearman test.

The relationship between quantum and redeployability and quantum and transaction-specificity of assets for investments motivated by raw material-seeking reasons was not performed inasmuch as none of the respondees reported their original investment to be small (under $1,000,000) and only one of the nine

			Table 8.5	

DIRECTIONAL CORRELATION
CAPITAL RISK ELEMENTS - TRANSACTION COST THEORY
EMPIRICAL EVIDENCE

No.		Invest-ment	RANGE AVERAGE Redeploy-ability	Transaction Specificity
72	**TOTAL SURVEY**			
36	<$1.0MM	1.00	1.92	2.19
36	>$1.0MM	2.39	2.55	2.79
36	<$1.0MM	1.00	1.92	2.19
22	$1-20 MM	2.00	2.32	2.73
14	>$20.0MM	3.00	3.00	2.91
44	**HOST MARKET**			
24	<$1.0MM	1.00	2.00	2.13
20	>$1.0MM	2.30	2.29	2.76
24	<$1.0MM	1.00	2.00	2.13
14	$1-20 MM	2.00	2.14	2.71
6	>$20.0MM	3.00	3.00	3.00
9	**RAW MATERIALS**			
1	<$1.0MM	1.00	3.00	3.00
8	>$1.0MM	2.63	3.00	3.00
1	<$1.0MM	1.00	3.00	3.00
3	$1-20 MM	2.00	3.00	3.00
5	>$20.0MM	3.00	3.00	3.00
19	**COST REDUCTION**			
11	<$1.0MM	1.00	1.64	2.27
8	>$1.0MM	2.38	2.63	2.75
11	<$1.0MM	1.00	1.64	2.27
5	$1-20 MM	2.00	2.40	2.60
3	>$20.0MM	3.00	3.00	3.00

FINDING: IN EVERY COMPARISON, AS QUANTUM OF INVESTMENT INCREASED, ASSET RIGIDITY INCREASED.
(Asset rigidity represented by decreasing redepolyability of assets and increasing transaction-specificity of assets.)

Note: Raw Material comparison suffers from inadequate small (<$1.0MM) population. However, asset rigidity remains at range maximum as investment quantum increases.

reported an initial investment under $20,000,000. All reported the redeployability of the investment to be less than 34% and the transaction-specificity of the investment in excess of 67%. Therefore, the general characteristic of the reported raw material-seeking investments can be described as large and reasonably immobile ("sunk").

Findings

Starting from a base of small investment (under $1,000,000), there was no real pattern of redeployability or transaction-specificity apparent at that level of investment. This is not surprising as small investments may be either generalized and portable or specific in nature depending upon the function to be performed. Examples such as general garment manufacture versus precision tool fabrication come to mind. However, once the investments rose above a million dollars, the pattern of increasing specificity and decreasing redeployability became readily apparent. The uniformity in the results - both total survey and survey segmented-by-reason for investment - supports a finding that transaction-specificity of assets tends to increase and redeployability of assets tend to decrease as quantum of investment increases. Therefore, the null hypotheses (H1A - H1F) are rejected. The general research hypothesis is accepted as the evidence supports the proposition that, as non-trivial investment increases, transaction-specificity tends to increase and redeployability of assets tends to decrease. .

Interpretations

Given the finding of a fixed directional relationship existing among and between the capital risk elements of transaction cost theory, then the use of the most measurable risk - non-triviality of the investment - as a single surrogate for the capital risk elements appears to be justifiable procedure.

The relationship between quantum and redeployability in cost reduction motivated investments requires further comment. Although the critical values of the observed sample appears slightly weaker than the values generated by host country market motivation, it is nevertheless strongly supportive that the relationship is monotonic-increasing. This invites the conclusion that, although the "footloose" reputation of cost reduction motivated FDI has been demonstrated on a number of occasions, the degree of redeployability nevertheless tends to remain inversely related to the quantum, after a certain threshold of investment has been reached. Potential use of these findings will be commented upon in the Policy Recommendations section.

Hypothesis #2 - FDI Motivation & MNC Preferences

MNCs preferences for the elements of the subject countries Investment Attraction Packages were compared on the basis of the motivations of MNCs for conducting initial FDI into the host country. The paired groups of motivations tested were Host Country Market-seeking vs. Raw Material-seeking (H2A), Host Country Market-seeking vs. Cost Reduction-seeking (H2B), and Raw Material-seeking vs. Cost Reduction-seeking (H2C).The proposition examined was whether MNCs with different FDI motivations prefer differently configured Investment Attraction Packages. *t*-distribution tests, analysis of variance procedure (ANOVA) and Duncan's Multiple Range test were conducted to determine whether the difference in the means and variances of the paired groups was statistically significant. See Table 8.6. - Segmentation By FDI Motivation: Host Country Market - Raw Materials - Cost Reduction - for results of these tests.

Findings

The findings for this hypothesis will be examined separately for the Direct and Indirect Control Groups and concurrently for the sub-parts H2A, H2B and H2C. A finding for the overall hypothesis is not made for the reasons detailed.

As a refresher from Chapter VI, the Direct Control Group is made up of those elements of the IAP that concern the laws, regulations, and incentives promulgated by the host country. The host country government exercises direct control over these elements, can institute unilateral and effective change over any and all such elements, as they deem appropriate, and the content of the elements generally have an immediate and direct effect upon the financial performance of MNCs. The Indirect Control Group is made up of those elements representing conditions existing within the host country over which the government-of-the-day can exercise only limited control or has non-existent control. The contents of these elements generally have a more long term and indirect effect upon the financial performance of MNCs.

Findings in Direct Control Group

Utilizing *t* - distribution, Anova, and Duncan's, the number of elements showing statistically significant difference in the test of the overall Direct Control Group, at the .05 confidence level, were: *t*-distribution - 14 (50.0%); Anova - 16 (57.1%); and Duncan - 18 (64.3%). Findings in the Financial Restrictions Classification showed statistically significant differences occuring in 60 - 70% of the tests of the individual elements of the comparisons of host country market-seeking, raw material-seeking, and cost reduction-seeking MNCs. For the Inverstment & Ownership Classification, the comparable statistically significant

TABLE 8.6

SEGMENTATION OF MNCs PREFERENCES BY FDI MOTIVATION

	TOTAL SURVEY			HOST COUNTRY MARKET			RAW MATERIALS			COST REDUCTION			t-DIST			ANOVA	DUNCAN		
	RELATIVE		ABSL.	RELATIVE		ABSL.	RELATIVE		ABSL.	RELATIVE		ABSL.							
	MEAN SCORE	RK	MED-IAN	MEAN SCORE	RK	MED-IAN	MEAN SCORE	RK	MED-IAN	MEAN SCORE	RK	MED-IAN	HCM RM	HCM CR	RM CR		HCM RM	HCM CR	RM CR
FINANCIAL RESTRICTIONS																			
PROFIT REPATRIATION	1.79	1	1	1.70	1	1	1.44	1	1	2.17	1	1							
CAPITAL REPATRIATION	2.94	2	1	2.88	4	1	2.56	2	2	3.33	2	1				++			x
FOREX CONTROL	3.33	3	1	2.76	3	1	3.78	3	2	4.44	3	2		**		+++	x	x	x
DIVIDEND REPATRIATION	3.43	4	1	2.72	2	1	4.78	5	1	4.44	3	2		***		+++	x		x
FOREIGN PERSONNEL	5.15	5	2	5.26	6	2	4.44	4	2	5.29	6	2				+++	x		
FOREX BALANCING REQUIRED	5.25	6	2	5.21	5	2	5.50	6	2	5.20	5	2							
FINANCE FROM ABROAD	7.12	7	3	7.19	8	3	8.63	8	3	6.25	7	3	*		***	+++	x	x	x
LOCAL CONTENT MINIMA	7.30	8	3	6.90	7	3	8.50	7	3	7.65	8	3	**			+++	x	x	x
EXPORT MINIMA	8.19	9	3	8.08	10	3	9.33	10	3	7.82	9	3		**		+++	x	x	x
R&D MINIMA	8.19	10	3	7.74	9	3	8.88	9	3	8.88	10	3		**		+++	x	x	
INVESTMENT & OWNERSHIP																			
EQUITY LIMITS	2.05	1	1	1.79	1	1	5.26	6	3	1.11	1	1	**	***	**				
PROFIT REINVEST LIMITS	3.31	2	1	3.26	3	1	3.50	2	2	3.31	2	2							
DIVEST OWNERSHIP REQUIRED	3.44	3	1	3.09	2	1	4.38	4	3	3.75	3	1				+++	x	x	x
EXPAND/DIVERSIFY LIMITS	4.04	4	2	3.73	4	2	3.50	2	2	4.94	6	2	*			+++	x	x	
BOARD APPOINTMENTS LIMITED	4.41	5	2	4.23	5	2	4.50	5	3	4.75	4	1							
OWN LAND/BUILDINGS LIMITED	5.17	6	2	5.26	7	2	5.38	7	3	4.88	5	2							
INTELLECTUAL PROP. PROTECT	5.36	7	2	5.54	8	3	3.00	1	1	6.20	7	2	*		***	+++		x	x
SECTORS EXCLUDED	5.69	8	3	5.20	6	2	5.63	8	3	6.87	8	3			***	+++		x	x
TAXES & SUBSIDIES INCENTIVES																			
INCOME TAX - LOW	2.57	1	2	2.33	1	2	2.67	1	3	3.00	2	2							
DUTY FREE IMPORT	3.18	2	2	2.82	2	2	5.67	6	3	2.63	1	2	*		*	+++	x		x
TAX HOLIDAYS	4.46	3	2	4.83	3	3	4.11	2	2	3.89	3	2							
NO WITHHOLDING TAX	5.07	4	2	5.09	4	2	6.11	8	3	4.47	4	3			*	+			x
ACCELERATED DEPRECIATION	5.58	5	3	5.38	5	3	4.56	3	3	6.59	8	3		*	***	+		x	x
LOW RENT FTZ	5.98	6	3	6.66	9	3	6.00	7	3	4.67	5	2		***		+++		x	x
CAPITAL GRANTS	6.10	7	3	6.11	7	3	5.33	4	3	6.44	6	3							
SUBSIDIES	6.29	8	3	5.94	6	3	5.56	5	3	7.41	9	3		**	**	+++		x	x
GOVT TENDER PREFERENCE	6.60	9	3	6.16	8	3	6.67	9	3	7.63	10	3		***	***	++		x	
PROTECTED MARKET	7.08	10	3	6.86	10	3	9.38	10	3	6.53	7	3	***		***	+++	x		x
ECONOMIC CONDITIONS																			
FOREX FLUCTUATION	1.89	1	2	1.74	1	2	2.50	3	3	1.95	2	2	*						
TARIFF LEVELS	2.35	2	2	2.62	3	2	2.22	1	3	1.83	1	1	**						
INFLATION TREND	2.39	3	2	2.28	1	2	2.44	2	3	2.61	3	2							
GDP GROWTH	3.00	4	3	2.87	4	2	2.67	4	3	3.50	4	3	***						
LEGAL CONDITIONS																			
EXPROPRIATION PROTECTION	1.68	1	2	1.79	2	2	1.33	1	2	1.62	1	2	*						
LAW CLARITY	1.73	2	2	1.53	1	1	2.56	3	2	1.77	2	2	***		***				
DISPUTE RESOLUTION	2.30	3	2	2.26	3	2	2.00	2	2	2.62	3	2			**				
POLITICAL CONDITIONS																			
COUNTRY STABILITY	1.36	1	1	1.28	1	1	1.11	1	1	1.67	2	1		***	***				
CIVIL DISTURBANCE	1.82	2	1	1.85	2	1	2.33	2	2	1.50	1	1			**				
LEADERSHIP TURNOVER	2.48	3	2	2.42	3	2	2.44	3	2	2.61	3	2							
LABOUR CONDITIONS																			
SKILLS AVAILABLE	1.83	1	2	1.71	1	2	1.67	1	2	2.16	1	2							
WAGE LEVELS	2.21	2	2	2.18	2	2	2.22	2	2	2.26	2	2							
HIRE/FIRE RESTRICTIONS	2.55	3	2	2.63	3	2	2.67	3	2	2.32	3	2							
EDUCATION FACILITIES	3.06	4	2	2.92	4	3	3.44	4	3	3.16	4	2							
INFRASTRUCTURE CONDITIONS																			
TELECOMMUNICATIONS FACILITIES	1.88	1	2	1.89	1	2	2.33	3	2	1.63	1	1		**					
TRANSPORT SYSTEM	2.00	2	2	1.97	2	2	1.44	1	1	2.32	3	2		**					
ELECTRICITY RELIABILITY	2.26	3	2	2.53	3	2	2.00	2	2	1.84	2	2		***					
ADMINISTRATION CONDITIONS																			
INTEGRITY OF OFFICIALS	1.68	1	2	1.83	1	2	1.67	1	1	1.38	1	2		***					
EFFECTIVE ADMINISTRATION	2.25	2	2	1.95	2	2	2.33	3	2	2.94	3	2		***					
FDI SCREENING	2.78	3	2	2.91	3	2	3.44	4	2	2.13	2	2		***	***				
PUBLIC SAFETY	2.97	4	2	3.03	4	2	2.22	2	2	3.25	4	2	***		***				

Legend:

	t-Dist	Anova	Duncan	Importance				
Prob. < .10	*	+		Highest	9	10	6	9
Prob. < .05	**	++	X	Moderate	28	26	20	28
Prob. < .01	***	+++		Lesser	12	13	23	12

Summary of "Absolute Importance" Response Medians

Relative (Importance within Classification):
"Mean Score" within Classification
"RK" = Element Rank within Classification

differences were 37.5 - 50%, and for the Taxes and Subsidies Classification the percentages ranged from 50 - 70%.. Review of Table 8.6, "Segmentation by FDI Motivation: Host Country Market - Raw Materials - Cost Redcution", reveals that statistically significant differences exists between and among the three strategic motivations and that they exist in significant numbers of the individual elements. Without further ado, it seems appropriate to reject the null hypothesis for the Direct Control Group. This leads to the acceptance of the propositions that different motivations for FDI (host market, raw materials, cost reduction) result in MNCs having significantly different preferences for the various financial performance-effecting elements of the host country's IAP (Direct Control Group

H2A, H2B, H2C). Guisinger (1985)[1], Contractor (1991)[2], Cable and Persaud (1987)[3] detail that different incentives have differing effects upon different investors and suggest that the importance attached to financial performance-impacting legislation is likely to depend upon the reason for investment. Attention was specifically called to the different requirements of investors seeking access to host country market and of investors in export-oriented industries. Thus, for the Direct Control Group, acceptance of the hypotheses confirms in practice the potential implied by the above researchers. See Table 8.7 - "MNC Ranking of Host Country Investment Attraction Packages, Segmented for Motivation for FDI".

Findings in Indirect Control Group

Utilizing *t* - distribution, Anova, and Duncan's, the number of elements showing statistically significant difference in the overall Indirect Control Group, at the .05 confidence level, were: *t*-distribution - 13 (61.9%); Anova - 0 (0.0%); and Duncan - 0 (0.0%).

It is particularly noteworthy that the more robust Duncan's and Anova registered no significant differences in the preferences being accorded to any of the elements of any of the classifications making up the Indirect Control Group. The weaker *t*-distribution recorded the following percentage of elements reflecting significant difference in the named classifications:

> Economic Conditions : 50%
>
> Legal Conditions : 66.7%
>
> Political Conditions : 66.7%
>
> Labour Conditions : 0%
>
> Infrastructure Conditions : 100%
>
> Administrative Conditions : 100%

See Table 8.6 -" Segmentation By FDI Motivation: Host Country Market, Raw Materials - Cost Reduction".

Applying the more severe Duncan test to the Indirect Control Group and supported fully by the ANOVA test - but not the less demanding *t*-distribution, a finding is made that preferences of investors motivated by host country market-seeking reasons do not differ significantly from those motivated by raw material-seeking reasons or cost reduction-seeking reasons nor does the raw material-seeking investor differ significantly in his IAP preferences from those of the cost reduction-seeking investor. Therefore, for the individual classifications and for the

Indirect Control Group as a whole, the null hypotheses are accepted that investors respond to the same configuration of IAP without regard to motivation - host country market-seeking or raw material-seeking (H2A); host country market-seeking or cost reduction (H2B); raw material-seeking or cost reduction-seeking (H2C).

The lack of weight given to the *t*-distribution test results in making the findings for the Indirect Control group is occasioned by the small number of relative rankings required within each classification (3 to 4). Use of forced ranking, coupled with a small number of items to be ranked, appears to have a tendency to cause large relative variations in means - certainly as compared to the 8 and 10 item forced rankings required of the Direct Control Group. Since *t* - distribution is a test of means only and does not possess the capability of taking into account the spread within the paired items, it seems particularly vulnerable in this small number, forced ranked situation. Accordingly, the more robust tests of Duncan and ANOVA were given controlling weight in this circumstance.

Acceptance of the null hypothesis for the Indirect Control Group, which group itself is a collection of conditions existing within a prospective host country, is a rejection of the research hypotheses for H2A, H2B, H2C that different motivations for FDI result in MNCs having significantly different preferences for these country-conditions. Root and Ahmed (1978)[4], Group of Thirty (1984)[5], and Lim (1983)[6] suggest that it is country conditions such as GNP growth direction, inflation rate, market size, that determine where MNCs locate their FDI. Implied in their findings is the presumption that MNCs apply their prime focus to host country conditions across-the-sectrum of investment purposes, motivations, size, etc. Acceptance of the null hypothesis for the Indirect Control Group confirms that such a presumption is supported at least as far as consistently applying focus to host country conditions in the face of differing motivations for FDI. See Table 8.7- "MNC Ranking of Host Country Investment Attraction Packages, Segmented for Motivation for FDI".

Hypothesis #2 General Finding

Hypothesis #2 was stated in its general form:

> "It is proposed that investment attraction packages preferred by MNCs
>
> conducting initial-investment in the specified countries differ depending

TABLE 8.7

MNC RANKING OF HOST COUNTRY INVESTMENT ATTRACTION PACKAGES
SEGMENTED BY MOTIVATION FOR FDI

DIRECT CONTROL GROUP

HOST COUNTRY MARKET

	cl	REL	ABS
PROFIT REPATRIATION	F	1	1
DIVIDEND REPATRIATION	F	2	1
FOREX CONTROL	F	3	1
CAPITAL REPATRIATION	F	4	1
EQUITY LIMITS	I	1	1
DIVEST OWNERSHIP REQUIRED	I	2	1
PROFIT REINVEST LIMITS	I	3	1
FOREX BALANCING REQUIRED	F	5	2
FOREIGN PERSONNEL	F	6	2
EXPAND/DIVERSIFY LIMITS	I	4	2
BOARD APPOINTMENTS LIMITED	I	5	2
SECTORS EXCLUDED	I	6	2
OWN LAND/BUILDINGS LIMITED	I	7	2
INCOME TAX - LOW	T	1	2
DUTY FREE IMPORT	T	2	2
NO WITHHOLDING TAX	T	4	2
LOCAL CONTENT MINIMA	F	7	3
FINANCE FROM ABROAD	F	8	3
R&D MINIMA	F	9	3
EXPORT MINIMA	F	10	3
INTELLECTUAL PROP. PROTECT	I	8	3
TAX HOLIDAYS	T	3	3
ACCELERATED DEPRECIATION	T	5	3
SUBSIDIES	T	6	3
CAPITAL GRANTS	T	7	3
GOVT TENDER PREFERENCE	T	8	3
LOW RENT FTZ	T	9	3
PROTECTED MARKET	T	10	3

RAW MATERIALS

	cl	REL	ABS
PROFIT REPATRIATION	F	1	1
DIVIDEND REPATRIATION	F	5	1
INTELLECTUAL PROP. PROTECT	I	1	1
CAPITAL REPATRIATION	F	2	2
FOREX CONTROL	F	3	2
FOREIGN PERSONNEL	F	4	2
FOREX BALANCING REQUIRED	F	6	2
PROFIT REINVEST LIMITS	I	2	2
EXPAND/DIVERSIFY LIMITS	I	2	2
EQUITY LIMITS	I	6	3
TAX HOLIDAYS	I	2	2
LOCAL CONTENT MINIMA	F	7	3
FINANCE FROM ABROAD	F	8	3
R&D MINIMA	F	9	3
EXPORT MINIMA	F	10	3
DIVEST OWNERSHIP REQUIRED	I	4	3
BOARD APPOINTMENTS LIMITED	I	5	3
OWN LAND/BUILDINGS LIMITED	I	7	3
SECTORS EXCLUDED	I	8	3
INCOME TAX - LOW	T	1	3
ACCELERATED DEPRECIATION	T	3	3
CAPITAL GRANTS	T	4	3
SUBSIDIES	T	5	3
DUTY FREE IMPORT	T	6	3
LOW RENT FTZ	T	7	3
NO WITHHOLDING TAX	T	8	3
GOVT TENDER PREFERENCE	T	9	3
PROTECTED MARKET	T	10	3

COST REDUCTION

	cl	REL	ABS
PROFIT REPATRIATION	F	1	1
CAPITAL REPATRIATION	F	2	1
EQUITY LIMITS	I	1	1
DIVEST OWNERSHIP REQUIRED	I	3	1
BOARD APPOINTMENTS LIMITED	I	4	1
DIVIDEND REPATRIATION	F	3	2
FOREX CONTROL	F	3	2
FOREX BALANCING REQUIRED	F	5	2
FOREIGN PERSONNEL	F	6	2
PROFIT REINVEST LIMITS	I	2	2
OWN LAND/BUILDINGS LIMITED	I	5	2
EXPAND/DIVERSIFY LIMITS	I	6	2
INTELLECTUAL PROP. PROTECT	I	7	2
DUTY FREE IMPORT	T	1	2
INCOME TAX - LOW	T	2	2
TAX HOLIDAYS	T	3	2
LOW RENT FTZ	T	5	2
FINANCE FROM ABROAD	F	7	3
LOCAL CONTENT MINIMA	F	8	3
EXPORT MINIMA	F	9	3
R&D MINIMA	F	10	3
SECTORS EXCLUDED	I	8	3
NO WITHHOLDING TAX	T	4	3
CAPITAL GRANTS	T	6	3
PROTECTED MARKET	T	7	3
ACCELERATED DEPRECIATION	T	8	3
SUBSIDIES	T	9	3
GOVT TENDER PREFERENCE	T	10	3

cl = classifications
F = Financial Restriction
I = Investment & Ownership
T = Taxes & Subsidies Incentives

INDIRECT CONTROL GROUP

HOST COUNTRY MARKET

	REL	ABS
COUNTRY STABILITY	1	1
CIVIL DISTURBANCE	2	1
LAW CLARITY	1	1
FOREX FLUCTUATION	1	2
TARIFF LEVELS	3	2
INFLATION TREND	1	2
EXPROPRIATION PROTECTION	2	2
DISPUTE RESOLUTION	3	2
LEADERSHIP TURNOVER	3	2
SKILLS AVAILABLE	1	2
WAGE LEVELS	2	2
HIRE/FIRE RESTRICTIONS	3	2
TELECOMMUNICATIONS FACILITIES	1	2
TRANSPORT SYSTEM	2	2
ELECTRICITY RELIABILITY	3	2
INTEGRITY OF OFFICIALS	1	2
EFFECTIVE ADMINISTRATION	2	2
FDI SCREENING	3	2
PUBLIC SAFETY	4	2
GDP GROWTH	4	2
EDUCATION FACILITIES	4	3

RAW MATERIALS

	REL	ABS
COUNTRY STABILITY	1	1
TRANSPORT SYSTEM	1	1
INTEGRITY OF OFFICIALS	1	1
CIVIL DISTURBANCE	2	2
LAW CLARITY	3	2
EXPROPRIATION PROTECTION	1	2
DISPUTE RESOLUTION	2	2
LEADERSHIP TURNOVER	3	2
SKILLS AVAILABLE	1	2
WAGE LEVELS	2	2
HIRE/FIRE RESTRICTIONS	3	2
TELECOMMUNICATIONS FACILITIES	3	2
ELECTRICITY RELIABILITY	2	2
EFFECTIVE ADMINISTRATION	3	2
FDI SCREENING	4	2
PUBLIC SAFETY	2	2
FOREX FLUCTUATION	3	3
TARIFF LEVELS	1	3
INFLATION TREND	2	3
GDP GROWTH	4	3
EDUCATION FACILITIES	4	3

COST REDUCTION

	REL	ABS
CIVIL DISTURBANCE	1	1
COUNTRY STABILITY	2	1
TARIFF LEVELS	1	1
TELECOMMUNICATIONS FACILITIES	1	1
TRANSPORT SYSTEM	3	2
INTEGRITY OF OFFICIALS	1	2
LAW CLARITY	2	2
EXPROPRIATION PROTECTION	1	2
DISPUTE RESOLUTION	3	2
LEADERSHIP TURNOVER	3	2
SKILLS AVAILABLE	1	2
WAGE LEVELS	2	2
HIRE/FIRE RESTRICTIONS	3	2
ELECTRICITY RELIABILITY	2	2
EFFECTIVE ADMINISTRATION	3	2
FDI SCREENING	2	2
PUBLIC SAFETY	4	2
FOREX FLUCTUATION	2	2
INFLATION TREND	3	2
EDUCATION FACILITIES	4	2
GDP GROWTH	4	3

upon the MNC motivation for undertaking the investment"

A finding concerning the null hypothesis was made under each of the classifications making up the IAP. These classifications have been brought together under the two groupings - Direct Control Group and Indirect Control Group. A uniformity exists among the classification findings <u>within</u> each of the two groups that make up the IAP yet there is no consistency of findings <u>between</u> the two groups - in fact, the findings for the two groups are diametrically opposed to each other.

The uniform finding for the classifications making up the Direct Control group is a rejection of the null hypothesis. The uniform finding in the Indirect Control group is acceptance of the null hypothesis. Although the latter finding is partially against expectations, such opposed findings are consistent with the existence of disagreement in the findings of other researchers. The delineation of the findings of this study into Direct Control and Indirect Control groups may assist in the better understanding of the conflict in findings of prior researchers.

Having made a finding for each of the basic two groups, and with the finding for one group being in opposition to that of the other group, it appears counterproductive and potentially misleading to make an overall finding for the general hypothesis:

> Counterproductive - because the essence of this study is to encourage the segmentation of FDI into its meaningful parts. As such, "forcing" a general finding to the general hypothesis, in the face of different findings for different segments, would produce an academic equivalent to the medical oxymoron: the operation was a success but the patient died.

> Misleading - because a general finding, even if the exceptions were strongly noted, runs the risk of being repeated without the caveats. Thus, false impressions would be encouraged. In the area of cost reduction-seeking investments research to-date that focuses on this motivation for FDI is scarce and misinterpretation becomes particularly damaging when abundant other views are not available for refutation.

Although a technical finding for accepting the general hypothesis could perhaps be supported by the weight of the statistical evidence outlined in Direct Control Group, such a finding would mask - or worse - the more important finding:

MNC strategic motivation for FDI changes the lens, the target and the focus through which MNCs view selected government-legislated actions which directly effect the financial performance of MNCs but does not significantly change the preferences MNCs hold for specified general conditions within a potential host country.

Comparison of Findings With Other Researchers

Many researchers have speculated that MNC preferences for host country incentives and conditions-precedent within a potential host country may differ with the MNC's reason for investment. Most have called for research on the point. Few appear to have done so. An exception is Rolfe et al. (1993)[7], who found that export-oriented investors preferred tax holidays and tariff concessions while Host Country Market investors preferred incentives protecting their market and the relaxation of foreign exchange restrictions on profit repatriation. The findings of research hypothesis #2 appear to bear witness to the accuracy of the speculation. The preferences of MNCs making initial investments into the specified three Caribbean countries significantly differ when segmented for host country market-seeking motivation, cost reduction-seeking motivation (export-oriented investment) and raw material-seeking. Although conceptually treated collectively as cost reduction-seeking motivation by some writers - Williamson (1986)[8], Brewer (1993)[9], Woodward and Rolfe (1993)[10] among others - the study data pointed to significant difference in MNC perceptions of host country restrictions and incentives between raw material-seeking investors and export-oriented, non-raw material-seeking investors - in addition to significant differences between each of these motivations and the host country market-seeking motivation.

Further segmentation of the preferences denoted in the responses of MNCs with differing strategic motivations revealed that, while significant difference does exist in their preferences for specified government restrictions and incentives that directly effect the financial performance of the MNCs (Direct Control Group of elements), no significant difference existed among MNCs of different motivations in their preferences for specified conditions existing within host countries that are not within the direct control of government and for which the effect upon MNC financial performance could be more indirect.(Indirect Control elements). The true finding for research hypothesis #2, then, is "yes" and "no".

This "split decision" demonstrates the dangers inherent in generalizations based on observations of amalgamations of similar yet distinctively different entities. To this degree, it offers support for the

Contractor (1991)[11] admonition concerning the inappropriateness of general statements regarding the effectiveness of FDI policies. The finding, in itself, contributes little to the resolution of the debate concerning whether incentives given by host countries to attract FDI are effective, nor does it attempt to indicate the relative importance to MNCs as between the two separate groups of elements within the Investment Attraction package - incentives / restrictions or general conditions within the country. The focus of this study has been investment attraction and the MNCs preferences for certain specified elements generally regarded as being of potential interest to the prospective investor. Findings concerning investor preferences, however, do not represent findings concerning the effectiveness of those preferences for either MNCs or host countries. The need for further research into Investment Attraction Package effectiveness is evident. It is hoped that such research will be aided by the type of segmentation utilized herein for distinguishing between the fiscal matters over which the government has control and the more general country conditions for which government is frequently a by-stander.

Evans and Doupnik (1986)[12] found profit repatriation to be the #1 concern of U.S. MNCs in their FDI's. Contractor (1990)[13] suggested that foreign exchange restrictions would primarily effect host country market-seeking investors. Rolfe et al. (1993)[14] found profit repatriation to be a priority with the Host Country Market-seeking investors. Rolfe and White (1992)[15] found that profit repatriation restrictions were not the primary concern of Caribbean Basin investors. Rolfe et al. (1993)[16] found all investors particularly concerned about host country foreign exchange restrictions. This study supported the Profit Repatriation as #1 concern finding across all of its segmentations (motivations - home country market, raw material, cost reduction; quantum-levels - large & small; host country market - large & small; cost reduction - large) with one exception. No support was evident for the unique category of initial investment- cost reduction motivation- small quantum.

Reuber et al.(1973)[17] cited protection of local markets in a developing country as being of major importance for market development and government-initiated projects. Rolfe et al. (1993)[18] postulated that market-penetration investors would prefer tariff and quota protection. While government-initiated products were not investigated during this study, the importance of a protected market to host country market-seeking investors was not confirmed by this study. In fact, in the relative rankings of importance within the classification of Taxes and Subsidies Incentives, the element of Protected Market ranked in 10th place out of a group of 10 and its absolute importance was ranked as "low" for both Host Country Market-seeking and Raw Materials-seeking motivations. Somewhat surprisingly, among the cost reduction-seeking investor, the protected market element ranked somewhat higher relatively (7th) but still retained the "low" absolute importance ranking. This finding of non-support is broadly in concert with the Rolfe et al. (1993) conclusion.

Guisinger (1985)[19] reported that for export-oriented subjects, financial incentives such as income tax holidays were more important. Helleiner (1973)[20] and Wells (1986)[21] observed that export-oriented investors are more likely to be influenced in their location decisions by tax holidays than are market oriented investors. Rolfe and White (1992)[22] investigated length of tax holiday and found some relationship between the presence of a 15 year holiday and attractiveness of a site. When comparing initial-investment host country market-seeking MNCs with cost reduction-seeking MNCs in the aggregate, little support is given the foregoing by this study. No statistically significant differences were found between initial investors of the different mstrategic otivations on Low Income Taxes, Tax Holidays, and No Withholding Tax. MNCs of Host Country Market-seeking and Cost Reduction-seeking investment motivations ranked Low Income Tax at the same level of absolute importance - "moderate", while Raw Materials-seeking investors recorded a "low" absolute ranking to the benefit. Tax Holidays (CR and RM) and No Withholding Tax (HCM) were ranked "moderate" to "low". (The motivation HCM, RM or CR appearing in the parentheses registered the level higher ranking denoted). Accelerated Depreciation ranked "low" for all three motivations. The finding of Bond and Samuelson (1986)[23] that tax holidays act as signals to identify high productivity countries receives some support in both the HCM and the CR application.

The preferences of MNCs making large and small investments for both host country market and cost reduction reasons are compared in Hypothesis #3.

Rolfe et al. (1993)[24] in their study of U.S. firms in the Caribbean Basin, speculated that firms making their initial investment into a country may place more emphasis on incentives that reduce their initial expenses, such as cash grants and feasibility studies than would firms that were already present in the country and were expanding their operations. This study provides no data on expansion investments but for initial investment, the two elements - Capital Grants and Subsidies - received lower order relative ranking within their classification (7th and 6th for HCM, and 6th and 9th for CR) and both received a "low" absolute ranking by MNCs of both host country market and cost reduction motivation.

Therefore, this study offers no support for the speculation that firms making initial investments place high value on Cash Grants and Subsidies.

Rolfe et al. (1993)[25] found the duty free import concession to be more highly prized by export oriented investors than by Host Country Market-seeking investors. In the aggregate, this study reveals no statistically significant difference existing between MNCs of the two different motivations - Host Country Market-seeking and Cost Reduction-seeking. Substantively, the "absolute" ranking data indicates that any difference in perceptions of the benefit may be said to be relatively minute. While MNCs of both motivations ranked the absolute importance of Duty Free Import as only "moderate", the relative ranking within the classification was #1 (out of 10) by cost reduction investors and #2 by host country marketers. Although this finding is somewhat surprising in the aggregate, the segmentation by quantum of investment in Hypothesis #3 clarifies this.

Interpretations of Findings

Although MNCs preferences for the various elements of the Investment Attraction Packages of the subject countries is found to vary with the strategic motivation of the MNC for conducting the FDI, one element stands out as a virtual "ticket to play" - the condition precedent, the quid quo pro - for those countries desiring to host FDI - Profit Repatriation. Of those MNCs responding to the survey, this was the sole element on which agreement of importance existed within the Direct Control Group. Each motivation denoted this element as being of the "highest" absolute importance, although an exception is referenced under Hypothesis #3 for the sub-category "initial investment - cost reduction - small investment". With virtual agreement between motivations that Profit Repatriation is #1 concern, a host country not offering this element faces serious questions as to whether its "hat" is effectively in the "ring" for FDI. To be sure, there are various degrees and permutations for Profit Repatriation - it may not have to be 100% each and every year - but for the first time investor into a given country, the established concept of return on investment (ROI) is likely to be associated with the developed country norm that parent corporations exercise their free and unfettered judgement in determining the use of its after-tax earnings. Until residence in the host country builds the confidence, the understanding, and, maybe, even the compassion for the country, indications that earnings will be subject to non-repatriation and, hence, non-inclusion in the parent "pool" of funds available for distribution as they deem appropriate, is likely to place the potential host country at serious disadvantage in attracting FDI. Profit Repatriation, as confirmed by the stated preferences of the MNCs responding to this study, appears to be a prime consideration in making the location decision regardless of strategic motivation. The avenues available for providing access to spendable reimbursement are greater for the raw material investor and the cost reduction investor since both have non-resident third party customers and/or have vertically intergrated structures at their command, both of which can facilitate the required transfer of funds or in-kind returns. The "alternate means" options for receiving profit repatriation by the host country market-seeking MNCs, of either large or small quantum, are more restricted.

The Indirect Control Group also netted one universal condition for FDI - Country Stability. Investment's aversion to uncertainty is well known. Although reward is a function of risk, at some level of country instability the risk apparently becomes unacceptable or, more accurately put for the context of this study, becomes a significantly negative factor in FDI location-decisions.

In the interests of reducing redundancy and increasing the specificity of the interpretations, further comment and interpretation is withheld until after the findings of Hypothesis #3 are discussed. Hypothesis #3 adds the dimension of quantum to Hypothesis #2's strategic motivation dimension. The resulting matrix identifies a series of "micro groups" whose absence from the more aggregated findings on strategic motivation would give rise to a confusing series of exceptions to generalized interpretations.

Hypothesis #3 -Quantum and FDI Motivation

MNCs preferences for the elements of the focus countries' Investment Attraction Packages were compared on the basis of the levels of quantum of initial investment made by MNCs and by the levels of quantum and motivations of MNCs for conducting initial FDI into the host country. The proposition examined was whether initial-investment MNCs with different motivations and different FDI quantum-levels prefer differently configured Investment Attraction Packages. Quantum of initial investment was segmented into two groupings: "small" - less than $1,000,000 - and "large" - $1,000,000 or more. Statistical tests (t-distribution) were conducted to determine whether the difference in the means of the paired groups was statistically significant. The paired groups of small versus large investment were tested against the total survey, against each other within the same motivation, and against host country market-seeking and cost reduction-seeking FDI motivations within the same level of quantum. Since the data to be tested was in paired groups only, it was inappropriate to invoke the Anova procedure and Duncan's Multiple Range test. See Table 8.8 - "Segmentation By FDI Motivation & Large vs. Small Quantum" - and Table 8.9 - "Segmentation By Large Quantum/FDI Motivation & Small Quantum/FDI Motivation" for results of these

TABLE 8.8

SEGMENTATION OF MNCs PREFERENCES BY FDI MOTIVATION & LARGE VS SMALL QUANTUM

ELEMENT	HOST COUNTRY MARKET SMALL (<$1.0 MM) RELATIVE MEAN SCORE	RK	ABSL. MED-IAN	LARGE (>$1.0MM) RELATIVE MEAN SCORE	RK	ABSL. MED IAN	T O S SM LG	COST REDUCTION SMALL (<$1.0MM) RELATIVE MEAN SCORE	RK	ABSL. MED-IAN	LARGE (>$1.0MM) RELATIVE MEAN SCORE	RK	ABSL. MED-IAN	T O S SM LG
DIRECT CONTROL GROUP														
FINANCIAL RESTRICTIONS														
PROFIT REPATRIATION	1.35	1	1	2.10	1	1	*	2.30	1	2	2.00	1	1	
CAPITAL REPATRIATION	2.74	3	1	3.00	4	2		3.20	2	2	3.40	2	1	
FOREX CONTROL	3.00	4	1	2.50	2	1		4.40	3	3	4.50	4	1	
DIVIDEND REPATRIATION	2.70	2	1	2.75	3	1		4.50	4	2	4.38	3	1.5	
FOREIGN PERSONNEL	4.78	6	2	5.84	5	2	*	5.78	6	3	4.75	5	1.5	
FOREX BALANCING REQUIRED	4.39	5	2	6.21	6	2	**	5.00	5	2	5.43	6	2	
FINANCE FROM ABROAD	7.22	8	3	7.16	10	3		6.33	7	3	6.13	7	3	
LOCAL CONTENT MINIMA	6.17	7	2	7.94	7	3	***	6.67	8	3	8.75	9	3	*
EXPORT MINIMA	8.10	10	3	8.06	8	3		7.78	9	3	7.88	8	3	
R&D MINIMA	7.35	9	3	8.31	9	3		9.00	10	3	8.75	10	3	
INVESTMENT & OWNERSHIP														
EQUITY LIMITS	1.80	1	1	1.77	1	1		1.10	1	2	1.13	1	1	
PROFIT REINVEST LIMITS	3.18	2	1	3.38	3	1		2.30	2	2	5.00	5	2	*
DIVEST OWNERSHIP REQUIRED	3.23	3	1	2.85	2	1		3.80	3	2	3.67	3	1	
EXPAND/DIVERSIFY LIMITS	3.90	4	2	3.46	4	2		4.40	4	2	5.63	6	2	
BOARD APPOINTMENTS LIMITED	4.00	5	2	4.62	5	2		5.50	6	2	3.50	2	1	**
OWN LAND/BUILDINGS LIMITED	5.36	7	2	5.08	7	2		5.40	5	3	4.80	4	1	
INTELLECTUAL PROP. PROTECT	5.41	8	2	5.77	8	3		6.22	7	3	6.17	7	1	
SECTORS EXCLUDED	5.32	6	2	5.00	6	3		7.00	8	3	6.67	8	2	
TAXES & SUBSIDIES INCENTIVES														
INCOME TAX - LOW	2.11	1	1	2.59	1	2		3.80	3	2	2.00	1	2	**
DUTY FREE IMPORT	2.53	2	2	3.12	2	2		1.82	1	1	3.75	2	2	
TAX HOLIDAYS	4.55	4	3	5.19	3	2		2.70	2	2	5.38	6	2	*
NO WITHHOLDING TAX	4.37	3	2	5.94	7	2	*	4.33	5	3	4.63	3	3	
ACCELERATED DEPRECIATION	5.26	5	3	5.50	4	3		7.78	8	3	5.25	5	3	**
LOW RENT FTZ	6.21	7	3	7.19	10	3		4.30	4	2	5.13	4	2.5	
CAPITAL GRANTS	6.32	8	3	5.88	6	3		5.20	6	3	8.00	10	3	*
SUBSIDIES	5.32	6	3	6.65	8	3		8.11	10	3	6.63	8	3	
GOVT TENDER PREFERENCE	6.53	9	3	5.79	5	2		7.88	9	3	7.38	9	3	
PROTECTED MARKET	6.84	10	3	6.85	9	3		7.11	7	3	5.88	7	3	
INDIRECT CONTROL GROUP														
ECONOMIC CONDITIONS														
FOREX FLUCTUATION	1.95	1	2	1.47	1	2		1.91	2	2	2.00	1	1.5	
TARIFF LEVELS	2.23	3	2	3.12	4	2	**	1.70	1	1	2.00	1	1.5	
INFLATION TREND	2.18	2	2	2.41	2	2		2.50	3	2	2.75	3	2	
GDP GROWTH	2.95	4	2	2.76	3	3		3.78	4	3	3.14	4	3	
LEGAL CONDITIONS														
EXPROPRIATION PROTECTION	1.77	2	2	1.81	2	2		2.00	2	2	1.29	1	2	
LAW CLARITY	1.50	1	1	1.54	1	1		1.67	1	1	1.86	2	2	
DISPUTE RESOLUTION	2.14	3	2	2.44	3	2		2.33	3	2	2.86	3	2	
POLITICAL CONDITIONS														
COUNTRY STABILITY	1.27	1	1	1.29	1	1		1.40	1	1	2.00	2	2	***
CIVIL DISTURBANCE	1.86	2	1	1.82	2	2		1.90	2	1	1.00	1	1	**
LEADERSHIP TURNOVER	2.09	3	2	2.88	3	2	***	2.30	3	2	3.00	3	2	*
LABOUR CONDITIONS														
SKILLS AVAILABLE	1.86	2	2	1.60	1	1.5		2.09	2	2	2.25	2	2	
WAGE LEVELS	1.77	1	2	2.75	3	2	**	2.00	1	1	2.43	3	2	
HIRE/FIRE RESTRICTIONS	2.68	4	2	2.56	2	2		2.64	3	2	1.86	1	2	
EDUCATION FACILITIES	2.64	3	3	3.31	4	2	**	3.09	4	2	3.25	4	3	
INFRASTRUCTURE CONDITIONS														
TELECOMMUNICATIONS FACILITIES	1.91	2	2	1.86	2	2		1.73	2	2	1.50	1	1	
TRANSPORT SYSTEM	2.23	2	2	1.63	1	2		2.45	3	2	2.13	2	1.5	
ELECTRICITY RELIABILITY	2.55	3	3	2.50	3	3		1.45	1	1	2.38	3	2	*
ADMINISTRATIVE CONDITIONS														
INTEGRITY OF OFFICIALS	1.89	1	2	1.75	1	1		1.26	1	2	1.50	1	2	
EFFECTIVE ADMINISTRATION	1.95	2	2	1.94	2	2		3.00	3	2	2.86	3	2	
FDI SCREENING	2.79	3	2	3.04	4	2		1.88	2	3	2.36	2	2	
PUBLIC SAFETY	3.05	4	2	3.00	3	2.5		3.03	4	3	2.86	3	2	*

Legend: Summary of "Absolute Importance" Response Medians

t-Dist		Importance				
Prob. < .10	*	Highest	11	9	7	10
Prob. < .05	* *	Moderate	26	23	23	28
Prob. < .01	***	Lesser	13	17	19	11

Relative (Importance within Classification)
"Mean Score" within Classification
"RK" = Element Rank within Classification

TABLE 8.9

SEGMENTATION OF MNCs PREFERENCES BY LARGE/FDI QUANTUM & SMALL QUANTUN/FDI MOTIVATION

	LARGE INVESTMENT (> $1.0 MM)							SMALL INVESTMENTS (< $1.0MM)						
	HOST MARKET			COST REDUCE			T O S HM CR	HOST MARKET			COST REDUCE			T O S HM CR
	RELATIVE MEAN SCORE	RK	ABSL. MEDIAN	RELATIVE MEAN SCORE	RK	ABSL. MEDIAN		RELATIVE MEAN SCORE	RK	ABSL. MEDIAN	RELATIVE MEAN SCORE	RK	ABSL. MEDIAN	
DIRECT CONTROL GROUP														
FINANCIAL RESTRICTIONS														
PROFIT REPATRIATION	2.10	1	1	2.00	1	1		1.35	1	1	2.30	1	2	
CAPITAL REPATRIATION	3.00	4	1	3.40	2	1		2.74	3	1	3.20	2	2	
FOREX CONTROL	2.50	2	1	4.50	4	1		3.00	4	1	4.40	3	3	
DIVIDEND REPATRIATION	2.75	3	1	4.38	3	1.5	*	2.70	2	1	4.50	4	2	**
FOREIGN PERSONNEL	5.84	5	2	4.75	5	1.5		4.78	6	2	5.78	6	3	
FOREX BALANCING REQUIRED	6.21	6	2	5.43	6	2		4.39	5	2	5.00	5	2	
FINANCE FROM ABROAD	7.16	7	3	6.13	7	3	*	7.22	8	3	6.17	7	3	
LOCAL CONTENT MINIMA	7.94	8	3	8.75	9	3		6.17	7	2	6.67	8	3	
EXPORT MINIMA	8.06	9	3	7.88	8	3		8.10	10	3	7.78	9	3	
R&D MINIMA	8.31	10	3	8.75	10	3		7.35	9	3	9.00	10	3	**
INVESTMENT & OWNERSHIP														
EQUITY LIMITS	1.77	1	1	1.13	1	1		1.80	1	1	1.10	1	2	***
PROFIT REINVEST LIMITS	3.38	3	1	5.00	5	2		3.18	2	1	2.30	2	2	
DIVEST OWNERSHIP REQUIRED	2.85	2	1	3.67	3	1	**	3.23	3	1	3.8	3	2	
EXPAND/DIVERSIFY LIMITS	3.46	4	1	5.63	6	2	**	3.90	4	2	4.40	4	2	
BOARD APPOINTMENTS LIMITED	4.62	5	2	3.50	2	1	***	4.00	5	2	5.5	6	2	
OWN LAND/BUILDINGS LIMITED	5.08	7	1.5	4.60	4	1		5.36	7	2	5.40	5	3	
INTELLECTUAL PROP. PROTECT	5.77	8	3	6.17	7	1		5.41	8	2	6.22	7	3	
SECTORS EXCLUDED	5.00	6	2	6.67	8	2	***	5.32	6	2	7.00	8	3	**
TAXES & SUBSIDIES INCENTIVES														
INCOME TAX - LOW	2.59	1	2	2.00	1	2	*	2.11	1	1	3.80	3	2	*
DUTY FREE IMPORT	3.12	2	2	3.75	2	2		2.53	2	2	1.82	1	1	
TAX HOLIDAYS	5.19	3	2.5	5.38	6	2		4.55	4	3	2.70	2	2	**
NO WITHHOLDING TAX	5.94	7	2	4.63	3	3		4.37	3	2	4.33	5	3	
ACCELERATED DEPRECIATION	5.50	4	3	5.25	5	3		5.26	5	3	7.78	8	3	***
LOW RENT FTZ	7.19	10	3	5.13	4	2.5	**	6.21	7	3	4.30	4	2	*
CAPITAL GRANTS	5.68	6	3	8.00	10	3	*	6.32	8	3	5.20	6	3	
SUBSIDIES	6.65	8	3	6.63	8	3		5.32	6	3	8.11	10	3	***
GOVT TENDER PREFERENCE	5.79	5	2	7.38	9	3	**	6.53	9	3	7.88	9	3	
PROTECTED MARKET	6.85	9	3	5.88	7	3		6.84	10	3	7.11	7	3	
INDIRECT CONTROL GROUP														
ECONOMIC CONDITIONS														
FOREX FLUCTUATION	1.47	1	2	2.00	1	1.5		1.95	1	2	1.91	2	2	
TARIFF LEVELS	3.12	4	2	2.00	1	1.5	**	2.33	3	2	1.70	1	1	
INFLATION TREND	2.41	2	2	2.75	3	2		2.16	2	2	2.50	3	2	
GDP GROWTH	2.76	3	2	3.14	4	3		2.95	4	2	3.78	4	3	***
LEGAL CONDITIONS														
EXPROPRIATION PROTECTION	1.81	2	1.5	1.29	1	2		1.77	2	2	2.00	2	2	
LAW CLARITY	1.54	1	1.5	1.86	2	2		1.50	1	1	1.67	1	1	
DISPUTE RESOLUTION	2.44	3	2	2.86	3	2	*	2.14	3	2	2.33	3	2	
POLITICAL CONDITIONS														
COUNTRY STABILITY	1.29	1	1	2.00	2	2	***	1.27	1	1	1.40	1	1	
CIVIL DISTURBANCE	1.82	2	1	1.00	1	1	***	1.86	2	1	1.90	2	1	
LEADERSHIP TURNOVER	2.68	3	2	3.00	3	2	***	2.09	3	2	2.30	3	2	
LABOUR CONDITIONS														
SKILLS AVAILABLE	1.50	1	1.5	2.25	2	2	*	1.86	2	2	2.09	2	2	
WAGE LEVELS	2.75	3	2	2.43	3	2		1.77	1	2	2.00	1	1	
HIRE/FIRE RESTRICTIONS	2.56	2	2	1.86	1	2		2.68	4	2	2.68	3	2	
EDUCATION FACILITIES	3.31	4	2	3.25	4	3		2.64	3	3	3.09	4	2	
INFRASTRUCTURE CONDITIONS														
TELECOMMUNICATIONS FACILITIES	1.86	2	2	1.50	1	1		1.91	1	2	1.73	2	2	
TRANSPORT SYSTEM	1.63	1	2	2.13	2	1.5		2.23	2	2	2.45	3	2	
ELECTRICITY RELIABILITY	2.50	3	2	2.36	3	2		2.55	3	3	1.45	1	1	***
ADMINISTRATION CONDITIONS														
INTEGRITY OF OFFICIALS	1.75	1	1	1.50	1	2		1.89	1	2	1.25	1	2	**
EFFECTIVE ADMINISTRATION	1.94	2	2	2.86	3	2	**	1.95	2	2	3.00	3	3	*
FDI SCREENING	3.04	4	2	2.36	2	2		2.78	3	2	1.88	2	3	**
PUBLIC SAFETY	3.00	3	2.5	2.86	3	2		3.05	4	2	3.03	4	3	

Legend:

Summary of "Absolute Importance" Response Medians

t-Dist		Importance				
Prob. < .10	*	Highest	15	15	11	7
Prob. < .05	**	Moderate	24	22	25	23
Prob. < .01	***	Lesser	10	12	13	19

Relative (importance within Classification)
"Mean Score" within Classification
"RK" = Element Rank within Classification

tests.

Findings

The findings are reported under each of the sub hypotheses (H3A - H3F) and conclude with the general finding.

H3A - Small vs. Large: Total Survey

Of the 49 elements listed in the Investment Attraction Package examined by this study, the number of individual elements showing statistically significant difference via the *t*-distribution test, at the .05 confidence level, was five (5),or 10.2%.

Findings in Direct Control Group

The responses from MNCs having different quantum levels of initial FDI in the subject countries show significant differences in the preferences accorded 10.7% of the individual elements making up the Direct Control Group, at the .05 level of confidence.

Statistically significant difference exists in a low number of the elements making up the Direct Control Group (3 of 28) and neither large nor small investing MNCs have ranked these elements as being of highest level of absolute ranking. The differences exhibited do not appear to be of sufficient strength to indicate basic divergence in focus of the two groups. (See Table 8.10 - "MNC Rankings of Host Country Investment Attraction Packages Segmented By Motivation, By Quantum of Investment"). It follows, then, that the null hypothesis of no significant difference existing between the large and small investing MNCs based on quantum invested should be accepted for the Direct Control Group.

Findings in Indirect Control Group

The responses from MNCs having different quantum levels of initial FDI in the subject countries show significant differences in the preferences accorded 9.5% of the individual elements making up the Indirect Control Group, at the .05 level of confidence.

The number of elements exhibiting statistically significant difference is small (2 of 21) and no support for substantive difference is received by either of the .05 level denoted elements (Leadership Turnover and Wage Levels) as the elements are ranked equally by both large and small investing MNCs on the importance scale. (See Table 8.10) Therefore, the null hypothesis of no significant difference existing between Total Survey - large and small investing MNCs - based on quantum invested is accepted for the Indirect Control Group.

TABLE 8.10

MNC RANKING OF HOST COUNTRY INVESTMENT ATTRACTION PACKAGES
SEGMENTED BY MOTIVATION, BY QUANTUM OF INVESTMENT

DIRECT CONTROL GROUP

HOST COUNTRY MARKET SMALL (LESS THAN $1,000,00	cl	REL	ABS	HOST COUNTRY MARKET LARGE ($1,000,000 OR MORE)	cl	REL	ABS	COST REDUCTION INVESTMENT SMALL (LESS THAN $1,000,00	cl	REL	ABS	COST REDUCTION INVESTMENT LARGE ($1,000,000 OR MORE)	cl	REL	ABS
PROFIT REPATRIATION	F	1	1	PROFIT REPATRIATION	F	1	1	DUTY FREE IMPORT	T	1	1	PROFIT REPATRIATION	F	1	1
DIVIDEND REPATRIATION	F	2	1	FOREX CONTROL	F	2	1					CAPITAL REPATRIATION	F	2	1
CAPITAL REPATRIATION	F	3	1	DIVIDEND REPATRIATION	F	3	1					FOREX CONTROL	F	4	1
FOREX CONTROL	F	4	1	CAPITAL REPATRIATION	F	4	1					DIVIDEND REPATRIATION	F	3	1.5
EQUITY LIMITS	I	1	1	EQUITY LIMITS	I	1	1					FOREIGN PERSONNEL	F	5	1.5
PROFIT REINVEST LIMITS	I	2	1	DIVEST OWNERSHIP REQUIRED	I	2	1					EQUITY LIMITS	I	1	1
DIVEST OWNERSHIP REQUIRED	I	3	1	PROFIT REINVEST LIMITS	I	3	1					BOARD APPOINTMENTS LIMITED	I	2	1
INCOME TAX - LOW	T	1	1	EXPAND/DIVERSIFY LIMITS	I	4	1					DIVEST OWNERSHIP REQUIRED	I	3	1
				OWN LAND/BUILDINGS LIMITED	I	7	1.5					OWN LAND/BUILDINGS LIMITED	I	4	1
												INTELLECTUAL PROP. PROTECT	I	7	1
FOREX BALANCING REQUIRED	F	5	2	FOREIGN PERSONNEL	F	5	2	PROFIT REPATRIATION	F	1	2	FOREX BALANCING REQUIRED	F	6	2
FOREIGN PERSONNEL	F	6	2	FOREX BALANCING REQUIRED	F	6	2	CAPITAL REPATRIATION	F	2	2	PROFIT REINVEST LIMITS	I	5	2
LOCAL CONTENT MINIMA	F	7	2	BOARD APPOINTMENTS LIMITED	I	5	2	DIVIDEND REPATRIATION	F	4	2	EXPAND/DIVERSIFY LIMITS	I	6	2
EXPAND/DIVERSIFY LIMITS	I	4	2	SECTORS EXCLUDED	I	6	2	FOREX BALANCING REQUIRED	F	5	2	SECTORS EXCLUDED	I	8	2
BOARD APPOINTMENTS LIMITED	I	5	2	INCOME TAX - LOW	T	1	2	EQUITY LIMITS	I	1	2	INCOME TAX - LOW	T	1	2
SECTORS EXCLUDED	I	6	2	DUTY FREE IMPORT	T	2	2	PROFIT REINVEST LIMITS	I	2	2	DUTY FREE IMPORT	T	2	2
OWN LAND/BUILDINGS LIMITED	I	7	2	TAX HOLIDAYS	T	3	2.5	DIVEST OWNERSHIP REQUIRED	I	3	2	TAX HOLIDAYS	T	6	2
INTELLECTUAL PROP. PROTECT	I	8	2	GOVT TENDER PREFERENCE	T	5	2	EXPAND/DIVERSIFY LIMITS	I	4	2	LOW RENT FTZ	T	4	2.5
DUTY FREE IMPORT	T	2	2	NO WITHHOLDING TAX	T	7	2	BOARD APPOINTMENTS LIMITED	I	6	2				
NO WITHHOLDING TAX	T	3	2					TAX HOLIDAYS	T	2	2				
								INCOME TAX - LOW	T	3	2				
								LOW RENT FTZ	T	4	2				
FINANCE FROM ABROAD	F	8	3	FINANCE FROM ABROAD	F	7	3	FOREX CONTROL	F	3	3	FINANCE FROM ABROAD	F	7	3
R&D MINIMA	F	9	3	LOCAL CONTENT MINIMA	F	8	3	FOREIGN PERSONNEL	F	6	3	EXPORT MINIMA	F	8	3
EXPORT MINIMA	F	10	3	EXPORT MINIMA	F	9	3	FINANCE FROM ABROAD	F	7	3	LOCAL CONTENT MINIMA	F	9	3
TAX HOLIDAYS	T	4	3	R&D MINIMA	F	10	3	LOCAL CONTENT MINIMA	F	8	3	R&D MINIMA	F	10	3
ACCELERATED DEPRECIATION	T	5	3	INTELLECTUAL PROP. PROTECT	I	8	3	EXPORT MINIMA	F	9	3	NO WITHHOLDING TAX	T	3	3
SUBSIDIES	T	6	3	ACCELERATED DEPRECIATION	T	4	3	R&D MINIMA	F	10	3	ACCELERATED DEPRECIATION	T	5	3
LOW RENT FTZ	T	7	3	CAPITAL GRANTS	T	6	3	OWN LAND/BUILDINGS LIMITED	I	5	3	PROTECTED MARKET	T	7	3
CAPITAL GRANTS	T	8	3	SUBSIDIES	T	8	3	INTELLECTUAL PROP. PROTECT	I	7	3	SUBSIDIES	T	8	3
GOVT TENDER PREFERENCE	T	9	3	PROTECTED MARKET	T	9	3	SECTORS EXCLUDED	I	8	3	GOVT TENDER PREFERENCE	T	9	3
PROTECTED MARKET	T	10	3	LOW RENT FTZ	T	10	3	NO WITHHOLDING TAX	T	5	3	CAPITAL GRANTS	T	10	3
								CAPITAL GRANTS	T	6	3				
								PROTECTED MARKET	T	7	3				
								ACCELERATED DEPRECIATION	T	8	3				
								GOVT TENDER PREFERENCE	T	9	3				
								SUBSIDIES	T	10	3				

cl = classifications
F = Financial Restrictions
I = Investment & Ownership
T = Taxes & Subsidies Incentives

INDIRECT CONTROL GROUP

HOST COUNTRY MARKET SMALL (LESS THAN $1,000,00	REL	ABS	HOST COUNTRY MARKET LARGE ($1,000,000 OR MORE)	REL	ABS	COST REDUCTION INVESTMENT SMALL (LESS THAN $1,000,00	REL	ABS	COST REDUCTION INVESTMENT LARGE ($1,000,000 OR MORE)	REL	ABS
COUNTRY STABILITY	1	1	COUNTRY STABILITY	1	1	TARIFF LEVELS	1	1	CIVIL DISTURBANCE	1	1
LAW CLARITY	1	1	CIVIL DISTURBANCE	2	1	LAW CLARITY	1	1	TARIFF LEVELS	1	1
CIVIL DISTURBANCE	2	1	INTEGRITY OF OFFICIALS	1	1	COUNTRY STABILITY	1	1	TELECOMMUNICATIONS FACILITIES	1	1.5
			LAW CLARITY	1	1.5	CIVIL DISTURBANCE	2	1	FOREX FLUCTUATION	1	1.5
			EXPROPRIATION PROTECTION	2	1.5	WAGE LEVELS	1	1	TRANSPORT SYSTEM	2	1.5
			SKILLS AVAILABLE	1	1.5	ELECTRICITY RELIABILITY	1	1			
FOREX FLUCTUATION	1	2	TRANSPORT SYSTEM	1	2	INTEGRITY OF OFFICIALS	1	2	EXPROPRIATION PROTECTION	1	2
WAGE LEVELS	1	2	FOREX FLUCTUATION	1	2	FOREX FLUCTUATION	2	2	HIRE/FIRE RESTRICTIONS	1	2
INTEGRITY OF OFFICIALS	1	2	INFLATION TREND	2	2	EXPROPRIATION PROTECTION	2	2	INTEGRITY OF OFFICIALS	1	2
TRANSPORT SYSTEM	2	2	TELECOMMUNICATIONS FACILITIES	2	2	SKILLS AVAILABLE	2	2	LAW CLARITY	2	2
INFLATION TREND	2	2	EFFECTIVE ADMINISTRATION	2	2	TELECOMMUNICATIONS FACILITIES	2	2	SKILLS AVAILABLE	2	2
EXPROPRIATION PROTECTION	2	2	HIRE/FIRE RESTRICTIONS	2	2	INFLATION TREND	3	2	COUNTRY STABILITY	2	2
EFFECTIVE ADMINISTRATION	2	2	DISPUTE RESOLUTION	3	2	DISPUTE RESOLUTION	3	2	FDI SCREENING	2	2
SKILLS AVAILABLE	2	2	LEADERSHIP TURNOVER	3	2	LEADERSHIP TURNOVER	3	2	WAGE LEVELS	3	2
TELECOMMUNICATIONS FACILITIES	2	2	GDP GROWTH	3	2	TRANSPORT SYSTEM	3	2	ELECTRICITY RELIABILITY	3	2
LEADERSHIP TURNOVER	3	2	ELECTRICITY RELIABILITY	3	2	HIRE/FIRE RESTRICTIONS	3	2	WAGE LEVELS	3	2
TARIFF LEVELS	3	2	FDI SCREENING	4	2	EDUCATION FACILITIES	4	2	INFLATION TREND	3	2
DISPUTE RESOLUTION	3	2	EDUCATION FACILITIES	4	2				DISPUTE RESOLUTION	3	2
FDI SCREENING	3	2	TARIFF LEVELS	4	2				LEADERSHIP TURNOVER	3	2
PUBLIC SAFETY	4	2	PUBLIC SAFETY	3	2.5				ELECTRICITY RELIABILITY	3	2
GDP GROWTH	4	2							EFFECTIVE ADMINISTRATION	3	2
									PUBLIC SAFETY	3	2
ELECTRICITY RELIABILITY	3	3				FDI SCREENING	2	3	GDP GROWTH	4	3
EDUCATION FACILITIES	3	3				EFFECTIVE ADMINISTRATION	3	3	EDUCATION FACILITIES	4	3
HIRE/FIRE RESTRICTIONS	4	3				GDP GROWTH	4	3			
						PUBLIC SAFETY	4	3			

H3B - Small vs. Large: Host Country Market

Six (6) of the individual elements making up the Investment Attraction Package showed showed statistically significant difference, at the .05 confidence level. This represented 12.4% of the total elements.

Findings in Direct Control Group

The responses from MNCs having different quantum levels of initial FDI in the subject countries and who invested for host country market-seeking reasons show significant differences in the preferences accorded 7.1% of the individual elements making up the Direct Control Group, at the .05 level of confidence.

Statistically significant difference exists in a low number of the elements making up the Direct Control Group (2 of 28) and neither large nor small investing MNCs have ranked these elements as being of highest level of absolute importance. The differences exhibited do not appear to be of sufficient strength to indicate basic divergence in focus of the two groups. (See Table 8.10). It follows, then, that the null hypothesis of no significant difference existing between Host Country Market-seeking large and small investing MNCs based on quantum invested should be accepted for the Direct Control Group.

Findings in Indirect Control Group

The responses from MNCs having different quantum levels of initial FDI in the subject countries and who invested for host country market-seeking reasons show significant differences in the preferences accorded 19.0% of the individual elements making up the Indirect Control Group, at the .05 level of confidence

The number of elements exhibiting statistically significant difference is not insignificant (4 of 21), yet little support for substantive difference is received by any of the denoted elements. Only one element - Education Facilities - shows a difference in absolute level of importance (large ranking "moderate" and small ranking "low") and the other three elements were agreed as being moderately important. (See Table 8.10) Therefore, the null hypothesis of no significant difference existing between Host Country Market-seeking large and small investing MNCs based on quantum invested is accepted for the Indirect Control Group.

H3C - Small vs. Large: Cost Reduction

10.2% of the individual elements of the total IAP showed statistically significant difference, at the .05 confidence level, when subjected to the *t*-distribution test.

Findings in Direct Control Group

The responses from MNCs having different quantum levels of initial FDI in the subject countries and who invested for cost reduction-seeking reasons show significant differences in the preferences accorded 10.7% of the individual elements making up the Direct Control Group, at the .05 level of confidence.

The existence of significant difference in three (3) of the 28 elements of the Direct Control Group is underscored by the highest relative importance attached to one of the elements (Board Appointments Limitations) by the small quantum cost reduction investor. Such high absolute ranking provides corroborated evidence that difference in focus exists between the two groups. This presumption is boosted by the differences expressed in several of the absolute rankings accorded the various elements of the Direct Control Group. Tables 8.10 shows the divergence of views on levels of absolute importance rankings attached by small and large MNCs to the IAP elements. Importance level of ranking of four elements (Foreign Exchange Control, Foreign Personnel, Ownership of Land/Buildings, and Intellectual Property Protection) recorded the maximum two-level difference with each of these elements being ranked "highest" by the large investment MNCs and "low" by the small investor. Although it is evident that the number of elements containing statistically significant difference is relatively small in comparison to the total number of elements involved, the differences appear to be reasonably sharp when viewed in the light of the evidence presented by the absolute importance rankings as determined by the median of the MNCs responses in the Direct Control Group. Accordingly, for the Direct Control Group, the null hypothesis (H3C), that MNCs making large investments in the focus countries for cost reduction seeking reasons respond to the same configuration of investment attraction package as do those making smaller investments, is rejected.

Findings in Indirect Control Group

The responses from MNCs having different quantum levels of initial FDI in the subject countries and who invested for cost reduction-seeking reasons show significant differences in the preferences accorded 9.5% of the individual elements making up the Indirect Control Group, at the .05 level of confidence.

Evidence of statistically significant difference occurred in two elements out of the 21 of the Indirect Control Group at the .05 level, and in three additional elements at the .10 level. Of the nine elements whose medians level of absolute importance was denoted as "highest", aggreement on importance levels was achieved between large investing and small investing MNCs for only two elements. Disagreement on ranking level was restricted to a one-level difference against a two-level maximum potential. A significant difference in the focus appears to exist between the small investing MNCs and the large investors when both are motivated to conduct FDI by cost reduction reasons. This difference attracts both statistical and substantive support. Accordingly, for the Indirect Control Group, the null hypothesis (H3C), that MNCs making large investments in the focus countries for cost reduction seeking reasons respond to the same configuration of investment attraction package as do those making smaller investments, is rejected.

H3D - Host Country Market vs. Cost Reduction: All Quantums

This sub-hypothesis, which compares the IAP preferences of MNCs with an initial investment of any quantum denomination and having Host Country Market-seeking as motivation with those of similarly situated Cost Reduction-seeking MNCs, is a repeat of H2B in that the inclusion of a parameter that is universal to all participants -"initial investment of <u>any</u> quantum denomination" - gives the identical result as does a comparison which excludes that parameter. The purpose of including the sub-hypothesis is to render completeness to the analyses conducted under this sub-section. The findings of H2B concerning different strategic motivations for FDI result in MNCs having significantly different preferences for the financially impacting elements of the IAP are adopted for H3D and will be repeated here in summary form only:

Null hypothesis for Direct Control Group rejected.

Null hypothesis for Indirect Control Group accepted.

H3E - Host Country Market-seeking vs. Cost Reduction-seeking: Small Quantum

Eleven (11) or 22.4% of the elements making up the Investment Attraction Package showed statistically significant difference, at the .05 confidence level.

Findings in Direct Control Group

The responses from MNCs having different initial strategic motivations - host country market or cost reduction - for FDI in the focus countries and who made small initial investments show significant differences in the preferences accorded 25.0% (7 of 28) of the individual elements making up the Direct Control Group, at the .05 level of confidence. See Table 8.9.

The existence of significant difference in seven (7) elements of the Direct Control Group, combined with both the level of the absolute rankings and the difference in importance attached to these elements by the host country market-seeking MNCs with small initial investments in comparison with the similarly situated cost reduction-seeking MNCs provides clear, corroborated evidence that difference in focus exists between the two compared motivations of similar quantum level. See Table 8.11 entitled: "MNC Rankings of Investment Attraction Packages - Comparison of Large Investments, By Motivation - Comparison of Small Investments, By Motivation". Therefore, the null hypothesis for the Direct Control Group - that MNCs making small investments in the focus countries for Host Country Market-seeking reasons respond to the same configuration of investment attraction package as do those making small investments for Cost Reduction-seeking reasons - is rejected.

TABLE 8.11

MNC RANKING OF HOST COUNTRY INVESTMENT ATTRACTION PACKAGES

COMPARISON OF LARGE INVESTMENTS, BY MOTIVATION   COMPARISON OF SMALL INVESTMENTS, BY MOTIVATION

DIRECT CONTROL GROUP

LARGE INVESTMENTS — HOST COUNTRY MARKET

	cl	REL	ABS
PROFIT REPATRIATION	F	1	1
FOREX CONTROL	F	2	1
DIVIDEND REPATRIATION	F	3	1
CAPITAL REPATRIATION	F	4	1
EQUITY LIMITS	I	1	1
PROFIT REINVEST LIMITS	I	3	1
DIVEST OWNERSHIP REQUIRE	I	2	1
EXPAND/DIVERSIFY LIMITS	I	4	1
OWN LAND/BUILDINGS LIMITE	I	7	1.5
FOREIGN PERSONNEL	F	5	2
FOREX BALANCING REQUIRED	F	6	2
BOARD APPOINTMENTS LIMIT	I	5	2
SECTORS EXCLUDED	I	6	2
INCOME TAX - LOW	T	1	2
DUTY FREE IMPORT	T	2	2
TAX HOLIDAYS	T	3	2
GOVT TENDER PREFERENCE	T	5	2
NO WITHHOLDING TAX	T	7	2
FINANCE FROM ABROAD	F	7	3
LOCAL CONTENT MINIMA	F	8	3
EXPORT MINIMA	F	9	3
R&D MINIMA	F	10	3
INTELLECTUAL PROP. PROTE	I	8	3
ACCELERATED DEPRECIATION	T	4	3
CAPITAL GRANTS	T	6	3
SUBSIDIES	T	8	3
PROTECTED MARKET	T	9	3
LOW RENT FTZ	T	10	3

LARGE INVESTMENTS — COST REDUCTION

	cl	REL	ABS
PROFIT REPATRIATION	F	1	1
CAPITAL REPATRIATION	F	2	1
FOREX CONTROL	F	4	1
DIVIDEND REPATRIATION	F	3	1.5
FOREIGN PERSONNEL	F	5	1.5
EQUITY LIMITS	I	1	1
BOARD APPOINTMENTS LIMIT	I	2	1
DIVEST OWNERSHIP REQUIRE	I	3	1
OWN LAND/BUILDINGS LIMITE	I	4	1
INTELLECTUAL PROP. PROTE	I	7	1
FOREX BALANCING REQUIRED	F	6	2
PROFIT REINVEST LIMITS	I	5	2
EXPAND/DIVERSIFY LIMITS	I	6	2
SECTORS EXCLUDED	I	8	2
INCOME TAX - LOW	T	1	2
DUTY FREE IMPORT	T	2	2
LOW RENT FTZ	T	4	2.5
TAX HOLIDAYS	T	6	2
FINANCE FROM ABROAD	F	7	3
EXPORT MINIMA	F	8	3
LOCAL CONTENT MINIMA	F	9	3
R&D MINIMA	F	10	3
NO WITHHOLDING TAX	T	3	3
ACCELERATED DEPRECIATION	T	5	3
PROTECTED MARKET	T	7	3
SUBSIDIES	T	8	3
GOVT TENDER PREFERENCE	T	9	3
CAPITAL GRANTS	T	10	3

SMALL INVESTMENTS — HOST COUNTRY MARKET

	cl	REL	ABS
PROFIT REPATRIATION	F	1	1
DIVIDEND REPATRIATION	F	2	1
CAPITAL REPATRIATION	F	3	1
FOREX CONTROL	F	4	1
EQUITY LIMITS	I	1	1
PROFIT REINVEST LIMITS	I	2	1
DIVEST OWNERSHIP REQUIRE	I	3	1
INCOME TAX - LOW	T	1	1
FOREX BALANCING REQUIRED	F	5	2
FOREIGN PERSONNEL	F	6	2
LOCAL CONTENT MINIMA	F	7	2
EXPAND/DIVERSIFY LIMITS	I	4	2
BOARD APPOINTMENTS LIMIT	I	5	2
SECTORS EXCLUDED	I	6	2
OWN LAND/BUILDINGS LIMITE	I	7	2
INTELLECTUAL PROP. PROTE	I	8	2
DUTY FREE IMPORT	T	2	2
NO WITHHOLDING TAX	T	3	2
FINANCE FROM ABROAD	F	8	3
R&D MINIMA	F	9	3
EXPORT MINIMA	F	10	3
TAX HOLIDAYS	T	4	3
ACCELERATED DEPRECIATION	T	5	3
SUBSIDIES	T	6	3
LOW RENT FTZ	T	7	3
CAPITAL GRANTS	T	8	3
GOVT TENDER PREFERENCE	T	9	3
PROTECTED MARKET	T	10	3

SMALL INVESTMENTS — COST REDUCTION

	cl	REL	ABS
DUTY FREE IMPORT	T	1	1
PROFIT REPATRIATION	F	1	2
CAPITAL REPATRIATION	F	2	2
DIVIDEND REPATRIATION	F	4	2
FOREX BALANCING REQUIRED	F	5	2
EQUITY LIMITS	I	1	2
PROFIT REINVEST LIMITS	I	2	2
DIVEST OWNERSHIP REQUIRE	I	3	2
EXPAND/DIVERSIFY LIMITS	I	4	2
BOARD APPOINTMENTS LIMIT	I	6	2
TAX HOLIDAYS	T	2	2
INCOME TAX - LOW	T	3	2
LOW RENT FTZ	T	4	2
FOREX CONTROL	F	3	3
FOREIGN PERSONNEL	F	6	3
FINANCE FROM ABROAD	F	7	3
LOCAL CONTENT MINIMA	F	8	3
EXPORT MINIMA	F	9	3
R&D MINIMA	F	10	3
OWN LAND/BUILDINGS LIMITE	I	5	3
INTELLECTUAL PROP. PROTEC	I	7	3
SECTORS EXCLUDED	I	8	3
NO WITHHOLDING TAX	T	5	3
CAPITAL GRANTS	T	6	3
PROTECTED MARKET	T	7	3
ACCELERATED DEPRECIATION	T	8	3
GOVT TENDER PREFERENCE	T	9	3
SUBSIDIES	T	10	3

cl = classifications
F = Financial Restriction
I = Investment & Ownership
T = Taxes & Subsidies Incentives

INDIRECT CONTROL GROUP

LARGE INVESTMENTS — HOST COUNTRY MARKET

	REL	ABS
COUNTRY STABILITY	1	1
CIVIL DISTURBANCE	2	1
INTEGRITY OF OFFICIALS	1	1
LAW CLARITY	1	1.5
EXPROPRIATION PROTECTION	2	1.5
SKILLS AVAILABLE	1	1.5
TRANSPORT SYSTEM	1	2
FOREX FLUCTUATION	1	2
INFLATION TREND	2	2
HIRE/FIRE RESTRICTIONS	2	2
TELECOMMUNICATIONS FACILITI	2	2
EFFECTIVE ADMINISTRATION	2	2
GDP GROWTH	3	2
DISPUTE RESOLUTION	3	2
LEADERSHIP TURNOVER	3	2
WAGE LEVELS	3	2
ELECTRICITY RELIABILITY	3	2
TARIFF LEVELS	4	2
FDI SCREENING	4	2
EDUCATION FACILITIES	4	2
PUBLIC SAFETY	3	2.5

LARGE INVESTMENTS — COST REDUCTION

	REL	ABS
CIVIL DISTURBANCE	1	1
TELECOMMUNICATIONS FACILITI	1	1
FOREX FLUCTUATION	1	1
TARIFF LEVELS	1	1.5
TRANSPORT SYSTEM	2	1.5
HIRE/FIRE RESTRICTIONS	1	2
INTEGRITY OF OFFICIALS	1	2
EXPROPRIATION PROTECTION	1	2
LAW CLARITY	2	2
COUNTRY STABILITY	2	2
SKILLS AVAILABLE	2	2
FDI SCREENING	2	2
DISPUTE RESOLUTION	3	2
INFLATION TREND	3	2
LEADERSHIP TURNOVER	3	2
WAGE LEVELS	3	2
ELECTRICITY RELIABILITY	3	2
EFFECTIVE ADMINISTRATION	3	2
PUBLIC SAFETY	3	2
GDP GROWTH	4	3
EDUCATION FACILITIES	4	3

SMALL INVESTMENTS — HOST COUNTRY MARKET

	REL	ABS
COUNTRY STABILITY	1	1
LAW CLARITY	1	1
CIVIL DISTURBANCE	2	1
FOREX FLUCTUATION	1	2
WAGE LEVELS	1	2
TELECOMMUNICATIONS FACILITI	1	2
INTEGRITY OF OFFICIALS	1	2
TRANSPORT SYSTEM	2	2
INFLATION TREND	2	2
EXPROPRIATION PROTECTION	2	2
SKILLS AVAILABLE	2	2
EFFECTIVE ADMINISTRATION	2	2
TARIFF LEVELS	3	2
DISPUTE RESOLUTION	3	2
LEADERSHIP TURNOVER	3	2
FDI SCREENING	3	2
GDP GROWTH	4	2
PUBLIC SAFETY	4	2
ELECTRICITY RELIABILITY	3	3
EDUCATION FACILITIES	3	3
HIRE/FIRE RESTRICTIONS	4	3

SMALL INVESTMENTS — COST REDUCTION

	REL	ABS
TARIFF LEVELS	1	1
LAW CLARITY	1	1
COUNTRY STABILITY	1	1
CIVIL DISTURBANCE	2	1
WAGE LEVELS	1	1
ELECTRICITY RELIABILITY	1	1
INTEGRITY OF OFFICIALS	1	2
FOREX FLUCTUATION	2	2
EXPROPRIATION PROTECTION	2	2
SKILLS AVAILABLE	2	2
TELECOMMUNICATIONS FACILITIES	2	2
DISPUTE RESOLUTION	3	2
TRANSPORT SYSTEM	3	2
INFLATION TREND	3	2
HIRE/FIRE RESTRICTIONS	3	2
LEADERSHIP TURNOVER	3	2
EDUCATION FACILITIES	4	2
FDI SCREENING	2	3
EFFECTIVE ADMINISTRATION	3	3
GDP GROWTH	4	3
PUBLIC SAFETY	4	3

Findings in Indirect Control Group

The responses from MNCs having different strategic motivations - host country market or cost reduction - for initial FDI in the focus countries and who made small initial investments show significant differences in the preferences accorded 19.0% of the individual elements making up the Indirect Control Group, at the .05 level of confidence.

The existence of significant difference in four (4) elements (out of 21) of the Indirect Control Group, combined with both the level of the absolute rankings and the difference in importance attached to these elements by the host country market-seeking MNCs with small initial investments in comparison with the similarly situated cost reduction-seeking MNCs, (See Table 8.11) provides corroborated evidence that difference in focus exists between the two compared motivations of similar quantum level. Therefore, the null hypothesis for the Indirect Control Group - that MNCs making small investments in the focus countries for Host Country Market-seeking reasons respond to the same configuration of investment attraction package as do those making small investments for Cost Reduction-seeking reasons - is rejected.

H3F - Host Country Market-seeking vs. Cost Reduction-seeking: Large Quantum

The number of individual IAP elements showing statistically significant difference, at the .05 confidence level, was 11, (22.4%). (See Table 8.9).

Findings in Direct Control Group

The responses from MNCs having different motivations - host country market or cost reduction - for initial FDI in the subject countries and who made large initial investments show significant differences in the preferences accorded 21.4% of the individual elements making up the Direct Control Group, at the .05 level of confidence.

The existence of statistically significant difference in six (6) of the 28 elements of the Direct Control Group, combined with both the level of the absolute rankings and the difference in importance attached to these elements by the large investing MNCs with Host Country Market-seeking motivations in comparison with the large investing MNCs with Cost Reduction-seeking motivations, provides an appropriate degree of meaningful evidence that difference in focus exists between the two compared motivations of similar quantum level. Therefore, for the Direct Control Group, the null hypothesis - that MNCs making large investments in the focus countries for Host Country Market-seeking reasons respond to the same configuration of investment attraction package as do those making large investments for Cost Reduction-seeking reasons - is rejected.

Findings in Indirect Control Group

The responses from MNCs having different motivations - host country market or cost reduction - for initial FDI in the subject countries and who made large initial investments show significant differences in the preferences accorded 23.8% of the individual elements making up the Indirect Control Group, at the .05 level of confidence.

The existence of significant difference in five (5) of 21 elements of the Indirect Control Group, combined with both the level of the absolute rankings and the difference in importance attached to these elements by the host country market-seeking MNCs with large initial investments in comparison with the similarly situated cost reduction-seeking MNCs provides corroborated evidence that difference in focus exists between the two compared motivations of similar quantum level. (See Table 8.11) Therefore, the null hypothesis for the Indirect Control Group that MNCs making large investments in the focus countries for Host Country Market-seeking reasons respond to the same configuration of investment attraction package as do those making large investments for Cost Reduction-seeking reasons is rejected.

Hypothesis #3 General Finding

Hypothesis #3 was stated in its general form:

"It is proposed that investment attraction packages preferred by MNCs operating in the specified countries differ depending upon the quantum-level of MNC investment and the strategic motivation for MNC investment."

Before making a finding on the general hypothesis, the sub-hypotheses findings (H3A - H2F) must be examined as the foregoing examination of the parts appear to confirm a key premise of this study. Unlike Hypothesis #2, wherein directional consistency in the parts is required to give creditability of a finding for the whole, different findings for the sub-hypotheses of Hypothesis #3 can add sharpness to the larger purposes of this investigation. Recall that a basic objective of the study was to determine whether segmentation of investor parameters along the lines suggested by transaction cost theory and MNC strategic motivations can lead to the identification of "micro-groups" of FDI investors that possess homogeneous attributes and unique investment attraction preferences.

A finding concerning the null hypothesis has already been made under each of the sub-hypotheses. A listing of these findings on the null hypotheses reveals:

H3A: Small vs. Large: Total Response
Direct Control Group: accepted.
Indirect Control Group: accepted.

H3B: Small vs. Large: Host Country Market-seeking
Direct Control Group: accepted.
Indirect Control Group: accepted.

H3C: Small vs. Large: Cost Reduction-seeking
Direct Control Group: rejected.
Indirect Control Group: rejected.

H3D: HCM* vs. CR**: All Quantums (Restated H2B)
Direct Control Group: rejected.
Indirect Control Group: accepted.

H3E: HCM H3E: * vs. CR**: Small Quantum
Direct Control Group: rejected.
Indirect Control Group: rejected.

H3F: HCM* vs. CR**: Large Quantum
Direct Control Group: rejected.
Indirect Control Group: rejected

*   Host Country Market-seeking
** Cost Reduction-seeking

Inasmuch as H3A - Total Survey: Quantum - is an amalgamation of all responses from the survey undifferentiated for initial motivation, acceptance of the null hypothesis is a finding that differences in levels of quantum of investment, in and of themselves, are unlikely to evoke significantly different preferences by MNCs for those elements of the IAP that the MNCs themselves have identified as being of high priority. This finding is admittedly theoretical since no FDI is made without a strategic motivation on the part of the MNC. Sub-hypotheses H3B-H3F shed the practical light upon the significance of quantum-level of investment and its impact upon the decision-making of MNCs.

The distinguishing characteristic separating Hypotheses H3B - H3F is the introduction of investor strategic motivation into the investigation of the effect of quantum-level of investment. There is no consistency of MNC preference findings on the effects of quantum-level of investment as between small and large investors having the same investment motivation yet there is consistency of findings as between host country market and cost reduction motivations having the same investment quantum-level. It is in the consistency/inconsistency itself wherein the "micro groups with homogeneous attributes and unique investment attraction preferences" can be found.

Different Quantum-Levels / Same Motivation

H3B - Small vs. Large - Host Country Market: acceptance of the null hypothesis (for both Direct Control and Indirect Control Groups of elements) is a finding that differences in quantum-level of investment by Host Country Market-seeking MNCs are unlikely to evoke significantly different preferences for those elements of the IAP that the MNCs themselves have identified as being of high priority. This result was somewhat unexpected. However, given that the preponderance of MNC replies to the survey listed host country market as the investment motivation, H3B also provides a mathematical explanation of the amalgamated result reported for the Total Survey sub-hypothesis (H3A).

H3C - Small vs. Large - Cost Reduction: rejection of the null hypothesis for both the Direct Control and the Indirect Control groups leads to a finding of acceptance for the research hypothesis which proposed that investors making large investments and who were motivated by cost reduction-seeking (export-oriented) reasons respond to a differently configured investment attraction package than those smaller investors who are motivated by cost reduction-seeking reasons.

The dichotomy in the findings for Cost Reduction (H3C) with Total Survey (H3A) is mathematically induced but is no less real in its message. The distribution of the survey responses is in accord with the literature on developing country inward flow of FDI - host country market-seeking is the most common reason for FDI. (UNCTAD, 1993a). [26] Of the 72 responses to the survey, 44 responses were from host country market seekers and 19 from cost reduction seekers. The Total Survey finding that no significant difference in MNC preferences for the elements of the IAP could be attributed to differences in quantum-level of investment is basically a function of the legitimate skewness in the survey respondees motivation for initial FDI. Total Survey finding reflected the 2+-to-1 weighting favoring host country market-seeking motivation. It should be recalled that "Small vs. Large : Host Country Market-seeking (H3B)" failed to reveal significant differences attributable to investment size. While Small vs. Large Cost Reduction (H3C) did reveal significant differences, Total Survey (H3A) averaged out the diversity shown by the minority (Cost Reduction-seeking - H3C) with the more homogeneous large majority (Host Country Market-seeking - H3B). Thus the dangers of over-aggregation are illustrated.

Different Motivations / Same Quantum-Levels

H3D - Different Motivations / Undifferentiated Quantum-Levels - is a restatement of H2B. As such, it is a test for motivation only and is reported under Hypothesis #2..

H3E - Host Country Market-seeking vs. Cost Reduction-seeking - Small: <u>and</u>

H3F - Host Country Market-seeking vs. Cost Reduction-seeking - Large:

Rejection of the null hypothesis for both the Direct Control and the Indirect Control Groups for <u>both</u> H3E and H3F leads to a finding of acceptance for the two research hypotheses. The proposition is accepted that initial investors making same-level quantum of investments (small level or large level) and who are motivated by host country market-seeking reasons respond to a differently configured investment attraction package than those same-level investors (small level or large level) who are motivated by cost reduction-seeking reasons.

A finding has been made for two of the basic three FDI motivations - Host Country Market-seeking and Cost Reduction-Seeking (export-oriented). It will be recalled that respondees having the third strategic motivation - Raw Material-seeking - evidenced no investments in the small quantum category and, thus, no comparisons for statistically significant difference between small and large investors could be made.

The evidence seems clear for the adoption of a generalized finding since the segmentations of that finding are also clear and reinforced by the general direction indicated in Hypothesis #2. The evidence indicates that:

> For MNCs making first-time investments for <u>host country market-seeking</u> reasons, quantum-level of investment (small or large) <u>is not</u> a significant factor effecting MNC preferences for the elements of the subject countries' investment attraction packages.

> For MNCs making first-time investments for <u>cost reduction-seeking</u> reasons, quantum-level of investment (small or large) <u>is</u> a significant factor effecting MNC preferences for the elements of the subject countries' investment attraction packages.

> MNCs making initial investments of <u>similar quantum-levels</u> (small/large) and possessing <u>different investment motivations</u> (host country market or cost reduction) exhibit significantly <u>different preferences</u> for the elements of the subject countries' Investment Attraction Packages.

Summary of Hypothesis #3 Findings

Different quantum-levels of investment can result in MNCs exhibiting different preferences for the elements of a country's IAP when:

a) the motivation for investing is different,

or

b) the motivation for the investment is cost reduction.

Hypothesis #2 (segmentation for motivation) netted findings for the various sub-hypotheses that were uniform within the individual Control Group and in opposition between the two Control Groups. Hypothesis #3 (segmentation for motivation and quantum-level of investment) turns Hypothesis #2 on its head with findings for the various sub-hypotheses that are in opposition to each other but uniform between the two Control Groups. Table 8.12, titled "Summary of Research Hypotheses Findings" depicts these complex results. The complexity is spearheaded by the non-uniformity represented in the Host Country Market-seeking findings.

SUMMARY OF FINDINGS AND IAP PREFERENCES

MNCs conducting initial FDI in the three focus Caribbean countries appear to evidence significant differences in their preferences for those elements of an Investment Attraction Package that directly affect their financial performance when the MNCs are segregated into homogeneous micro-groups based on strategic motivation for FDI.

MNCs conducting initial FDI in the three Caribbean focus countries do not appear to evidence significant differences in their preferences for those elements of an Investment Attraction Package that indirectly affect their financial performance when the MNCs are segregated into homogeneous micro-groups based on strategic motivation for FDI.

MNCs conducting initial FDI in the three Caribbean focus countries appear to evidence significant differences in their preferences for elements of an Investment Attraction Package when the MNCs are segregated into homogeneous micro-groups based on strategic motivation and quantum-level of FDI.

An exception exists: MNCs motivated to invest for Host Country Market-seeking reasons did not display significant differences in their preferences for elements of the Investment Attraction Packages of the three Caribbean when segmented into the two groups - large-level & small-level

Table 8.12

SUMMARY OF RESEARCH HYPOTHESES FINDINGS

HYPOTHESES: MNCs preferences for elements of host countries IAP
               will DIFFER depending upon the motivation for the FDI
               and the quantum of FDI.

RESEARCH HYPOTHESIS	DIRECT CONTROL GROUP		INDIRECT CONTROL GROUP	
	Support	No Support	Support	No Support
#2 - FDI Motivation				
#2A - HCM vs. RM	X			X
#2B - HCM vs. CR	X			X
#2C - RM vs. CR	X			X
#3-FDI Quantum & Motivation				
#3A - Total Survey (Large vs. Small)		X		X
#3B - Host Country Market (Large vs. Small)		X		X
#3C - Cost Reduction (Large vs. Small)	X		X	
#3E - Small Quantum (HCM vs CR)	X		X	
#3F - Large Quantum (HCM vs CR)	X		X	

Legend:
  HCM = Host Country Market-seeking
  RM   = Raw Materials-seeking
  CR   = Cost Reduction-seeking
  IAP = Investment Attraction Package
  "Support" = Research Hypothesis supported
  "No Support" = Research Hypothesis not supported
  Direct Control Group = Portion of IAP that Gov't can directly influence .
  Indirect Control Group = Portion of IAP wherein Gov't exercises indirect or nil control.

Notes:
  #3A - Large vs. Small only. No segmentation for FDI motivation.
  #3D - Total Unsegmented for Quantum omitted. Duplicates #2B.
  #3A & #3D included for completeness only.

initial investment. The preferences of large and small Host Country Market-seeking MNCs do show some differences but, on the whole, their interests appear reasonably well aligned.

An additional exception is Total Survey - Undifferentiated for Motivation. This is a mathematically induced exception based upon legitimate skewness in the population of MNC motivation for investment: Total Survey reflects the heavy bias generated by the more numerous Host Country Market group. Although not a useful exception for the purpose of determining investor preferences within identifiable groups, the exception is useful for its illustrative power concerning the drawing of conclusions from generalized data.

Until relatively recent times, the Secondary Sector (largely Host Country Market-seeking motivated) has been the predominent motivation for FDI in the developed countries and remains so today in the developing countries. (UNCTAD, 1993a)[27] Today, the Tertiary Sector (of which a substantial element includes the Cost Reduction motivation) represents over 50% of developed countries FDI and is increasing rapidly in the developing countries.[28] Given the past preponderance of investment for Host Country Market-seeking, the concentration of research thereon, and the relative uniformity of Host Country Market-seeking research findings that can be grouped under the Direct Control and Indirect Control rubric, the odd-man-out has been the cost reduction motivation. Given the accuracy of UNCTAD reported trends, the uniqueness of the investment attraction needs of the cost reduction motivation will merit greater attention in the furture and the odd-man-out position may be up for grabs. Though somewhat few and far between, the remaining strategic motivation - raw materials-seeking - generally represents large to very large investment, travels its own path, and has its own unique set of preferences.

---

[1]Guisinger, S. 1985. *Investment incentives and performance requirements: Patterns of international trade, production and investment.* Westport, CN.: Praeger, Greenwood Press, p.48.

[2]Contractor, F. 1991. "Government policies and foreign direct investment". *UNCTC Studies, Series No. 17,* N.Y.: United Nations, p.23.

[3]Cable, V. and Persaud, B. 1987. "New trends and policy problems in foreign investment: The experience of Commonwealth developing countries" in *Developing With Foreign Investment.* The Commonwealth Secretariat, Kent: Croom Helm Ltd, p.8.

[4]Root, F. and Ahmed, A. 1978. "The influence of policy instruments on manufacturing foreign direct investment in developing countries". *Journal of International Business Studies,* Winter 1987, pp. 81-94.

[5]Group of Thirty. 1984. *Foreign direct investment 1973-87.* N.Y.: Group of Thirty, p.31.

[6]Lim, D. 1983. "Fiscal incentives and direct foreign investment in less developed countries". *Journal of Development Studies.* Jan. pp. 207-12.

[7]Rolfe, R.; Ricks, D.; Pointer, M.; and McCarthy, M. 1993. "Determinants of FDI preferences of MNEs". *Journal of International Business Studies,* Vol 24, No. 2 (Spring, 1993), p.349.

[8]Williamson, O. 1986. *Economic organization. Firms, markets and policy control.* N.Y.: University Press, p. 176.

[9]Brewer, T. 1993."Government policies, market imperfections, and foreign direct investment". *Journal of International Business Studies,* Vol 24, No. 1, p.113.

[10]Woodward, D., and Rolfe, R. 1993. "The location of export oriented foreign direct investment in the Caribbean basin". *Journal of International Business Studies,* Vol.24, No.1, p. 121.

[11]Contractor, F. 1990. "Government policies towards foreign investment. An empirical investigation of the link between national policies and FDI flows". A paper presented to Annual Conference, Academy of International Business, Miami: p. 21.

[12]Evans, T., and Doupnik, T. 1986. "Foreign exchange risk management under Standard 53.83". Stamford, CN.: *Financial Accounting Standards Board.*

[12]Guisinger. 1985. *op cit*, p. 41.

[13]Contractor. 1991. *op cit*, p.23.

[14]Rolfe et al. 1993. *op cit*, p.344.

[15]Rolfe, R., and White, R. 1992. "The influence of tax incentives in determining the location of foreign direct investment in developing countries." *Journal of American Taxation Association*, Vol.13, No. 2, pp. 39-57.

[16]Rolfe et al. 1993. *op cit*, p.342.

[17]Reuber, G., Crookell, H., Emerson, M., and Gallais-Hamonno, G. 1973. *Private foreign investment in development*. Oxford: Clarendon Press, p.22.

[18]Rolfe et al. 1993. *op cit*, p.338.

[19]Guisinger. 1985. *op cit*, p.41.

[20]Helleiner, G. 1987. "Direct foreign investment and manufacturing for export: A review of the issues" in *Developing With Foreign Investment*. The Commonwealth Secretariat, Kent: Croom Helm, Ltd, p. 76.

[21]Wells, L. 1986. "Investment incentives: An unnecessary debate." *CTC Reporter*, Autumn, pp. 58-60.

[22]Rolfe and White. 1992. *op cit*, pp.39-57.

[23]Bond, E., and Samuelson, L. 1986. "Tax holidays as signals". *The American Economic Review*, Vol 16, No.4., Sept, 1986, p.820.

[24]Rolfe et al. 1993. *op cit*, p.338

[25]Rolfe et al. 1993. *op cit*, p.345.

[26]UNCTAD. 1993a. *World investment report 1993. Transnational corporations and integrated international production*. N.Y.: p.61

[27]*loc cit*.

[28]*loc cit*.

Chapter IX

WHO SAID WHAT ?

Comparison of Findings with Other Researchers

> 'All discussion, debate, all dissidence tends
> to question, and in consequence to upset
> existing convictions"
>
> Learned Hand
> 1872 - 1961

To-date few studies have examined the influence of the quantum of investment on the preferences MNCs harbor for specific elements of the Investment Attraction Package nor has quantum of investment frequently been included in studies of incentive effectiveness. Lim (1983)[1] has mentioned that large sized raw material investments may be an exception to his generally pessimistic view of the attraction effectiveness of incentives, and others have commented in passing that very large scale investment into developing countries may require special incentives. Recently, Rolfe et al. (1993)[2] included quantum - (small / large) - in their study of FDI incentive preferences. Although the majority of investments examined by Rolfe et al. were of the small quantum, expansion-investment type and the differentiation by investor strategic motivation was not provided, definition of "small" and "large" was similar, plus a Table segmenting the preferences of initial investors (26 respondees) and expansion/acquisition investors (70 respondees) was provided. Responses included five (5) from Jamaica, two (2) from Trinidad-Tobago and none from Barbados. As the findings were reported on the basis of their "small vs. large" proposition, they provide a useful point of departure for this study.

Rolfe et al. summarized their findings by stating "investment size made more difference on incentive preferences than did any other single factor".[3] While noting that the overall ranking showed highest investor concern to be with foreign exchange restrictions and taxation of profits, their study concluded that small firms placed more emphasis on two (2) incentives - relaxation of restrictions on dividends and intercompany payments. Larger investor emphasis was reported as being on those elements whose benefits increased with investment size, such as, cash grants, land grants, job training subsidies, and real estate tax concessions. Holding motivation constant, that is, comparison within host country market-seeking motivation and within cost reduction-seeking motivation, this study offers no support to the Rolfe et al. findings in the instance of initial investors for host country market motivation and raises the specter of a reversed finding for the cost reduction (export) investor contention.

Small quantum initial investments within the host country market motivation attracted no significantly greater preference than larger quantum investments in the elements of Dividend Repatriation, Profit Repatriation and Foreign Exchange Control nor did larger quantum investors evidence greater preference than smaller quantum investors in the Capital Grants and Subsidies elements for this motivation. Low Income Tax reflected the "highest" absolute rating from small investors and "moderate" rating from large investors.

In the dividend and intercompany payments areas, small quantum initial investments within the cost reduction motivation evidenced no statistically significant differences to larger quantum investments but some substantive differences of lesser preference than larger quantum investments were revealed in the elements of Profit Repatriation and Foreign Exchange Control. Large quantum investors level-ranked both items as being of "highest" absolute importance with small quantum investors denoting "moderate" and "low", respectively. Larger quantum investors evidenced no greater preference than smaller quantum investments in the Capital Grants and Subsidies elements for this motivation as both large and small quantum initial investors for cost reduction motivation ranked the two items as being of "low" level absolute importance.

When comparing small investment preference with large investment preference - in the aggregate for all investor motivations - the findings of this study generally support the overall findings of Rolfe et al. that the highest investor concern appears to be with foreign exchange restrictions and taxation of profits. Small and large investors were basically in agreement in according highest preference - both relative ranking and absolute importance ranking within the Financial Restrictions elements - to Profit Repatriation, Capital Repatriation, Dividend Repatriation and Foreign Exchange Control. Some difference was noted when small investors placed Low Income Tax within their "highest" absolute importance category while large investors denoted this as "moderate". Statistically significant difference at the .05 level was recorded on the No Withholding Tax element with large investors according the element as being of "moderate" absolute importance and small recording "low" importance. As these reported similarities and differences in small and large investor preferences are disaggregated for investor strategic motivation - both within the same motivation and between the different motivations - their directional impact is clarified. Due to the scarcity of prior research into investor diversity, the question of support of prior research, in some cases, becomes moot.

Inasmuch as Hypothesis #2 found that MNCs did not differentiate according to motivation in their preferences for the elements included under the Indirect Control Group and the findings of this H3B that Host Country Market-seeking MNCs do not differentiate in their preferences based on the quantum-level of their investment (both Direct or Indirect Control Groups), the findings lend some support - in the aggregate - to researchers, such as Reuber et al. (1973)[4], Shaw and Toye (1978)[5], Root and Ahmed (1978),[6] Lim (1983)[7], , the Group of Thirty (1984)[8], and Cable and Persaud (1987)[9]. These researchers have maintained that a country's overall attractiveness is the key factor for those contemplating FDI and that low labour costs and tax/financial incentives are relatively unimportant. To the degree that a consistent evluation of the preferences concerned with country conditions is maintained across the different motivations (H2), and within the host country market-seeking motivation when examined for quantum effect (H3B), such consistency could be said to be supportive. It does not address the relative worth question directly - it only supports that a consistency of evaluative-thought is applied to country conditions but not to the financial restrictions / incentives (H2 - Direct Control Findings). It should be noted, however, that at the time when the majority of these researchers addressed the issue, cost reduction (export-oriented investment) was in relative infancy, and the researchers' focus tended to be host country markets with occasional comment directed toward raw material investment attraction.

Opposing this thread of support, however, are the specifics produced by segmentation. The micro group "initial investor - host country market - small investment" lists Low Income Tax as "highest" level absolute importance and Wage Levels as "moderate" absolute importance, #1 in its classification for relative importance, and statistically, registered as significantly different from similiarly constituted large investments, at the .01 level of confidence. Wage rates were denoted as the "highest" absolute importance level by the micro group "initial investor - cost reduction motivation - small investment" and Low Income Tax reflected "moderate" absolute importance level for both small and large cost reduction investments. Such findings are consistent with the findings of Rolfe et al. (1993) [10]concerning large and small investors in the Caribbean and supply some clues to the unanswered questions posed by Woodward and Rolfe (1993)[11] concerning the response of export- oriented investors to the factors that normally govern the location of MNCs facilities in LDCs. Further, the findings offer reinforcement to several other researchers - Wells (1987)[12], that export-oriented investment requires inexpensive labour and reasonable infrastructure, transport and communications facilities; Austin (1990)[13], that wage cost is the primary reason for MNCs to integrate developing countries into their global plans; Rolfe and White (1992)[14], that a country's infrastructure and wages effected its attractiveness for export-oriented FDI; Kumar (1994)[15], that countries possessing a pool of low cost labour have an advantage in attracting export-oriented production. Small quantum - cost reduction-seeking investors ranked Wage Levels and Electricity Relaibility as "highest" level of absolute importance. Their larger investing counterparts gave the "highest" ranking to Telecommunications Facilities and Transport System. Each micro-group listed the other's "highest" preferences as its "moderate" absolute preference. It bears repeating, however, that the support is limited to the two micro groups: initial investors, small & large quantum investments, cost reduction motivation. When these two micro groups were amalgamated in the Hypothesis #2 findings for cost reduction motivation (without sub grouping for investment quantum), only the Telecommunications Facility element was designated as "highest" absolute importance.

Although these findings of the referenced researchers did not address the issue of relative importance viv-a-vis country conditions, their statements that low labour costs and tax/financial incentives are relatively unimportant are not substanciated by this study.

Rolfe et al. (1993) found the duty free import concession to be more highly prized by export oriented investors than by Host Country Market-seeking investors. In the aggregate, this study reveals no statistically significant difference existing between MNCs of the two different motivations - Host Country Market-seeking and Cost Reduction-seeking. However, when segmented both for quantum of investment (small vs. large) and for same-quantum / different-motivation, the initial investment - cost reduction motivation - small quantum investment is significantly different both from cost reduction - large quantum and from small investment - host country market. For this "micro group" of <u>initial investors - cost reduction motivation - small quantum investments</u>, the #1 concern was Duty Free Import, with Profit Repatriation ranked as first concern among the Financial elements of the IAP but relegated to the second level of importance - "moderate" - in the absolute ranking of importance. Accordingly, support is offered for Rolfe et al. from the "Initial, Cost Reduction, Small" micro-group.

The general lack of support from this study for the various propositions that exporters display a higher preference for tax related incentives than do host country market investors has been commented upon under Hypothesis #2 - FDI Motivations. However, when segmented into micro groups, little substantive difference is shown to exist on the tax related elements as between initial investors - large quantum investment - cost reduction motivation and those similarly situated investors with host country motivation. However, <u>initial investors - small quantum investment - host country market motivation</u> registered higher preference than their counterparts with cost reduction motivation on Low Income Tax (at the .10 level of confidence), Accelerated Depreciation (at the .01 level) and rank No Withholding Tax at the higher level, both relatively and in absolute importance. Pointedly, however, this cost reduction micro group showed the higher preference (at the .05 level) for Tax Holidays and level-ranked the absolute importance of the element at "moderate" - above that of their host country market counterparts "low" ranking. When segmented into micro groups, support for the greater interest in tax related incentives does appear in one quarter: <u>Initial investors - cost reduction motivation - large quantum investment group</u> which expresses higher preferences than the small investment - cost reduction group on the elements of Low Income Tax and Accelerated Depreciation (both significant at the .05 level) and Tax Holidays (at the .10 level). In summary, there is no support from this study for the propositions that exporters display a higher preference for tax related incentives than do host country market investors. Results from this study tend to support a contrasting conclusion in one specific micro group - "<u>initial investors- host country market motivation - small quantum investment</u>" vis-a-vis their counterpart of small investor-cost reduction motivated investors. Micro group segmentation does permit focused support of the Rolfe et al. proposition re investment size making a difference in the restricted area of tax preferences and for the specific micro group "<u>initial investors - cost reduction motivation - large quantum investment</u>".

SUMMARY

The contrasts in Hypothesis #2 (FDI motivation) findings from those reached or advocated by other researchers are:

1. Although Williamson (1986), Brewer (1987) and Rolfe (1993), among others, have advocated that raw materials motivation should be considered as being included in the strategic category of cost reduction, the instant study finding is that the data pointed to significant difference in MNC preferences for the elements of the IAP between raw material-seeking and export-oriented investment.

2. Protected market was cited as being of major importance for market development projects by Rueber (1973). Host country market-seeking MNCs ranked this factor quite low in the instant study.

3. Tax holidays are reported to be important to export-oriented investors by Guisinger (1985), Helleiner (1973)[16], Bond and Samuelson (1986)[17], Wells (1986) and Rolfe and White (1992). In the aggregate of host country market-seeking motivations, no support was found for tax holidays to be held in higher value by export-oriented investors. In the micro-groups of Hypothesis #3, tax holidays were held in higher regard by the "initial investor-cost reduction-small" but in lower regard by "cost reduction-large".

4. The instant study offers no support to the findings of Rolfe et al (1993) that export-oriented firms making initial investments place high value on cash grants and subsidies.

There were no directly comparable findings to the micro-group analysis of Hypothesis #3 (preferences segmented by initial investment, motivation, and quantum). However, the findings based on micro-groups revealed some contrasts with the preferences depicted in the literature review. Some of the more notable contrasts are:

1. Micro-group "Initial-Cost Reduction-Small": No support was evident that Profit Repatriation (foreign exchange restrictions) was #1 concern, as found by Evans and Doupnik (1986) - strong support was evident in all other micro-groups. In reverse, weak support for Contractor (1990) and Rolfe and White (1992) contention that profit repatriation was of no primary concern with small Cost Reduction investors, and non-support for the contention with large Cost reduction investors.

2. Micro group "Initial-HCM & CR-Small": The finding that low income tax, wage levels, and tax/financial incentives are important to these two groups contrasts with the characterizations of relative unimportance by Shaw and Toye (1978), Lim (1983), Rueber (1973), Root and Ahmed (1978),

the Group of Thirty (1984), and Cable and Persaud (1987). However, support is found for the contentions in other micro-groups.

3. Micro-group "Initial-Cost Reduction-Small". Rolfe et al. (1993) found the duty free concession to be more highly prized by the export-oriented investors than by the host country market-seeking investors. This study strongly supports Rolfe et al. finding re: initial-cost reduction-small, but found relatively equal - and high - preferences for this element exists among host country market-seeking, both small and large investors, and cost reduction-large.

Rolfe et al. provides a useful reference point to this study's call for the utilization of greater segmentation of the specific situation of the investor when pursuing the needed additional research. As an example: Rolfe et al. concluded that small firms placed more emphasis on relaxation of restrictions on dividends and inter-company payments and larger firms placed more emphasis in the capital grants and tax and subsidy areas. The instant study found:

> Micro-group "Initial-Host Country Market-Small": no support for Rolfe.et al.

> Micro-group "Initial-Cost Reduction-Small": in contrast to Rolfe et al.

> Aggregated for all motivations: general support for Rolfe et al.

---

[1]Lim, D. 1983. "Fiscal incentives and direct foreign investment in less developed countries". *Journal of Development Studies*. Jan. pp. 207-12.

[2]Rolfe, R.; Ricks, D.; Pointer, M.; and McCarthy, M. 1993. "Determinants of FDI preferences of MNEs". *Journal of International Business Studies*, Vol 24, No. 2 (Spring, 1993), p.349.

[3]*Ibid.*

[4]Reuber, G., Crookell,H., Emerson,M., and Gallais-Hamonno, G. 1973. *Private foreign investment in development*. Oxford: Clarendon Press, p.22.

[5]Shah, S. and Toye, J. 1978. "Fiscal incentives for firms in some developing countries: Survey and critique" in *Taxation and Economic Development*. J.F.T.Toye,(Ed.). London: Frank Cass. p.209.

[6]Root, F. and Ahmed, A. 1978. "The influence of policy instruments on manufacturing foreign direct investment in developing countries". *Journal of International Business Studies*, Winter 1987, pp. 81-94.

[7]Lim. 1983. *op cit*, pp.207-12.

[8]Group of Thirty. 1984. *Foreign direct investment 1973-87*. N.Y.: Group of Thirty, p.31.

[9]Cable, V. and Persaud, B. 1987. "New trends and policy problems in foreign investment: The experience of commonwealth developing countries" in *Developing with Foreign Investment*. The Commonwealth Secretariat, Kent: Croom Helm Ltd, p.8.

[10]*Ibid.*

[11]Woodward, D. and Rolfe, R. 1993. "The location of export oriented foreign direct investment in the Caribbean basin". *Journal of International Business Studies*, Vol.24, No.1, p. 121-44.

[12]Wells, L. 1986. "Investment incentives: An unnecessary debate." *CTC Reporter*, Autumn, p. 32

[13]Austin, J. 1990. *Managing in developing countries*. N.Y.: Free Press.

[14]Rolfe, R., and White, R. 1992. "The influence of tax incentives in determining the location of foreign direct investment in developing countries.". *Journal of American Taxation Association*, Vol.13, No. 2, pp. 39-57.

[15]Kumar, N. 1994. "Determinants of export orientation of foreign production by U.S. multinationals: An inter-country analysis". *Journal of International Business Studies*, Vol 25, No. 1, p.152.

[16]Helleiner, G. 1987. "Direct foreign investment and manufacturing for export: A review of the issues." *Developing With Foreign Investment*. The Commonwealth Secretariat, Kent: Croom Helm, p. 76.

[17]Bond, E., Samuelson, L. 1986. "Tax holidays as signals". *The American Economic Review*, Vol. 16, No. 4, Sept., 1986. p.820.

Chapter X

WHAT IT ALL MEANS

Interpretations of Findings

'To rest upon a formula is a blunder, that
prolonged, means death"

Oliver Wendell Holmes Jr.
June 4, 1928

INTERPRETATIONS OF MICRO-GROUP PREFERENCES

The differences denoted by the MNCs in their preferences for the various elements of the Investment Attraction Package of the three focus countries have been commented upon under the foregoing headings related to initial investors motivation and quantum-level of investment. It is via the comparison of segmented groups that the significance of the dependent variables are brought to light. It is the differences in the dependent variables that are the object of the search. Discovery of differences permits focus on customers needs and fosters the attempts to understand. For continuity and focus of this section, the findings of differences in the IAP preferences of initial-investment MNCs as related to strategic motivation, to quantum, and to quantum/motivation are discussed under the appropriate "Motivation" heading. The interpretations of findings for Hypothesis #2 (motivation) are included with the findings of Hypothesis #3 (quantum-level and motivation) in order to increase their specificity and to add dimension.

Total Survey - Undifferentiated For Strategic Motivation.

Acceptance of the null hypothesis for H3A - Total Survey - is consistent with, and reinforcing of, the acceptance of Research Hypothesis #2 for the Direct Control Group and the acceptance of the null hypothesis for the Indirect Control Group in Hypothesis #2. Based upon the particular demographics of those MNCs responding to this survey, quantum <u>alone</u>, when viewed in unsegmented Total Survey terms, has insufficient impact upon the IAP preferences of investing MNCs to warrant a finding of significant difference.

At maximum, a conservative interpretation of the findings for H3A - Total Survey: Quantum - when read in conjunction with the findings of Hypothesis #2 - appears to be: whether or not different quantum-levels of investment result in MNCs exhibiting different preferences for the elements of a country's IAP is primarily dependent upon the strategic motivation of the investor. However, the findings of H3C, H3E and H3F (quantum-level compared within cost reduction motivation and between cost reduction and host country market motivations) support the proposition that the preferences accorded by initial investing MNCs of cost reduction motivated investments are unique both between quantums and between motivations and thereby the limits of this maximum interpretation are revealed.

Aside from the concensus on Priority #1 - Profit Repatriation - each motivation seems to march to the beat of its own drummer. Further, within and between each motivation, some discernable counter beats can also be recognized. See Table 10.1, entitled "Important Initial-Investment Attraction Preferences of MNCs in Barbados, Jamaica and Trinidad-Tobago", and Table 10.2, entitled "Lesser Important Initial-Investment Attraction Preferences of MNCs in Barbados, Jamaica and Trinidad-Tobago". These Figures reflect the priority order of the "absolute importance" responses of the initial-investing MNCs, shown by strategic motivation for investment and quantum-level of investment. The two Figures indicate the areas of "highest" preference and high-moderate preference (both suggestive of the need for positive response from the host country) and the areas of "low" importance derived from responses indicating "low" or "low-moderate" importance (suggestive of possible opportunities for self-serving action from the host country).

Host Country Market-seeking MNCs

First-time investors into the subject Caribbean countries seeking Host Country Market tend to be in for the long-pull (average residence of respondees - 33 years). This supports a belief that MNCs recognize that developing local markets requires time and that entry for a short time period would require a diversion of management attention likely to be inappropriate in relation to expected financial returns. Their preferences of "highest" absolute importance reflect three (3) major priority areas, and several notable "moderate" priorities - each consistent with a longer term focus.

1) Financial priorities - Repatriation of Profit, Dividend, and Capital coupled with Foreign Exchange Control.

TABLE 10.1

IMPORTANT INITIAL - INVESTMENT ATTRACTION PREFERENCES OF MNCs
IN
BARBADOS, JAMAICA, TRINIDAD & TOBAGO

HOST COUNTRY MARKET

SMALL INVESTMENTS

DIRECT CONTROL
HIGHEST IMPORTANCE
PROFIT REPATRIATION
DIVIDEND REPATRIATION
FOREX CONTROL
CAPITAL REPATRIATION
EQUITY LIMITS
PROFIT REINVEST LIMITS
DIVEST OWNERSHIP REQUIRED
INCOME TAX - LOW

HIGH-MODERATE IMPORTANCE
FOREX BALANCING REQUIRED
EXPAND/DIVERSIFY LIMITS
BOARD APPOINTMENTS LIMITED
DUTY FREE IMPORT
TAX HOLIDAYS
NO WITHHOLDING TAX

INDIRECT CONTROL
HIGHEST IMPORTANCE
COUNTRY STABILITY
CIVIL DISTURBANCE
LAW CLARITY

HIGH-MODERATE IMPORTANCE
FOREX FLUCTUATION
WAGE LEVELS
TELECOMMUNICATIONS FACILITIES
INTEGRITY OF OFFICIALS
INFLATION TREND
SKILLS AVAILABLE
EFFECTIVE ADMINISTRATION

LARGE INVESTMENTS

DIRECT CONTROL
HIGHEST IMPORTANCE
PROFIT REPATRIATION
FOREX CONTROL
DIVIDEND REPATRIATION
CAPITAL REPATRIATION
EQUITY LIMITS
PROFIT REINVEST LIMITS
DIVEST OWNERSHIP REQUIRED
EXPAND/DIVERSIFY LIMITS
OWN LAND/BUILDINGS LIMITED

HIGH-MODERATE IMPORTANCE
FOREIGN PERSONNEL
BOARD APPOINTMENTS LIMITED
INCOME TAX - LOW
DUTY FREE IMPORT
TAX HOLIDAYS
GOVT TENDER PREFERENCE

INDIRECT CONTROL
HIGHEST IMPORTANCE
COUNTRY STABILITY
CIVIL DISTURBANCE
INTEGRITY OF OFFICIALS
LAW CLARITY
EXPROPRIATION PROTECTION
SKILLS AVAILABLE

HIGH-MODERATE IMPORTANCE
TRANSPORT SYSTEM
FOREX FLUCTUATION
INFLATION TREND
HIRE/FIRE RESTRICTIONS
EFFECTIVE ADMINISTRATION

RAW MATERIALS

LARGE INVESTMENTS

DIRECT CONTROL
HIGHEST IMPORTANCE
PROFIT REPATRIATION
DIVIDEND REPATRIATION
INTELLECTUAL PROP. PROTECT

HIGH-MODERATE IMPORTANCE
CAPITAL REPATRIATION
FOREX CONTROL
FOREIGN PERSONNEL
PROFIT REINVEST LIMITS
EXPAND/DIVERSIFY LIMITS
TAX HOLIDAYS

INDIRECT CONTROL
HIGHEST IMPORTANCE
COUNTRY STABILITY
TRANSPORTATION SYSTEM
INTEGRITY OF OFFICIALS

HIGH-MODERATE IMPORTANCE
EXPROPRIATION PROTECTION
SKILLS AVAILABLE
WAGE LEVELS
PUBLIC SAFETY

COST REDUCTION

SMALL INVESTMENTS

DIRECT CONTROL
HIGHEST IMPORTANCE
DUTY FREE IMPORT

HIGH-MODERATE IMPORTANCE
PROFIT REPATRIATION
CAPITAL REPATRIATION
DIVIDEND REPATRIATION
FOREX BALANCING REQUIRED
EQUITY LIMITS
PROFIT REINVEST LIMITS
DIVEST OWNERSHIP REQUIRED
EXPAND/DIVERSIFY LIMITS
TAX HOLIDAYS
INCOME TAX - LOW
LOW RENT FTZ

INDIRECT CONTROL
HIGHEST IMPORTANCE
TARIFF LEVELS
LAW CLARITY
COUNTRY STABILITY
CIVIL DISTURBANCE
WAGE LEVELS
ELECTRICITY RELIABILITY

HIGH-MODERATE IMPORTANCE
INTEGRITY OF OFFICIALS
FOREX FLUCTUATION
SKILLS AVAILABLE

LARGE INVESTMENTS

DIRECT CONTROL
HIGHEST IMPORTANCE
PROFIT REPATRIATION
CAPITAL REPATRIATION
FOREX CONTROL
DIVIDEND REPATRIATION
FOREIGN PERSONNEL
EQUITY LIMITS
BOARD APPOINTMENTS LIMITED
DIVEST OWNERSHIP REQUIRED
OWN LAND/BUILDINGS LIMITED
INTELLECTUAL PROP. PROTECT

HIGH-MODERATE IMPORTANCE
INCOME TAX - LOW
DUTY FREE IMPORT
LOW RENT FTZ

INDIRECT CONTROL
HIGHEST IMPORTANCE
CIVIL DISTURBANCE
TELECOMMUNICATIONS FACILITIES
FOREX FLUCTUATION
TARIFF LEVELS
TRANSPORT SYSTEM

HIGH-MODERATE IMPORTANCE
HIRE/FIRE RESTRICTIONS
INTEGRITY OF OFFICIALS
EXPROPRIATION PROTECTION
SKILLS AVAILABLE
FDI SCREENING

Inclusion Parameters:
"Highest" - As ranked by the MNCs on the Absolute Importance Scale.
"High-Moderate" - Ranked "Moderate" on the Absolute Importance Scale and in the top 50% of the Classification's Relative Scale.

TABLE 10.2

LESSER IMPORTANT INITIAL INVESTMENT PREFERENCES OF MNCs
IN
BARBADOS, JAMAICA, TRINIDAD & TOBAGO

HOST COUNTRY MARKET		RAW MATERIALS	COST REDUCTION	
SMALL INVESTMENTS	**LARGE INVESTMENTS**	*LESSER CONCERNS* **LARGE INVESTMENTS**	**SMALL INVESTMENTS**	**LARGE INVESTMENTS**

HOST COUNTRY MARKET — SMALL INVESTMENTS

DIRECT CONTROL
- FOREIGN PERSONNEL
- LOCAL CONTENT MINIMA
- SECTORS EXCLUDED
- OWN LAND/BUILDINGS LIMITED
- INTELLECTUAL PROP. PROTECT
- FINANCE FROM ABROAD
- R&D MINIMA
- EXPORT MINIMA
- TAX HOLIDAYS
- ACCELERATED DEPRECIATION
- SUBSIDIES
- LOW RENT FTZ
- CAPITAL GRANTS
- GOVT TENDER PREFERENCE
- PROTECTED MARKET

INDIRECT CONTROL
- TRANSPORT SYSTEM
- EXPROPRIATION PROTECTION
- TARIFF LEVELS
- DISPUTE RESOLUTION
- LEADERSHIP TURNOVER
- FDI SCREENING
- GDP GROWTH
- PUBLIC SAFETY
- ELECTRICITY RELIABILITY
- EDUCATION FACILITIES
- HIRE/FIRE RESTRICTIONS

HOST COUNTRY MARKET — LARGE INVESTMENTS

DIRECT CONTROL
- FOREX BALANCING REQUIRED
- SECTORS EXCLUDED
- NO WITHHOLDING TAX
- FINANCE FROM ABROAD
- LOCAL CONTENT MINIMA
- EXPORT MINIMA
- R&D MINIMA
- INTELLECTUAL PROP. PROTECT
- ACCELERATED DEPRECIATION
- CAPITAL GRANTS
- SUBSIDIES
- PROTECTED MARKET
- LOW RENT FTZ

INDIRECT CONTROL
- TELECOMMUNICATIONS FACILITIES
- GDP GROWTH
- DISPUTE RESOLUTION
- LEADERSHIP TURNOVER
- WAGE LEVELS
- ELECTRICITY RELIABILITY
- TARIFF LEVELS
- FDI SCREENING
- EDUCATION FACILITIES
- PUBLIC SAFETY

RAW MATERIALS — LARGE INVESTMENTS (*LESSER CONCERNS*)

DIRECT CONTROL
- FOREX BALANCING REQUIRED
- EQUITY LIMITS
- LOCAL CONTENT MINIMA
- FINANCE FROM ABROAD
- R&D MINIMA
- EXPORT MINIMA
- BOARD APPOINTMENTS LIMITED
- OWN LAND/BUILDINGS LIMITED
- SECTORS LIMITED
- INCOME TAX - LOW
- ACCELERATED DEPRECIATION
- CAPITAL GRANTS
- SUBSIDIES
- DUTY FREE IMPORT
- LOW RENT FTZ
- NO WITHHOLDING TAX
- GOVT TENDER PREFERENCE
- PROTECTED MARKET

INDIRECT CONTROL
- CIVIL DISTURBANCE
- LAW CLARITY
- DISPUTE RESOLUTION
- LEADERSHIP TURNOVER
- HIRE/FIRE RESTRICTIONS
- TELECOMMUNICATIONS FACILITIES
- ELECTRICITY AVAILABILITY
- EFFECTIVE ADMINISTRATION
- FDI SCREENING
- FOREX FLUCTUATION
- TARIFF LEVELS
- INFLATION GROWTH
- GDP TREND

COST REDUCTION — SMALL INVESTMENTS

DIRECT CONTROL
- BOARD APPOINTMENTS LIMITED
- FOREX CONTROL
- FOREIGN PERSONNEL
- FINANCE FROM ABROAD
- LOCAL CONTENT MINIMA
- EXPORT MINIMA
- R&D MINIMA
- OWN LAND/BUILDINGS LIMITED
- INTELLECTUAL PROP. PROTECTION
- SECTORS EXCLUDED
- NO WITHHOLDING TAX
- CAPITAL GRANTS
- PROTECTED MARKET
- ACCELERATED DEPRECIATION
- GOVT TENDER PREFERENCE
- SUBSIDIES

INDIRECT CONTROL
- EXPROPRIATION PROTECTION
- TELECOMMUNICATIONS FACILITIES
- DISPUTE RESOLUTION
- TRANSPORT SYSTEM
- INFLATION TREND
- HIRE/FIRE RESTRICTIONS
- LEADERSHIP TURNOVER
- EDUCATION FACILITIES
- FDI SCREENING
- EFFECTIVE ADMINISTRATION
- GDP GROWTH
- PUBLIC SAFETY

COST REDUCTION — LARGE INVESTMENTS

DIRECT CONTROL
- FOREX BALANCING REQUIRED
- PROFIT REINVEST LIMITS
- EXPAND/DIVERSIFY LIMITS
- SECTORS EXCLUDED
- TAX HOLIDAYS
- FINANCE FROM ABROAD
- EXPORT MINIMA
- LOCAL CONTENT MINIMA
- R&D MINIMA
- NO WITHHOLDING TAX
- ACCELERATED DEPRECIATION
- PROTECTED MARKET
- SUBSIDIES
- GOVT TENDER PREFERENCE
- CAPITAL GRANTS

INDIRECT CONTROL
- LAW CLARITY
- COUNTRY STABILITY
- DISPUTE RESOLUTION
- INFLATION TREND
- LEADERSHIP TURNOVER
- WAGE LEVELS
- ELECTRICITY RELIABILITY
- EFFECTIVE ADMINISTRATION
- PUBLIC SAFETY
- GDP GROWTH
- EDUCATION FACILITIES

Inclusion Parameters:

"Lesser Concerns" -- Ranked by the MNCs on the Absolute Importance Scale as "Low", OR
Ranked "Moderate" on the Absolute Importance Scale and in the bottom 50% of the Classification's Relative Scale.

Particularly with initial investment - before financial, emotional, and organizational interest-block ties to a particular location have been formed - the belief that the return on the investment will be available for servicing the corporate best interests is likely to be paramount in securing a location decision. The other avenues for obtaining a de facto, unfettered return on investment, such as favorable transfer pricing or reimbursement from downstream independent customers, are generally closed to the initial investor for home country market. Additionally, defacto investment return boosters, in the form of favorable home or host country tax treatment for expansion-via-reinvestment, are a function of initial investment success and realization is not assured. While the magnitude of the host market can confer relative barganing power upon the host having such endowments, the focus three small Caribbean countries (and potentially other small economy countries) would appear to possess little of such countervailing bargaining strength for ameliorating demands that initial MNC investment be able to reap the financial return warranted by its performance.

2) Ownership & Investment priorities - Equity Limitations, Divestiture of Ownership Requirements, Profit Reinvestment.

To initial investors, these restrictions are tantamount to a type of expropriation of their equity and/or the fruits of their risk taking. Before the investment is made, MNCs have control over their investment equity and borrowing power. In the absence of an unusually large opportunity, initial investors into a new market-location are likely to be skeptical that the expected overall returns on the investment will justify a mandated dilution of investment control or that restrictions on the use of profit are in the best interest of original investment performance. The host markets of the focus three countries are unlikely to be able to offer such an unusually large opportunity on other than the most infrequent of occasions.

3) Country Conditions priorities - Country Stability, Civil Disturbance, Law Clarity, Integrity of Officials.

For markets to operate, there must be a reasonable degree of peace and order (certainty) in the nation. Generally, investment shies away from uncertainty. Specifically, when the reason for investment is restricted to the host country market, some degree of order must prevail in the country itself for investors to have the confidence that the investment activity will proceed in some predictable and profitable fashion. The law, the legal process and those occupying positions of authority created by the law, are not immune from the need for predictability as investors shy away from unacceptable degrees of uncertainty in this area also.

Immediately following the "highest" preferences of the host market initial investor for reassurance that the parent corporation can reap the benefits for the risks undertaken, there follows a group of preferences ranking in the upper half of each classifications relative rankings and reinforced by an absolute importance ranking of at least "moderate". (See Figure 10.1). For both the small and the large quantum-level MNC investor motivated by Host Country Market-seeking, the preferences of Duty Free Entry and Board Appointments Limitations, reflect areas of mutual concern with profit and control, regardless of amount invested. Duty Free Importation for Host Country Market-seeking FDI can be a mixed blessing. It lowers cost but it can potentially increase competition from non-producer local importers (unless compensating non-tariff barriers are erected). However, when limited to capital goods utilized in the production process, duty free entry can increase the useage of more effective technology by reducing the cost of capital equipment - thereby increasing the cost competitiveness of the producer. This mixed blessing aspect is likely to have led to the "high/moderate" priority ranking. The other area of mutual concern between the small and large investing MNC - the Board Appointment Limitations - appears to indicate continuing concern with the major control issues outlined under "highest" priority.

The last group of mutual preferences of the small and large quantum-level investors- the least preferred (See Figure 10.2) - would appear to indicate a preference for competitive neutrality by government. At minimum, the preferences indicate an acceptance that it is unlikely that first time   investors into a host country market can reasonably expect to obtain a competitive advantage over indigenous competitors by voluntary act of the host country government. A review of the items of the IAP not appearing in the foregoing higher rated preferences would appear to confirm this. Lesser mutual concern was expressed for Direct Control items of Subsidies, Capital Grants, Accelerated Depreciation, Sectors Excluded, Intellectual Property Protection, Finance From Abroad, and Export, Local Content and R&D Minima. These would appear to indicate an MNC approach to entering the local market that is focused on the competitive environment : if the existance of a requirement or the absence of an incentive does not disadvantage the firm in comparison to its local competitors, then it is not perceived as being of a priority with the firm. Perhaps the yard stick for concern focuses on the ability to "pass on" the costs to the customer or represents an assessment that all competitors are exposed to the same relative degree of costs.

Small vs. Large Investments - Host Country Market-seeking

As noted earlier, the differences exhibited in the preferences of large investment quantum and small investment quantum MNCs making an initial investment into one of the three focus countries and having host country market motivation do not appear to be of sufficient strength to indicate basic divergence of focus between the two groups. This is not to say that there were no differences that could merit the attention of the host countries.

Small investors did place "highest" absolute importance on Low Income Tax and on Capital Repatriation where as large investors rated them as "moderate" The small initial investor is likely to be less able to take investment risk, is more cash strapped and is probably operating with less margin for error than his larger investing MNC. Should the small investment be made by a large MNC, the concern for a low income tax may be driven by the need to generate a superior return on investment (ROI) in order to justify the diversion of management attention occasioned by operating in an additional country.

Large quantum-level MNCs showed two (2) "highest" concern areas - Expansion / Diversification Limitations and Own Land/Buildings Limitations. These areas attracted the lower ratings of "high-moderate" and "lesser" concern, respectively, with the smaller quantum-level investor. The former - Expansion/Diversification Limitations - can reflect greater large investor concern for a strategy of widening the scope of their opportunities or possibly a greater need for the availability of profitable local-investment opportunities as a hedge against uncertainties of dividend and capital repatriation or other adverse foreign exchange restrictions. The latter - Own Land/Buildings Limitations - would appear to be a continuation of control concerns by the larger investor with the smaller quantum investor reflecting possibly the reality of limited capital availability or a designed limitation-of-risk strategy.

Two other differences in the perceptions of small and large MNCs may be noted. Small, initial investment for Host Country Market-seeking appears more concerned with the Wage levels, while large investments attach the greater concern to Skill Levels. Again, the small investor would appear to be operating with less margin for error and the larger investor is more able or willing to take a "comparison with competition" approach. If larger investment size can be correlated with greater equipment complexity, the higher concern by the larger investor for the host country's skill level would not be surprising.

Cost Reduction-seeking MNCs:

Significant difference was found to exist between the preferences for elements of the Investment Attraction Package recorded by initial investors - cost reduction motivation - small investment and similarly situated large investments. There were no mutually agreed preferences ranked in the "highest" importance category by both small and large quantum-level investors. Therefore, the interpretations surrounding each quantum-level of investment level within the cost reduction (export-oriented) motivation will be treated separately.

Small Investments - Cost Reduction-seeking

First-time investors into the focus Caribbean countries whose motivation is cost reduction (export-market) are of relatively recent arrival into the Caribbean (average year of establishment: 1980). The relative newness of cost reduction motivated investment in significant numbers may help explain the limited amount of research conducted to-date on this subdivision of FDI. The element denoted as being of "highest" absolute importance to this group of MNCs stands alone in its #1 ranking for elements of the Direct Control Group - Duty Free Import. For the small investment cost reduction-seeker, no other element was regarded as "highest" importance. In no other subdivision of motivation / quantum-level did the respondees reach such agreement for nominating a single item as their "highest" preference. In all other subdivisions, Profit Repatriation is #1 concern. While ranking Profit Repatriation as first within its classification, the median of this small investor micro-group accorded Profit Repatriation the "moderate" absolute importance position. It seems obvious that, for the small cost reduction group, Duty Free Import occupies the sine qua non position. It is not surprising that this micro-group ranks Wage Levels, Tariff Levels and Electricity Reliability as being of "highest" absolute importance in the Indirect Control Group elements. Again, they are the odd-man-out among the subdivisions in the rankings accorded these three conditions. In fact, these investors join with the majority of the other subdivisions of investors only in the nomination of Country Stability, Civil Disturbance and Law Clarity elements to the "highest" preference position. By definition, export is the cost reduction-seeker's game. Preoccupation with costs and conditions directly effecting their cost is expected. Low Wages are an obvious attraction, particularly if the jobs are unskilled or an appropriately skilled work force is available. Preference for this element nets less training cost to be carried by each item produced. Tariff Levels on equipment must either be rolled into the cost and amortized over the volume or not purchased and labour substituted therefor. Both add to the operating cost per item produced and lessen the competitive attraction of the country for the small Cost Reduction investor. Electricity Reliability, taken mostly for granted in the developed world, is a productivity factor that must be weighed. Crews sitting idle add to the per item cost, even if low paid. Purchase of stand-by generating capacity adds disproportionately to the small quantum investment capital requirements and/or deflects capital away from more directly contributing investments. The initial investor - cost reduction motivation - small investment MNC is very focused in his preferences and the narrowness of range of his host country interests reflect the realities of the business situation: survival depends upon low cost production. His low level of concern with the country's GDP Growth Rate, Effectiveness of Government Administration, Public Safety, even Expropriation Protection tend to reflect the single focus, enclave feature of the business (whether located in an FTZ or not).

Large Investments - Cost Reduction-seeking

Unlike their smaller cousins, the first time investor - cost reduction motivation - large investment MNCs are long term investors in the focus countries (average year of establishment - 1949). In many ways, the preferences of this micro group track more closely with (but are significantly different from) the host country market-seeker than with the small investment cost reduction - seeker. Some of this similarity with the market-seeker may relate to the length of residence, wherein longer residence may be associated with deeper interest in the host country per se, or possibly with the longer term strategic view expected of a large investment. However, the presence of a large number (87.5%) of vertically integrated firms in this group may provide the greater explanatory basis. Be that as it may, the elements denoted as "highest" absolute importance by the large investment CR micro group reflect four (4) major priorities - each consistent with their cost reduction purpose:

1) Financial priorities. Although de facto transfer of funds via favorable transfer pricing is a technique wherein the vertically integrated MNC may have unique opportunities - repatriation of profit, capital, dividends, and the availability of foreign exchange were nevertheless denoted as "highest" preference.

2) Control priorities. As vertically integrated companies, it is not surprising that the micro-group would register "highest" importance to elements that had the potential for adversely effecting MNCs accustomed structure, such as, Equity Limits, Board Appointment Limitations, Divestiture of Ownership.

3) Cost performance priorities. Consistent with investment purpose and longer term general nature of these investments, the "highest" preference was on the elements which offer system support for cost reduction - Foreign Personnel Limitations, Tariff Levels, Transportation System, Telecommunications Facilities - rather than the more direct contributors.

4) Security priorities. These concerns are manifested in "highest" concerns being accorded to proprietary matters (Intellectual Property Protection), property (Land/Buildings Ownership) and of facilities and personnel (Civil Disturbance).

Raw Materials-seeking MNCs

The principle of segregating potential investors into "Micro-Groups" that reflect the needs/benefits/cost for both MNCs and host countries is already well established in the raw materials (natural resources) motivation group. Many nations, including Barbados, Jamaica, and Trinidad-Tobago, have seperate investment attraction packages that apply to the Hotel industry, and where appropriate, to the Mining Industry and the Petroleum Industry. It has long been recognized that the needs, costs and benefits for both host and investor are unique in each of these three groups and action has been initiated by many governments to shape a customized IAP for the attraction of investments within those industries. In the instant survey, the results of the raw material group have been aggregated due to the small population of firms within the focus countries with this motivation.

Since there were no "small" initial investments reported in the raw materials-seeking group, the interpretations for the raw materials group are made against the host country market-seeking and cost reduction-seeking groups without the further subdivisions for quantum-level.

Similar to the host country market-seeking group, raw materials-seeking MNCs tend to be in for the long haul. Average date of original investment into the subject Caribbean countries is 1961, with only one investment having been made since 1966. This is principally indicactive of the shortage of marketable raw materials in the area. Recent first-time investment by MNCs into oil and bauxite extraction have been rare for the area as many of the established players have been involved over long periods and the market (for other than prospecting for oil) has not been bouyant enough to attract new investors. The exception is in the natural resources that are attractive to tourists.

Raw materials investing is assocoated with large investments by large, usually vertically integrated corporations and is known for its long term committments. The differences in investment package preferences between the raw material motivated MNCs and the MNCs of the other two basic motivations are primarily manifested in three areas:

1) Ownership Approach. Raw Material MNCs appear far more relaxed on the elements of Divestment of Ownership , Equity Limits and Board Appointments. Whereas Host Country Market and Cost Reduction-seeking motivated MNCs placed these concerns in the "highest" absolute importance level, the Raw Material investor placed them as "low" absolute importance.(Differences significant at the .01, .05, .01 level of confidence, respectively.) Unlike the other motivations, the ability to provide the large scale market for a relatively abundant commodity (bauxite) or a commodity available world-wide and generally in abundance (oil), and oft-times accompanied by processing pecularities of the raw material (bauxite and oil), has apparently given the raw material producer a level of confidence concerning security-of-supply unaccompanied by the felt-need for total or even majority ownership. Equity Limits and Ownership Divestments may represent much less of a threat to the continuation and control of the downstream enterprise for the vertically integrated raw material MNC. Divestment requirements and equity limits have the effect of either returning or lessening the parent corporations capital requirements and risk exposure, apparently without generating an unacceptable level of risk for the security of the coveted supply of the raw material. While more relaxed on ownership and equity in the entity of the host country subsidiary, the raw material motivated investor evidenced much stronger feeling concerning the ownership of ideas - Intellectual Property Protection. Here, the raw material MNCs reflected "highest" level absolute importance against "low" and "moderate" for Host Country Market and Cost Reduction respectively, with the difference with HCM and CR being significant at the .10 and .01 level, respectively. Proprietary knowledge accumulated by the MNC is regarded as a significant competitive advantage. The feeling seems to be particularly strong in those raw material industries of high volume, commodity type product that utilize technology generally perceived as "mature". Accordingly, each competitor in the industry seeks assurances that any special "twists" developed will be adequately protected.

2) Finance. Raw material seeking MNCs register "low" preferences for the financially impacting Low Income Tax, No Withholding Tax, Foreign Exchange Fluctuation and Duty Free Imports, and rank Capital Repatriation as being of "moderate" absolute importance. This contrasts with the Host Country Market and Cost Reduction MNCs who both ranked Capital Repatriation as "highest" level absolute importance and the elements of Low Income Tax and Foreign Exchange as "moderate" importance (with HCM difference to Raw Materials being significant at the .10 level). Duty Free Import also attracted a "moderate" ranking by both Host Country Market and Cost Reduction, with the CR difference to Raw Materials significant at the .10 level. A "moderate" level preference was shown for Tax Holidays by Raw Materials and Cost Reduction motivated MNCs while Host Country Market MNCs registered "low" level importance. The raw material-seeker, being generally large, integrated, and with multiple-nation investments, are likely to be well positioned to take advantage of the home country tax codes that allow tax credits for income taxes paid abroad. Some pay income tax on an assumed profit basis. In addition, those that are vertically integrated have transfer pricing opportunities. Thus their low regard for the level of corportate income taxes assessed by the host country reflect these advantages. Not all Raw Material-seeking subsidiaries pay taxible "dividends" to the parent and they frequently have negotiated duty concessions for bringing in production connected capital goods. As vertically integrated entities, they do not necessarily pay in foreign exchange for their product, but do bring in foreign exchange for payment for local goods, services and wages. As such, exchange rate fluctuation apparently may trouble them little, particularly over the long haul, - and at times has favored them - since the local exchange rate in the focus countries has moved unfavorably in relation to the dollar and the pound sterling. The "moderate" level ranking accorded Tax Holidays is a somewhat higher ranking than expected, particulaly in the light of U.S. tax law, but the specific situation for each MNC is likely to be required to gain a fuller appreciation of the ranking's meaning.

3) Administration. Difference at the .05 level exists between Raw Material-seekers and Host Country Market and Cost Reduction-seekers on the element of Law Clarity, with Host Country Market denoting a "highest" level of absolute importance and the other two motivations denoting "moderate" level. One explanation for the difference could be that the large raw material-

seekers generally have explicit agreements with the host country and generally have sufficient home office and local legal advisers skilled in handling legal complexities. There may be other interpretations of this difference which could be equally valid. Civil Disturbance registers a .05 level difference between Raw Material and Cost Reduction investors, with Cost Reduction and Host Country Market according this element the "highest" level of absolute ranking and raw material MNCs recording at "moderate" importance. Large raw material producers are generally large foreign exchange earners for the host country - a fact that is generally known by the local population. With some notable exceptions, this frequently produces a type of informal acknowledgement by opposing political elements within the host country that it would not be seen as being in the national interest for these operations to be disrupted. As for criminal element civil disruption effecting raw material-seeking MNCs, such operations usually have more than the average security operations found in the typical host country firm plus the criminal element may also understand that the government-of-the-day would be likely to react with dispatch should these foreign exchange earners be seriously hindered. Raw material MNCs have placed the "highest" level of importance on the element of Transportation System, with the difference vis-a-vis Cost Reduction being significant at the .05 level. Both Cost Reduction and Host Country Market ranked this element as "moderate" level importance. For the bauxite element of the raw materials group, the transportation system is key in two areas - for some producers, the public railroad is the converyor of finished product to the ports for final shipment; for others, the public transportation needs of their employees is a prime concern. It can be speculated that for the tourist industry element of raw materials group, the public transportation needs of its guests, as well as its employees, is a prime concern.

From an economic definition viewpoint, the case has been argued for the inclusion of raw materials within the cost reduction motivation for FDI. (Williamson[1], Brewer[2], among others). Although not without its theoretical merit, the case for maintaining the separate identity for raw materials would appear to be compelling from the investment attraction viewpoint.

---

[1]Williamson, O. 1986\). *Economic organization. Firms, markets and policy control.* N.Y.: University Press, p.177.

[2]Brewer, T. 1993. "Government policies, market imperfections, and foreign direct investment". *Journal of International Business Studies*, Vol 24, No. 1, p.33.

CHAPTER XI

AND THEREFORE

Conclusions

*"Look to the essence of a thing, whether it
be a point of doctrine, of practice, or of
interpretation."*

Marcus Aurelius Antoninus
(121-180 A.D.)

For developing countries - especially small-economy developing countries - segmenting MNCs into discrete micro-groups that have relatively homogeneous attributes reveals that micro-grouped MNCs have unique preferences for the various elements making up the investment attraction packages of host countries. Further, these preferences are not necessarily uniform among and/or between the micro-groups. The evidence presented in this study supports the view that multinational corporation preference for various elements of the investment attraction packages of host developing countries depends upon the specific reason for the MNC's investment (strategic motivation), the amount of investment risk undertaken by the MNC (quantum or dollar size of investment) and the timing of the investment (initial investment).

A second investment cannot be made in a country when a first investment has not preceded it. Location decisions for initial investment into developing countries are projected as being made on a one-investment-at-a-time, project basis. When MNCs consider locating a foreign direct investment in a host country in which it has no previous direct investment experience, it is assumed that the project is being undertaken for a single strategic motivation rather than multiple, and that the investment is of known approximate monetary value (quantum). It would appear unusual indeed for a single MNC to conduct simultaneous, multiple initial investments covering the spectrum of investment strategic motivations and sizes into any country wherein it lacked operating experience, and all the more unlikely should that potential country be a developing country. Thus, a need exists for focused information on the investment attraction preferences of specific groups of investors conducting their initial investment into a developing country in order to supplement the present, more widely available information on the preferences of FDI investors studied as a whole, undifferentiated for the timing of the investment (initial or expansion).

This study utilized the capital risk elements of transaction costs theory and the recognized strategic motivations of FDI to form a matrix for segmenting MNCs into micro groups possessing specific homogeneous attributes in a search for micro-group uniqueness in their investment attraction preferences. Each country permitting FDI within their borders presents an assortment of laws, regulations, incentives and conditions to potential investors that collectively have been labeled in this study as the "Investment Attraction Package". The micro-groups examined in the study consisted of MNCs who had conducted FDI in one or more of the three Caribbean countries of Barbados, Jamaica, and Trinidad & Tobago, and was limited to the initial investment location-decision of the MNCs. The MNCs were divided into sub-groups determined by the individual MNC's strategic motivation for conducting FDI (host country market-seeking, raw material-seeking, or cost reduction-seeking) and by the quantum-level of the investment (small-level or large-level).

The approach of this study was to search the investment preferences of discrete units of FDI investors possessing homogenous attributes that had been identified via a two-dimensional research model based upon recognized theories and capable of replication should other studies be designed to extend the findings of the present work. The expectations for the study were that the subdivision of FDI investors into smaller groups (micro-groups) would reveal the identities of preferences that were unique unto the micro-groups and that such uniqueness had previously been masked from recognition by submersion of the micro-groups into larger groups of FDI investors. The hope of the study is that if such differences are agreed to exist and are identified by this and future studies, the specific needs of each FDI micro-group - once identified - can be addressed by the developing countries and the effectiveness of the total Investment Attraction Package enhanced for the developing countries, MNCs, and/or both. The goal of the study is to be of constructive assistance in improving the amount of FDI flowing into the developing countries - particularly the small-economy developing countries - for the benefit of the host countries, their people, and the MNCs.

GENERAL CONCLUSIONS

The evidence presented in this study suggests that the following general conclusions could be appropriate.

1. The element of non-triviality of investment (quantum), due to its relatively fixed directional relationship with redeployability of assets and transaction-specificity of assets - especially in larger investments, provides a reasonable and convenient surrogate for all three capital risks elements of transaction costs theory, thus making the theory more readily usable when applying it to investigations of FDI relationships.

2. The matrix formed by non-triviality of investment (quantum) and investment strategic motivation (reason) provides a useful diagnostic tool for disaggregating FDI investors into homogeneous micro groups for the purpose of examining preferences for various elements of the Investment Attraction Packages of host countries. A third dimension - timing of investment - should be added to the matrix in future studies as prima face evidence suggests that initial FDI and expansion FDI are likely to respond differently to the investment attraction packages of host countries. It seems clear that the risks of over-agglomerazation inherent in Stages I and II of FDI research to-date are unnecessarily high and that Stage III (this study) is incomplete as to the timing segmentor. (See Figure 1.1).

3. Evidence supports the view that significant differences do exist between the preferences of different micro groups of MNCs for the elements of the investment attraction packages of the focus three Caribbean countries.

Given few marketable raw materials, little purchasing power and less population, the focus countries have limited options in the competition for attracting FDI. Maximizing the effectiveness of those options is likely to require new and innovative approaches. Knowledge of the differing needs and preferences of unique groups of investors may permit the targeting of specific groups whose unmet needs have been masked by their inclusion in larger groups of investors.

Specific Conclusions
"Ticket To Play"

To be taken seriously as a candidate for FDI, a host country must provide some means for the investor to effectively receive the fruits of the investment risk undertaken, in a form spendable by the corporation outside of the host country, with disposition at the sole discretion of the corporation. i.e., Profit Repatriation.

To the degree that investment return is illiquid or shackled in some manner, the initial investor is likely to discount the return or adjust the required investment "hurdle rate" until a satisfactory liquid and unfettered real return is achieved. As the rate is adjusted, the comparative desirability of the host country as a location for FDI also undergoes adjustment. A second - and not unrelated - condition-precedent also exists for would-be host countries - Country Stability. In the extreme, total instability is anathema to behavior predictability and behavior predictability is the goal of most, if not all, investors. Admittedly, country stability is an imprecise and relative concept. It can cover the gamut from physical security and a sense of well-being to the cogent business concerns for currency stability, investment safety, and host country attitude toward FDI. Nevertheless, as investment reward is a function of perceived investment risk, the greater the perceived instability, the greater the risk, and the greater the reward demanded by the investor. As the quantum of reward demanded increases, the comparative desirability of the host country as a location for FDI decreases. The elements of Profit Repatriation and Country Stability, as perceived from the opinions of the MNCs responding to the survey, amount to a "Ticket-to-Play" for host countries seeking to participate in the FDI ball game. This ticket defines the boundaries of the FDI game for the MNCs as a whole, as well as for the specified micro-groups.

Other IAP Preferences

The desirability of the other 47 elements included in the Investment Attraction Package (IAP) specified in this study varies between "highest" absolute importance (the "deal killers") to "low" absolute importance ("nice but not really essential"). Desirability of the individual elements making up the IAP varied significantly between most of the micro-groups identified by the study.

Guarded by the twin-pillars of Profit Repatriation and Country Stability, the road beyond the FDI Attraction Gate immediately divides itself into a trio of highways, each leading to the domain of a particular FDI strategic motivation. Along each motivation's highway lies the destination of the journey - the motivation/quantum-level micro groups. The discovery of the micro-groups sometimes yields the identity of needs unique unto the group itself while at other times needs identified are more reflective of the motivation's domain. With the aid of the transaction cost/motivation matrix, Table 10.1 lists the micro groups present in the aggregated total of all MNCs responding to the Postal Interview that underpins this study and suggests those elements that are of "highest importance" and "high-moderate importance" to the named micro-groups. Table 10.2 lists those elements for which each micro-group appears to have "lesser concerns".

PROPOSED MODEL FOR FDI FUTURE RESEARCH

It is perhaps worth repeating that incentives given to those not valuing them represent squandered assets of the provider and windfall profits to the receiver. Valued incentives withheld or onerous restrictions applied to specific investor groups can represent missed opportunity for the provider and force second-best locations for the investor. The subject of FDI attraction into developing countries has been much discussed and debated over the years. Research to-date has cast a wide net but too often the catch has been marketed under the generic title of FDI. Few have sought to divide the catch into species that increase the value provided to the diverse consumer. It is evident that there has not been a great deal of consensus developed on the broad outlines of the appropriate focus areas for developing country expenditure for investment attraction, let alone on the details of what attracts and what doesn't. As ever, the devil is in the details.

For developing countries - especially small-economy developing countries - segmenting MNCs into discrete micro-groups that have relatively homogenous attributes unique unto the micro-group reveals that MNCs preferences for the various elements making up the investment attraction packages of host developing countries are not uniform. The evidence presented in the study supports the view that multinational corporation preference for the various elements of the investment attraction packages of host developing countries depends upon the specific strategic reason for the MNC's investment (motivation), the amount of investment risk undertaken by the MNC (quantum) and the timing of the investment (initial investment).

At minimum, the evidence from the reported study and other studies suggests that:

> * FDI investors constitute a market for host developing countries seeking to attract FDI.
>
> * Host developing countries are offering a product to the market.
>
> * Identifiable market niches of FDI investors DO exist.
>
> * These market niches have unique needs to be met.
>
> * The over-agglomeration risk in FDI research to-date is unnecessarily high.
>
> * The analytical framework used in the reported study is incomplete, especially in scope of the timing dimension.

The logic behind the speculations of Guisinger [1985][1], Evans and Doupnik [1986][2], Cable and Persaud [1987][3] and Contractor [1990][4], among others, seems overpowering - expansion investment and original investment may require different investment-attraction approaches. The differences between the attraction-requirements of host country market-seeking, raw material-seeking and cost reduction-seeking investment are already evident in Rolfe et al. [1993][5], Woodward and Rolfe [1993][6], and Kumar [1994][7] and the reported study. The importance of quantum of investment, as suggested in Rolfe et al. [1993] and the reported study, shows promise. Figure 11.1, entitled "FDI Attraction - Developing Countries - Proposed Research Model" sets forth a model that builds on the findings of the past and offers increased resolution power for the future.

The model segments FDI investors by their strategic motivation (host market, raw materials, cost reduction), the investment's size - quantum (large, small), and the investment timing (initial or expansion).

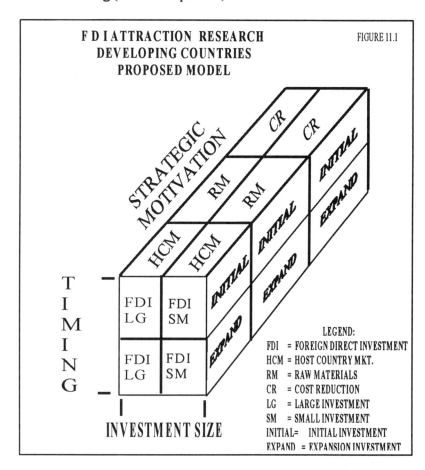

F D I ATTRACTION RESEARCH
DEVELOPING COUNTRIES
PROPOSED MODEL

FIGURE 11.1

LEGEND:
FDI = FOREIGN DIRECT INVESTMENT
HCM = HOST COUNTRY MKT.
RM = RAW MATERIALS
CR = COST REDUCTION
LG = LARGE INVESTMENT
SM = SMALL INVESTMENT
INITIAL= INITIAL INVESTMENT
EXPAND = EXPANSION INVESTMENT

It is suggested that acquisition investment be treated in accordance with the MNC's country-investment timing: initial or expansion. (Should further research reveal that acquisition nets a significantly different set of needs and/or tax effects for the MNC, then the framework can be modified to add this dimension to the timing plane). Further factors suggesting potential differences among investors, such as industry groupings, could also be considered for inclusion in the articulation. However, care needs to be given to the potential for excessive fragmentation of sample size which, especially in developing countries, is likely to be relatively small.

Knowledge of the differing needs and preferences of unique groups of investors may permit the targeting of specific groups whose unmet needs have been masked by their inclusion in larger groups of investors. Developing countries - especially the small economy, poorly endowed countries - need to be sure they retain the MNCs they have, expand them where they can, and seek both large and small investments of market-seekers, cost reducers, and natural resource consumers. Segregation of potential investors into reasonably homogeneous groups can lead to a closer "up front" approximation of fitting the needs of the individual investor into a framework of "equal particulars/ equal treatment" or "right things for like projects". Such a policy does not eliminate the need for individual case bargaining to "fine tune the fit" but it can reduce the scope of such bargaining which leads to the benefits of increased transparency.

GENERALIZABILITY POTENTIAL

The dangers of conclusions drawn from generalities lies in the details. While no claim can be made that the findings of this study represent anything more than an analysis of the preferences of MNCs making initial investments for the specified elements of the Investment Attraction Packages presented by Barbados, Jamaica, and Trinidad-Tobago, the number of instances wherein the findings of this study failed to support the findings of other researchers on points previously identified by them as being related to the FDI location decisions of MNCs is troubling. It is well within the realms of possibility that the subject three countries are sufficiently unique that the details surrounding them did not permit the application of principles drawn from a wider representation of nations. Should this be the case, the power of segmentation will have been illustrated from the outset.

Since many, if not most, of the multinational corporations responding to this survey have operations in other nations, it is unlikely that the MNCs themselves are the source of uniqueness to the degree required to skew the findings of this study away from the typicals as utilized in the prior studies.

An alternate explanation for the differences in the findings reported in this study from those of its predecessors is that the data utilized in the prior studies was in such an aggregated form that the conclusions drawn from the data could only be representative of the population represented by that data. Suspicion that greater segmentation of data could yield different results is well documented. Brewer (1993)[8] pointed to the different effects incentives could have upon investors depending upon whether the investment was original or expansion. Rolfe, et al,(1993)[9] tested this recently, and found that difference did exist but segmentation of preferences by motivation was not reported. Many have alluded to the potentially different effects of motivation on preferences.(Lim,1973[10]; Guisinger,1986[11]; Contractor,1991[12], among others). Most have reported on host country market-seeking investment. Recently, some have investigated cost reduction-seeking. Direct comparison of the two motivations has been scant. Quantum has been recently recognized (Rolfe et al.[13]) but investigated primarily for cost reduction motivation and in investor grouping unsegmented for timing - original or expansion.

The more likely explanation for differences in the findings of this study from those of prior researchers is a simple one: similar questions were addressed to dissimilar audiences. Put more accurately - while the questions being investigated appear broadly similar, differences in responses and findings originate from the unique and homogeneous identity of the respondents. Should this be the case, the value of segmentation will have been illustrated by the differing results.

There would appear to be general agreement that MNCs do evaluate their alternatives for investing capital. According to Grubert and Mutti (1991)[14]: "Economic theory suggests that a multinational corporation will allocate capital internationally so that its risk-adjusted marginal after-tax rate is equal across all alternatives." An assumption of this study is that MNCs - individually - have investment parameters for judging the comparative desirability of potential FDI locations and that these parameters are applied in a reasonably uniform manner across potential host countries.

Given only the three focus countries and their relative smallness, generalizability of results would be questionable at best. Given that the study is grounded in a primary research survey of multinational corporations, given that the responses emanated from the parent firms domiciled in the U.S. and U.K., given that the great majority of the responding firms conduct FDI in many countries -

including an array of developing countries, and given that these firms are likely to apply their location-decision parameters in a reasonably uniform manner across the spectrum of their potential location-choices, the potential for generalizability of results becomes increasingly difficult to dismiss.

ADDITIONAL RESEARCH SUGGESTED

In view of the study's suggestions of

1. lack of confirmation of significant elements of prior bench-mark studies by eminent researchers, and

2. demonstrated potential that disassembly of aggregated data can provide useful information for policy makers seeking to enlarge opportunities for attracting FDI,

additional research is required in order to assure the international community of the directions to be taken. It is assumed that the previously reported general findings are being utilized by policy makers in such investment influencing institutions as the IMF, The World Bank, and governments. Host country government - particularly developing country governments - are struggling to find solutions to the capital inflow shortages. Lack of FDI into these countries is playing some role in retarding the economic growth needed to raise the standard and quality of life in the developing countries. The urgings and recommendations of the influential international bodies may be being based in part upon findings formulated from aggregated data. In reality, investments are made (and attracted) one investment at a time.

The areas suggested for further investigation are primarily those pointed up by the differences in approach between this and prior research:

1. <u>Expansion investment versus initial investment</u>. Almost all prior studies have grouped the two together, yet it is logical to expect that they may march to different drummers. The thought is not new but the follow up has not as yet taken place on an appropriate scale. The present study appears to add some urgency to the need. Contractor (1990)[15] notes that developing nations have exhibited a very low rate of reinvested earnings by TNCs. For many countries, however, reinvestment can make up a significant portion (if not majority) of FDI, as was evident in Rolfe et al. (1993)[16]. There is growing suspicion that investor reaction to the total Attraction Package might well be different for the reinvestor than for the original investor. This raises the

question of the potential need for either "harmonizing" any known differences in the priorities of the two different types of investors, (with its attendant risks of satisfying neither), or of devising separate incentive schemes for each (with the attendant risk of unintended "spill over" effects). Specifically, some of the areas meriting further research would appear to include:

a. Identification of the key variables in the Investment Attraction Package for FDI by expansion investment. Specifically, the preferences related to the modes of expansion via new FDI injection, via reinvested profit and via acquisition, should be sought and defined

b. Examination of home country (specifically U.S.) tax law effects on the FDI investor. Generally speaking (yet there are some notable exceptions), present U.S. tax law does not tax corporations on their foreign earned profit until such profit is repatriated back to the U.S. Does such a provision encourage less than market return investments to be made? To the advantage or disadvantage of whom? Is management's and shareholders' interests in alignment on such investment? Is the test of "next best alternate use of funds" (pre-tax, post-tax) normally run on such reinvestments?

c. Does the greater familiarity with the host country result in higher or lower investment hurdles being set for reinvestment than for initial investment? In the more volatile Third World countries, country familiarity aids in defining differences between form and substance. As an example, many non-resident U.S. and U.K. home owners in Jamaica mistook rhetoric for substance in the 1972 change in the governing party and "gave away" their holdings only to find that foreign home owners were not expropriated and value returned in due course.

2. Quantum (dollar size) of investment differences - both within a particular motivation and between motivations.

3. Strategic motivation differences. This area has received much needed recent attention but the investigation of cost reduction motivated investments has too often been agglomerated into the investigation of its more numerous fellow-motivation - host country market. Since cost reduction-seeking MNCs are projected by some researchers to be the motivation in the ascendancy for small, low-wage nations, additional investigation is indicated - both for the evaluation of net benefits to the host country as well as for the identification of investment attraction parameters.

4. Do the micro-group results presented by this study have meaning for:

    a. Other poor, small, developing countries in the Caribbean.

    b. Large, poor, developing countries, with little potential for matching population with sufficient purchasing power to produce a large and attractive market. For example, the African nations.

    c. Large, poor, emerging but underdeveloped countries, with perceived future potential for presenting a large market, such as Eastern Europe, South America, Pacific Rim.

    d. Developed countries - of all sizes. As these countries try to reduce the sustained high unemployment levels that are believed to contribute to so many of the developed countries' social ills, the investment attraction needs of the job creating small entrepreneur may not be too different from the small FDI investor. Particular emphasis could be placed on those investigations segmenting for quantum of investment, and more particularly for the small investment - cost reduction or host country market.

The study of investor preferences for elements of an IAP and the effectiveness of such elements in attracting FDI are essentially two different subjects. While effectiveness may be inferred by some to be implicit in statements of relative preferences, "support" for such effectiveness is absent. Further, the effectiveness dispute surrounding FDI attraction policies is made up of several parts, including operational effectiveness in attracting the investors and cost effectiveness for the host country. Making the matter of effectiveness more complex is the comparative terms in which the framework of the debate has been held:- Country Conditions are more (or less) influential in bringing FDI to a host country than are Incentives. While the wisdom of Contractor (1991)[17] concerning the inappropriateness of general statements regarding the effectiveness of FDI policies needs to be borne in mind, it would assist the focus of future efforts directed toward improving the investment attraction capability of host developing countries if there was resolution of the dispute existing between   expressed or implied investor preferences and their effectiveness as attractors. The resolution needs to be sought both in terms of persuasive power to effect the location decision and in terms of overall cost/benefit for the host country. Without resolution, policy makers must continually be "looking over their shoulders" when considering various proposals grounded in either one of the two advocated-positions of relative attraction-superiority. Following the logic of Contractor, the search may be the more fruitful and the statements of results the more creditable if the investigation were confined to specific investor groups and the results confined to specific statements .

---

[1]Guisinger, S. 1985. *Investment incentives and performance requirements: Patterns of international trade, production and investment.* Westport, CN.: Praeger, Greenwood Press, p.48.

[2]Evans, Thomas, and Doupnik, Timothy (1986). "Foreign Exchange Risk Management Under Standard 53.83", Stamford, CN.: *Financial Accounting Standards Board.*

[3]Cable, V. and Persaud, B. 1987. "New trends and policy problems in foreign investment: The experience of Commonwealth developing countries" in *Developing with Foreign Investment.* The Commonwealth Secretariat, Kent: Croom Helm Ltd, p.8.

[4]Contractor, F. 1990. "Government policies towards foreign investment. An empirical investigation of the link between national policies and FDI flows". A paper presented to Annual Conference, Academy of International Business, Miami: p. 21.

[5]Rolfe, R.; Ricks, D.; Pointer, M.; and McCarthy, M. 1993. "Determinants of FDI preferences of MNEs". *Journal of International Business Studies*, Vol 24, No. 2 (Spring, 1993), p.352.

[6]Woodward, D. and Rolfe, R. 1993. "The location of export oriented foreign direct investment in the Caribbean basin". *Journal of International Business Studies*, Vol.24, No.1, p. 121.

[7]Kumar, N. 1994. "Determinants of export orientation of foreign production by U.S. multinationals: An inter-country analysis". *Journal of International Business Studies*, Vol 25, No. 1, p.152.

[8]Brewer, T. 1993. "Government policies, market imperfections, and foreign direct investment". *Journal of International Business Studies*, Vol 24, No. 1, p.133.

[9]Rolfe, et al.1993. *op cite.* p.347.

[10]Lim, D. 1983. "Fiscal incentives and direct foreign investment in less developed countries". *Journal of Development Studies*, Jan., pp. 207-12.

[11]Guisinger, S. 1985. *op cite.* p.48.

[12]Contractor, F. 1991. "Government policies and foreign direct investment". *UNCTC Studies, Series No. 17*, N.Y.: United Nations, p.23.

[13]Rolfe et al. 1993. *op cit*, p.349.

[14]Grubert, H. and Mutti, J. 1991. "Taxes, tariffs and transfer pricing in multinational corporate decision making". *The Review of Economics and Statistics*, p.288.

[15]Contractor. 1990. *op cite.* p. 21.

[16]Rolfe et al. 1993. *op cit*,. p.343.

[17]Contractor. 1991. *op cit*,. p.21.

Chapter XII

POLICY RECOMMENDATIONS

"We will either find a way or make one."

Hannibal
(247? - 183 B.C.)

Recommendations to policy makers should be approached with much caution. It is a truism that the further a person is from the center of responsibility the more irresponsible or inappropriate the suggestions can become. Not only is the suggester not as subject to the moderating hot coals of accountability for the "improvements" suggested, but there is frequently a large "expertise" gap created by the differing levels of insider - outsider background, training, and experience. In more recent times, there is also the considerable factor of "special interest" advocacy that tends to "color" the receptivity potential for "policy" recommendations. The "advocacy" contained in the following recommendations is simple, straight-forward, and declared up-front: the goal of the recommendations is to suggest ways in which the amount of FDI flowing into developing countries might be effectively increased. With profound humility, the following policy recommendations are submitted::

Articulated Investment Attraction Code

Developing countries seek to increase their stock of investment capital for the purpose of increasing economic activity within their boundaries. Of special concern for this study are the small, relatively poor, developing countries. With few marketable raw materials, little purchasing power and less population, the warnings of Beamish et al. (1991)[1] and Miller (1993)[2] ring in the ear : the days of small economies attracting FDI for host country market reasons are getting rarer. Conventional wisdom increasingly limits the future potential of these countries for attracting FDI to the single motivation of export-oriented investment. Such a projection is not challenged by this study, but its message for the small, relatively poor country may be in need of amplification. The corollary to this looming likelihood is that small-economy developing countries, such as Barbados, Jamaica, and Trinidad-Tobago, must wring every ounce of synergy out of their few endowments. Given their small market size, they cannot afford to cede the field for host country market-seeking MNCs to their larger market competitors. Nor can they simply do head-to-head battle with their larger rivals for the more limited benefits dispensed by the cost reduction-seeking investor. Although the principle of targeting is strongly embraced, and is the very essence of this study, the suggestion of Rolfe et al. (1993)[3] that countries seeking large companies should focus their efforts on incentives that are a function of the amount of investment is a high risk strategy for small countries - "great" if they hit but devastating if they "miss". Rather, small poorly endowed countries need to be sure they retain the MNCs they have, expand them where they can and seek both large and small investments of both market-seekers and cost reducers.

A policy of "judge each case on its merits" sounds eminently fair and reasonable but can lead to the chaos of administrative overload or worse - suspicions of "who's got a better deal" by the aggressive investor, "I can't get what I really need" by the more timid or inexperienced investor, and the temptations of corruption for both investor and host officials. The potential for segregation of recipients into reasonably homogeneous groups can lead to a closer "up front" approximation of fitting the needs of the individual investor into a framework of "equal particulars/equal treatment" or "right things for like people". Such a policy does not eliminate the need for individual case bargaining to "fine-tune the fit" but it can reduce the scope of such bargaining which leads to the benefits inherent in increased transparency. The pursuit of such a strategy is not an "all things to all people" approach, it is a "right things to right people" approach. Toward this end, the establishment of an articulated FDI code should be considered. Specific targeted incentives, regulations and laws should be fashioned for specific groups of investors possessing homogenous attributes and which display unique sets of needs and bring unique sets of benefits/costs. The search for both group identity and group needs could begin with the micro groups and their needs as identified by this study, but further more refined definitions of the homogenous attributes should be attempted.

A beneficial increase in transparency accompanies a policy of "all animals of a certain type are equal", with open admission that many types are welcome, especially when the policy replaces an "all animals are equal" policy which is usually accompanied by the sotto voce statement "but some are more equal than others". (with apologies to the late George Orwell and his masterpiece - "Animal Farm"[4]).

Conceptually, the smallness of a developing country might be an advantage in that 1) there are less special interests groups to upset when granting targeted favors to targeted groups and 2) there is the potential, though apparently not the current practice, that smaller countries can respond to opportunities in a quicker, surer fashion.

An added benefit of an articulated investment code is that, during the promulgation of the code, both the political directorate and the civil service will have had to "think through" each unique set of investors to which the separate sections of the code are addressed and the agreements reached could be expected to be codified by legislation. Thus, the responsible bureaucrat can respond to external inquiry and can negotiate with potential investors in that manner which reflects the certainty-of-approval so required of any effective negotiator. Such a condition might be especially valued by the higher level, permanent civil servant-type whose position-tenure is frequently dependent upon properly reflecting the philosophy of the government-of-the-day.

Tax Holidays - Mutually Supportive Approaches

Current tax law in some developed countries (notably, the U.S.) can have a neutralizing effect for the income tax holidays negotiated on behalf of an MNC's foreign operations by effectively increasing the parent corporation's tax liability by an amount equivalent to the tax holiday benefit. Tax credits are granted for income taxes paid to foreign countries and are not granted when foreign income tax is not paid. As such, when a qualified developing country grants a tax holiday as a matter of course to attract foreign investment, the developing country foregoes a source of revenue and the parent corporation may not be the benefit recipient. (If the corporation pays no foreign income taxes, it gains no tax credits for reducing its home country tax). The qualifications represented by the word "may" are several. For example, there exists a U.S. tax law provision postponing tax due on foreign profits until they are repatriated, under certain specified circumstances and provided an appropriate tax treaty exists between the two taxing countries. This postponement potential will not apply to all MNCs investing in the subject countries, may not apply to most and is unlikely to apply to one of the specific micro group - Small Quantum - Cost Reduction-seeker - since 1) such companies may not have large capability for shifting tax credits among several foreign subsidiaries and/or 2) such companies may repatriate profit annually. To the degree that the MNC is not able to take advantage of tax loopholes that allow deferral of tax liability until foreign profit is repatriated, then the recipient of the host country's tax holidays benefits may be the home country of the MNC (U.S.) and not the MNC itself. The policy implications are clear: host country and MNCs need to work together to formulate that set of mutually supportive approaches that insures that benefits demanded/given work to the benefit of the intended.

In implementing the suggestion, an articulated approach which, within a given micro group essentially treats all equally, may be of some benefit - particularly should MNC home country tax law require that the host country tax law reflect the mandatory nature of the tax.

Existing FDI Review

Host developing countries should regularly review the needs of those foreign direct investors presently resident within the territorial jurisdiction. The minimum purpose of review is to retain those who have already committed investment capital within the territory. However, this review should be from both the retention and the expansion perspective. The requirements for attracting the expansion candidate are likely to be different from those of the first time investor and should be confirmed by targeted survey.

Ownership & Control Limitations

Table 10.1 - Major Preferences of MNCs - reveals the ranking of "Highest" and "High-Moderate" absolute importance attached to the elements of Equity Limitations, Divestiture of Ownership and Board Appointments for the micro-groups Host Country Market-seeking - Large and Small, and for Cost Reduction-seeking - Large, with Cost Reduction-seeking-Small in agreement on the first two named elements. Hypothesis #1 revealed the directional relationship between quantum of investment and the "sunk" nature of the assets. Given that a significant portion of the assets of a large investment are likely to permanently reside in the host country, the country is enriched by the capital investment and the level of available local capital remains uncommitted and potentially available for application to additional nation enriching capital investments. The legal ownership entity of the "sunk" assets within the country does not change the nation's defacto capital enrichment achieved by having attracted the FDI. Further, the element "Finance from Abroad" attracted the importance ratings recorded as being of "lesser concerns" of all four micro groups. The policy implications would appear to be that due note should be taken that restrictions on ownership and control are a major negative when attracting FDI, that the nations permanent capital stock is enriched by some proportion of the investment regardless of nominal ownership title, and that most MNCs appear to be prepared to finance their capital requirements from abroad. As such, restrictions on ownership and control of equity holdings of MNCs runs the risk of location non-selection yet the opposite restriction of requiring finance from abroad would not appear to be detrimental to attracting FDI and would conserve local capital for additional growth opportunities.

Foreign Personnel Limitations

Cost Reduction-seeking - Large Quantum and Host Country Market-seeking - Large Quantum listed Foreign Personnel Restrictions as being of "Highest" and "High-Moderate" absolute importance. In some of the comments accompanying the survey, this was frequently connected to adverse remarks concerning the red tape and bureaucracy of the host country. As reflected in the importance rankings and in the interpretations section, limitation on the number of expatriate personnel seem to lack a risk/reward balance, particularly in a project where its justification for host country location is cost reduction. Anything running counter to the basic justification of the project (cost reduction) is likely to be evaluated negatively for that location and inability to have "experienced staff" goes to the heart of a cost reduction project. From a practical viewpoint, ex-pats are expensive. Especially in cost reduction motivated FDI, it would seem that the market mechanism can be relied upon to hold their number in check. However, a requirement for some stipulated length of service with the parent company might be justified as a bar against untrained 3rd country expatriates being brought in especially for the task.

"Slanting" Promotional Efforts - U.K. and U.S.

There may be some potential for "slanting" promotional material to take advantage of the differences in preferences expressed by the U.S. and the U.K. MNCs for the country conditions (Indirect Control Group). The U.K. MNCs placed the greater importance on Foreign Exchange Fluctuation, Inflation Trend, Law Clarity, Education Facilities, Transportation System and Integrity of Officials, whereas their counterparts in the U.S. placed the higher interest in Wage Levels and Public Safety. Suggestions of cultural closeness (language, laws, customs, etc.,) or geographic closeness could be utilized, especially with small MNCs and/or first time MNCs. So as not to overdraw the potential, host countries should be aware of the findings of Lorimo (1993) that there is no evidence to support the proposition that MNCs target host countries for FDI based on cultural distance.[5].

WRAP UP

To maximize the effective use of the limited resources of small developing economies for attracting the needed FDI, those resources must be targeted to the specific needs of identifiable MNC micro-groups. The study has sought the identity of those "different strokes" and those "different folks".

From earliest times it has been recognized that the first requirement for hitting a target is to know what the target is. "Targeting the Foreign Direct Investor" seeks to improve the identification process presently being used and suggests that the target is, in fact, multiple targets - each with unique traits and needs. The concept is neither new nor original. The "micro-groups" of MNC investors having unique and homogeneous attributes that are identified by applying the study research model can be said to be "market niches". The analysis of the preferences of each micro-group is an effort to determine the real needs and expectations of the individual niches. The task now shifts to host developing country - the "producer" - to determine how best to meet the needs and expectations of the customer - the FDI investor, i.e., what total IAP (the "product") is within the country's capability to present and is such offering competitive. Lastly, and most importantly, the host developing country must determine the viability of the offering - does the production and sale of the market-acceptable product meet the established minimum level of expected returns for the investment required.

Foreign direct investment (FDI) is only one avenue for attracting the capital needed to spur economic growth of the small-economy developing countries. However, its importance is growing as the former easy availability of other sources for financing economic growth recedes in the wake of a global embrace of market-driven solutions and privatization. Although Mahbub ul Hag (1974)[6] has powerfully reminded all that "market" is a combination of both population and purchasing power, and the fact will remain that the poorer developing nations are generally small-economies, poor, and possess few factor endowments other than a low-cost labor force. It is vital for them to make the most of what FDI they currently possess and to find ways and means for attracting more.

The "independence" concerns of the 1970s have given way to the "interdependence" reality of the 1990s. Liberalization of attitudes toward FDI in the late 1980s has spawned competition for FDI in the 1990s. Given the competitive environment and the supply of nations possessing only the low labour-cost factor, the search in the latter portion of the 1990s needs focus on effective ways of increasing the total FDI returns - both to host developing countries and to the investing MNCs.

---

[1]Beamish, P.; Killing, J.; Lecraw, D.; Crookell, H. 1991. *International management, Text and cases*. Homewood, IL.: Irwin, p. 95.
[2]Miller, R. 1993. "Determinants of U.S. manufacturing abroad", *Finance and Development*. March, 1993, p. 118.

[3]Rolfe, R.; Ricks, D.; Pointer, M.; and McCarthy, M. 1993. "Determinants of FDI preferences of MNEs". *Journal of International Business Studies*, Vol 24, No. 2 (Spring, 1993), p.352.

[4]Orwell, G. 1945. *Animal Farm: A fairy story*. London: Secker and Warburg.

[5]Larimo, J. 1993 . *Foreign direct investment behavior and performance*. Finland: Acta Wasaensia, University of Vaasa, p.38.

[6]Haq, Mahbub Ul. 1976. "The third world and the international economic order". *Development Paper #22*, Overseas Development Council, N.Y.: Random House, pp. 1-11.

APPENDIX A

FOREIGN DIRECT INVESTMENT IN BARBADOS, JAMAICA, AND
TRINIDAD-TOBAGO POSTAL INTERVIEW

CORPORATE NAME:_____

RESPONDENT'S NAME:_____

TITLE:_____

NB: ALL INFORMATION GIVEN IS REGARDED AS CONFIDENTIAL AND, IN THE FINAL REPORT
STAGE NOT BE IDENTIFIABLE WITH YOUR COMPANY.

1. WHAT IS THE PRINCIPAL INDUSTRY SECTOR OF YOUR AFFILIATED COMPANY IN
BARBADOS, JAMAICA, TRINIDAD & TOBAGO? (PLEASE UNDERLINE THE APPROPRIATE
COUNTRY OR COUNTRIES.) _____. *HEREAFTER, THE DESIGNATION
"(COUNTRY)" WILL REFER TO THE COUNTRY YOU HAVE UNDERLINED..

2. IS THE (COUNTRY) COMPANY OPERATION INTEGRATED WITH THAT OF THE PARENT OR
OTHER SUBSIDIARIES OF THE PARENT?
VERTICALLY ___ : HORIZONTALLY ___ : OTHER ___ : NOT AT ALL ___

3. DO YOU FEEL YOUR FIRM IS DIFFERENTIATED FROM YOUR COMPETITORS? IF SO,
CHARACTERIZE THE ADVANTAGE.
TECHNOLOGY BASED ___ : KNOW HOW BASED ___ : RAW MATERIALS BASED ___ : BRAND /
TRADE NAME ___ : OTHER ADVANTAGE ____

4. AT THE TIME OF MAKING THE ORIGINAL INVESTMENT IN (COUNTRY), WHAT WAS THE
PRINCIPAL BENEFIT YOUR FIRM WAS SEEKING?
A. MARKET ___ . FIRM'S PRINCIPAL MARKET IS: _____ INTRA-COMPANY:
    ___ HOST COUNTRY: ____ CARICOM: ____ EX -REGION EXPORT: ___
B. RAW MATERIAL ____ . RAW MATERIAL AVAILABILITY IS: ___ WORLD WIDE: ___
    SELECTIVELY AVAILABLE: ____ SCARCE
C. COST REDUCTION ___ . WHAT FACTOR WAS PRIMARY TARGET: ___ LABOR:
    ___ HOST COUNTRY TAXES: ___ HOME COUNTRY TAXES.
D. OTHER ___ . PLEASE SPECIFY, _____.

5. PLEASE DESCRIBE THE TYPE OF OWNERSHIP STRUCTURE OF YOUR AFFILIATE COMPANY
IN (COUNTRY).
____ WHOLLY-OWNED SUBSIDIARY
____ PARTIALLY OWNED SUBSIDIARY.
    PERCENT PARENT OWNERSHIP _____%
____ JOINT VENTURE
____ OTHER (PLEASE SPECIFY)
    PERCENT PARENT OWNERSHIP _____%

6. DESCRIBE THE PARENT COMPANY'S ABILITY TO EXERCISE ANY OPERATIONAL CONTROL OF (COUNTRY) COMPANY:

_____ PROPORTIONAL TO OWNERSHIP
_____ BOARD INPUT ONLY.
_____ MANAGEMENT CONTRACT.
_____ TECHNOLOGY.
_____ OTHER. (PLEASE DESCRIBE)

7. IN WHAT YEAR WAS YOUR FIRST INVESTMENT MADE IN COUNTRY? _____

8. AT THE TIME OF ORIGINAL INVESTMENT, THE PARENT FIRM ENVISIONED:
A. TOTAL INVESTMENT (1992 DOLLARS
OF APPROXIMATELY:
____ LESS THAN U.S. $1,000,000
____ BETWEEN U.S. $1,000,000
&   U.S. $20,000,000
____ OVER U.S. 20,000,000

B. INVESTMENT DEEMED REDEPLOY ABLE TO ANOTHER COUNTRY IF "THINGS DID NOT WORK OUT" WOULD HAVE BEEN:
____ OVER 67% REDEPLOY ABLE
____ BETWEEN 34 - 67% DEPLOYABLE
____ LESS THAN 34% REDEPLOY ABLE

C. SPECIFIC SITE, EQUIPMENT & LEARNING COSTS CONVERTIBLE TO ALTERNATE USE (PROFITABILITY) WITHIN THE COUNTRY:
_____ OVER 67% CONVERTIBLE
_____ BETWEEN 37 - 67% CONVERTIBLE
_____ LESS THAN 34% CONVERTIBLE

LISTED ON THE NEXT PAGE ARE SOME OF THE MORE COMMON PROVISIONS ESTABLISHED BY DEVELOPING COUNTRIES FOR THE PURPOSE OF AFFECTING FOREIGN DIRECT INVESTMENT WITHIN THEIR BORDERS. ALSO LISTED ARE SOME OF THE MORE COMMON SERVICES AND CONDITIONS WHICH CAN EXIST WITHIN DEVELOPING COUNTRIES AND WHICH MAY AFFECT FOREIGN DIRECT INVESTMENT WITHIN THEIR BORDERS.
PLEASE REVIEW EACH LIST AND INDICATE YOUR COMPANY'S CURRENT EVALUATION OF:

* THE RELATIVE IMPORTANCE OF EACH ITEM, WITHIN THE CATEGORY, TO YOUR COMPANY'S DECISION TO LOCATE IN (COUNTRY).
(PLEASE USE FORCED RANKING, I.E., NO TWO ITEMS OF EQUAL IMPORTANCE. RANK # 1 = HIGHEST IMPORTANCE)

* THE ABSOLUTE IMPORTANCE OF EACH ITEM TO YOUR COMPANY'S DECISION TO LOCATE IN (COUNTRY).

LEVEL OF IMPORTANCE TO BE INDICATED AS:
"A" = A "GO/ NO GO " ITEM. A " DEAL KILLER". FUNDAMENTAL TO THE
        INVESTMENT.
"B" = MODERATELY IMPORTANT. COULD BE "DEAL KILLER" BUT
        EXPECT TO REACH MUTUALLY   SATISFACTORY SOLUTION TO ITEM.
"C" = PREFERRED ITEM. LIKE TO HAVE BUT NO "DEAL KILLER.

THE WORD "RESTRICTIONS" IS USED TO INDICATE PRESENCE OF GOVERNMENT
LAWS/REGULATIONS LIMITING FOREIGN DIRECT INVESTMENT.

	IMPORTANCE	
FINANCIAL RESTRICTIONS	REL 1-10	ABSL A / B/ C
MANDATED MINIMUM EXPORTS	____	____
FOREIGN EXCH. CONTROL. CONVERSION	____	____
CAPITAL REPATRIATION	____	____
FOREIGN PERSONNEL & INPUTS LIMITS	____	____
PROFIT REPATRIATION	____	____
MANDATED LOCAL R&D MINIMUMS	____	____
MANDATED LOCAL CONTENT MINIMUMS	____	____
DIVIDEND REPATRIATION/ UTILIZATION	____	____
FOREIGN EXCHANGE BALANCING REQUIRED	____	____
(CASH INFLOWS = OR) CASH OUTFLOWS)		
FINANCING MUST COME FROM ABROAD	____	____
OTHER (SPECIFY)_____	____	____

THE WORD "INCENTIVES" IS USED TO INDICATE PRESENCE
OF GOVERNMENT LAWS/ REGULATIONS USUALLY REGARDED AS TO
FOREIGN DIRECT INVESTMENT.

	IMPORTANCE	
TAXES & SUBSIDIES INCENTIVES	REL 1-10	ABSL A/ B/ C
ACCELERATED DEPRECIATION SCHEDULES	____	____
SUBSIDIES (INCL. BELOW MARKET LOANS)	____	____
CORPORATE INCOME (LOW)	____	____
PROTECTION AGAINST IMPORTS	____	____
LOW RENT "FREE PORT" FACILITIES	____	____
GOVERNMENT TENDER PREFERENCE	____	____
WITHHOLDING TAX (NON EXISTENT)	____	____
TAX HOLIDAYS	____	____
CAPITAL GRANTS	____	____
DUTY FREE IMPORTATION OF INPUTS	____	____
OTHER (SPECIFY) _____	____	____
OTHER (SPECIFY) _____	____	____

	IMPORTANCE	
INVESTMENT & OWNERSHIP RESTRICTIONS	REL 1-8	ABSL A/ B /C
EQUITY OWNERSHIP LIMITATIONS	____	____
DIVERSIFICATION/ EXPANSION RESTRICTED	____	____
PROFIT REINVESTMENT RESTRICTED	____	____
DIVESTITURE OF OWNERSHIP REQUIRED	____	____
APPOINTMENTS TO BOARD RESTRICTED	____	____
CERTAIN SECTORS OF ECONOMY DENIED	____	____
INTELLECTUAL PROPERTY RIGHTS LIMITED	____	____
RIGHT TO OWN LAND/BUSINESS PREMISES	____	____
OTHER (SPECIFY)_____	____	____
OTHER (SPECIFY)_____	____	____

OTHER CONSIDERATIONS
(PLEASE DENOTE CORPORATE ESTIMATE OF EFFECT ON LOCATION DECISION SHOULD
LISTED BE DEEMED UNCOMPETITIVE WITH OTHER DEVELOPING COUNTRIES).

IMPORTANCE

	REL	ABSL
ECONOMIC	1- 4	A/ B/ C
EXCHANGE RATE FLUCTUATION	___	___
INFLATION TREND	___	___
GDP GROWTH RATE	___	___
LEVEL OF TARIFFS OR QUOTAS	___	___
OTHER (SPECIFY) _____	___	___
LEGAL 1-3		
EXPROPRIATION PROTECTION GUARANTEES	___	___
HOST CO. DISPUTE RESOLUTION REQ'D	___	___
CLARITY/ SIMPLICITY OF LAW/PROCEDURES	___	___
OTHER (SPECIFY) _____	___	___
POLITICAL 1-3		
POLITICAL LEADERSHIP TURNOVER	___	___
POLITICAL STABILITY OF COUNTRY	___	___
POTENTIAL FOR CIVIL DISTURBANCE	___	___
OTHER (SPECIFY) _____	___	___
LABOR 1-4		
AVAILABILITY OF SKILLS	___	___
EDUCATION FACILITIES	___	___
HIRE/ FIRE RESTRICTIONS	___	___
LOCAL WAGE LEVELS	___	___
OTHER (SPECIFY) _____	___	___
INFRASTRUCTURE 1-3		
TRANSPORTATION SYSTEM ADEQUACY	___	___
TELECOMMUNICATIONS FACILITIES	___	___
ELECTRICITY RELIABILITY	___	___
OTHER (SPECIFY) _____	___	___
ADMINISTRATION 1-4		
FDI SCREENING PROCEDURES ('RED TAPE')	___	___
PUBLIC SAFETY PROVISIONS	___	___
INTEGRITY OF OFFICIALS-CORRUPTION	___	___
EFFECTIVENESS OF HOST CO. ADMIN.	___	___
OTHER (SPECIFY)_____	___	___

IN YOUR OPINION, WHAT, IF ANY, ADDITIONAL ACTIONS BY HOST COUNTRY GOVERNMENTS WOULD BE EFFECTIVE IN INCREASING LEVELS OF PRIVATE INVESTMENT INTO (COUNTRY)?

IN YOUR OPINION, WHAT WERE THE THREE (3) MOST IMPORTANT THINGS THAT PERSUADED YOUR COMPANY TO INVEST IN (COUNTRY)?

IN YOUR OPINION, WHAT ARE THE THREE (3) GREATEST IMPEDIMENTS TO ATTRACTING FOREIGN INVESTMENT INTO (COUNTRY)?

THANK YOU FOR YOUR HELP!
EDWARD J. COYNE , SR. DIR. MIBA PROGRAM
NOVA UNIVERSITY 3301 COLLEGE AVENUE
FT. LAUDERDALE, FL 33314

BIBLIOGRAPHY

Aharoni, Yair (1966), *The Foreign Investment Decision Process*, Boston: Harvard University Press.

Arrow, Kenneth (1969), "The Organization of Economic Activity" *in The Analysis and Evaluation of Public Expenditure: the PPB System*, Joint Economic Committee, 91st U.S. Congress, 1st Session, p. 48.

Austin, James (1990), *Managing in Developing Countries*, New York: Free Press.

Ball, D A and McCulloch, Wendell H (1993*), International Business. Introduction and Essentials*, 5th Ed., Homewood, IL.: Irwin.

Babbie, Earl (1992), *The Practice of Social Research*, 6th Ed., Belmont, CA.: Wadsworth.

Beamish, Paul W ; Killing, J Peter; Lecraw, Donald J ; Crookell, Harold (1991), *International Management. Text and Cases*, Homewood, IL.: Irwin.

Behrman, Jack (1974), *Decision Criteria for Foreign Direct Investment in Latin America*, New York: Council of the Americas.

Bergsten, C Fred; Horst, Thomas; Moran, Thomas (1978), *American Multinationals and American Interests*, Wash., D.C.: Brookings Institution.

Bergsten, C. Fred, Noland, Marcus(1993), *Reconcilable Differences? United States - Japan Economic Conflict*, Washington, D.C.: Marcus Noland Institute, pp. 206-228.

Boddewyn, Jean J (1988), "Political Aspects of MNE Theory", *Journal of International Business Studies*, Vol. 19, No.3, pp. 341-63.

Bond, Eric W and Samuelson, Larry (1986), "Tax Holidays as Signals", *The American Economic Review*, Vol. 16, No. 4, p. 820

Brace, Charles and Brace, Corrinne (1991), *Understandable Statistics, Concepts and Methods*, Lexington, MA.: Heath.

Bradberry, William (1986), *U.S. Multinational Corporate Managers' Response to Investment Incentives and Performance Requirements*, PhD thesis, University of Texas at Dallas: p. 48.

Bradley, J (1968), *Distribution-Free Statistics*, Englewood Cliffs, N.J.: Prentice Hall, Ch. 2.

Brewer, Thomas; David, Kenneth; and Lim, Linda (1987), *Investing in the Developing Countries. A Guide for Executives*, Lexington, MA.: D.C. Heath & Co.

Brewer, Thomas (1993), "Government Policies, Market Imperfections, Foreign Direct Investment", *Journal of International Business Studies*, Vol.24, No. 1, p.82-104.

Buckley, Peter J and Casson, Marc (1976), *The Future of the Multinational Enterprise*, London: Macmillan.

Buckley, Peter J. (1985), "A Critical Review of the Theories of the Multinational Enterprise" in Buckley, Peter and Casson, Marc, (1985), *The Economic Theory of the Multinational Enterprise. Selected Papers*, Hong Kong: Macmillan.

Buckley, Peter J. (1989), *The Multinational Enterprise: Theory and Applications*, London: Macmillan.

Buckley, Peter J. (1992), *Studies in International Business*, New York: St. Martin Press.

Cable, Vincent and Persaud, Bishnodat (1987), "New Trends and Policy Problems" in "Foreign Investment: the Experience of Commonwealth Developing Countries" in Vincent Cable and Bishnodat Persaud, *Developing with Foreign Investment*, Kent: Croom Helm, p. 8.

Casson, Marc (1979), *Alternatives to the Multinationals*, New York: Holmes & Meier.

Clegg, Jeremy (1992), "Explaining Foreign Direct Investment Flows" in Peter Buckley and Marc Casson, *Multinational Enterprises in the World Economy*, Hants, England: Edward Elgar.

Coase, Ronald (1952), "The Nature of the Firm" in Stigler, George and Bouldings, Kenneth (Eds.) *Readings in Price Theory*, Homewood, IL.: Irwin.

Coase, Ronald, (1960), "The Problem of Social Cost", *Journal of Law and Economics*, p. 15.

Commons, John R (1934), *Institutional Economics*, Madison: University of Wisconsin Press.

Commonwealth Secretary-General (1974), *New Trends in Foreign Investment: The Experience of Commonwealth Countries*, Kent: Croom Helm, Foreword.

Contractor, Farok J (1990), "Government Policies Toward Foreign Investment. An Empirical Investigation of the Link Between National Policies and FDI Flows" in a paper presented to the Annual Conference, Academy of International Business, Miami: pp.21-26.

Contractor, Farok J., (1991), *Government Policies and Foreign Direct Investment*, UNCTC studies series No. 17, pp. 19-25.

Cornell, Robert (1989), *International Direct Investment and the New Economic Environment. Tokyo Round Table*, Organization for Economic Cooperation and Development, p.10 -11.

Davies, Leslie R (1987), *Senior Management Perceptions of the Foreign Direct Investment Decision*, PhD thesis, University of Bradford, p. 6.

Deere, Carmen; Antrobus, Peggy; Bolles, Lynn; Melendez, Edwin; Phillips, Peter; Rivera, Marcia; Safa, Helen (1990), *In the Shadows. Caribbean Development Alternatives and U.S. Policy*, Bolder, CO.: Westview Press.

Dun & Bradstreet Inc, USA (1992), *Million Dollar Directory. America's Leading Public and Private Companies Series*, New York: Dun & Bradstreet

Dunning, John H.(1988a), "The Electic Paradigm of International Production: A Restatement and Some Possible Extensions", *Journal of International Business*, Vol. XIX, No. 1, p. 1.

Dunning, John H., (1988b), *Explaining International Production*, London: Unwin Hyman.

Dunning H., (1994), "Reappraising the Eclectic Paradigm, in an Age of Alliance Capitalism", Memmograph, Newark, NJ.: Rutgers University.

Elizabeth, Regina II (1983), "Christmas Message to the Commonwealth", *The London Times*, 27 Dec., p.1.

Evans, Thomas and Doupnik, Timothy (1986), "Foreign Exchange Risk Management Under Standard 53.83", *Financial Accounting Standards Board*.

Flam, Harry and Flanders, M (1991), "Introduction" in Heckscher, Eli F and Ohlin, Bertil, *Heckscher-Ohlin trade Theory*, Cambridge, MA.: MIT Press, p. 25.

Folsom, Ralph; Gordon, Michael; and Spanogle, John (1988*), International Business Transactions in a Nutshell*, St. Paul, MN.: West Publishing.

Fusfeld, Daniel R (1990), *The Age of the Economist*, 6th Ed., London: Scott, Foresman & Co.

Gale Research Co. (1992), *Ward's Business Directory. America's Leading Private and Public Companies*, Detroit, MI.: Book Tower.

Gardiner, P (1975), "Scales and Statistics", *Review of Educational Research*, Vol. 45, pp. 43-57.

Geringer, J Michael and Herbert, Lewis (1989), "Control and Performance of International Joint Ventures", *Journal of International Business Studies*, Vol. XX, No. 2, p.236.

Glass, G; Peckman, P; Sanders, J (1972), "Consequences of Failure to Meet Assumptions Underlying the Fixed Effects Analysis of Variance and Covariance", Review of Educational Research, Vol. 42, pp.237-88.

Gold, David (1993), "World Investment Report 1993: Transnational Corporations and Integrated International Production. An Executive Summary", *Transnational Corporations*, Vol. 2, No. 2, p.99.

Grosse, Robert (1980), *Foreign Investment Codes and the Location of Direct Investment*, New York: Praeger.

Grosse, Robert and Behrman, Jack (1992), "Theory in International Business", *Transnational Corporations*, Vol. 1, No. 1.

Group of Thirty (1984), *Foreign Direct Investment 1973-87*, New York: Group of Thirty.

Grubert, Harry and Mutti, John (1991), "Taxes, Tariffs and Transfer Pricing in Multinational Decision Making", *Review of Economics and Statistics*, p. 288.

Guisinger, Stephen E (1985), *Investment Incentives and Performance Requirements: Patterns of International Trade, Production and Investment*, New York: Praeger.

Harris, Phillip R and Moran, Robert T (1991), *Managing Cultural Differences*, 3rd Ed., Houston, TX.: Gulf Publishing

Hennart, Jean-Francois (1989), "Can the 'New' Forms of Investment Substitute for the 'Old' Forms?", *Journal of International Business Studies*, Vol XX, No. 2, p. 217.

Helleiner, G K (1987), "Direct Foreign Investment and Manufacturing for Export: A Review of the Issues", in *Developing with Foreign Investment*, The Commonwealth Secretariat, Kent: Croom Helm, p. 76.

Hoover, Gary; Campbell, Alta and Spain, Patrick (1993), *Hoover's Handbook of American Business*, Austin, TX.: Reference Press.

Hope, Kemp (1986), *Economic Development in the Caribbean*, New York: Praeger.

Hymer, Stephen H. (1976), *The International Operations of National Firms: A study of Direct Foreign Investment*, Cambridge, MA.: MIT Press

Inter-American Development Bank (1993), *Economic and Social Progress in Latin America*, Special Section : Human Resources, Wash., D.C.: IDB

International Monetary Fund (1977), *Balance of Payments Manual*, Wash, D.C.: IMF para. 408.

International Monetary Fund (1992), *Balance of Payments Statistics Yearbook*,

Wash., D.C.: IMF.

Jobber, Davis (1990), "Maximizing Response Rates in Industrial Surveys: A review of the Evidence", *Advances in Business Marketing*, Vol 4, JAI Press, p. 122.

Johnson, Chalmers (1980), *MITI and the Japanese Miracle*, Stanford, CA.: Stanford University Press.

Kahler, Miles (1986), *The Politics of International Debt*, Ithaca, N.Y.: Cornell University Press.

Kanuk, Leslie and Sorenson, Conrad (1975), "Mail Surveys and Response Rates: A Literature Review", *Journal of Marketing Research*, Vol. XII, p. 141.

Kerlinger, Fred N. (1986), *Foundations of Behavioral Research*, 3rd Ed. Orlando, FL.: Holt, Rinehart & Winston.

Kline, John (1993), "Research Note: International Regulation of Transnational Business: Providing the Missing Leg of Global Investment Standards", *Transnational Corporations*, Vol. 2, No. 1, p.155.

Knight, Frank H (1965), *Risk, Uncertainty and Profit*, New York: Row.

Korten, David (1991), "Sustainable Development: A Review Essay", *World Policy Journal*, Vol. 9, No. 1, pp. 157-90.

Kreinin, Mordechai F (1991), *International Economics. A Policy Approach*, New York: Harcourt, Brace, Jovanovich.

Kumar, Nagesh (1994), "Determinants of Export Orientation on Foreign Production by U.S. Multinationals: An Inter-Country Analysis", *Journal of International Business Studies*, Vol. 25, No.1, p. 148.

Lane, Henry W and DiStafano, Joseph J (1992), *International Management Behavior*, 2nd Ed., Boston, MA.: PWS-Kent.

Larimo, Jorma (1993), *Foreign Direct Investment Behavior and Performance*, Acta Wasaensia, Finland: University of Vaasa.

Lecraw, Donald J (1992), "Multinational Enterprises and Developing Countries" in *New Directions in International Business: Research for the 1990s*, Peter Buckley (Ed.), Hants, England: Edward Elgar.

Leontief, Wassily (1954), "Domestic Production and Foreign Trade: The American Capital Position Re-Examined", *Economica Internazionale*, Vol. 7, pp. 3-32.

Lewis, William (1991), "Free market and the Prosperity Gap", *The McKinsey Quarterly*, No. 4, pp.116-132.

Lim, David (1983), "Fiscal Incentives and Direct Foreign Investment in Less Developed Countries", *Journal of Development Studies*, pp. 207-12.

Haq, Mahbub Ul (1976), "The Third World and the International Economic Order", Development paper #22, Overseas Development Council, New York: Random House, pp. 1-11.

Martyn, Howe (1970), *Multinational Business Management*, Lexington, MA.: Heath

Miller, Robert R (1993), "Determinants of U.S. Manufacturing Abroad", *Finance and Development*, Mar., p. 118.

Minor, Michael S (1994), "The Demise of Expropriation as an Instrument of LDC Policy, 1980 -1992", *Journal of International Business Studies*, Vol. 25, No. 1, p. 182.

Nakatani, Iwao (1992), "The Asymmetry of the Japanese-style vs. American-style Capitalism as the Fundamental Source of Japan-U.S. Imbalance Problems",

National Bureau of Economic Research and Japan Center for Economic, Research. Background paper for the U.S.-Japan Economic forum (February).

Okita, Saburo (1992), "Transition to Market Economy", Mimeograph.

Organization for Economic Cooperation and Development (1986), *The OECD Guidelines for Multinational Enterprises*, Paris: OECD.

Organization for Economic Cooperation and Development (1989), *International Direct Investment and the New Economic Environment. Tokyo Round Table*, Paris, OECD.

Orwell, George (1945), *Animal Farm: A Fairy Story*, London: Secker and Warburg

Ostry, Sylvia (1992), "The Domestic Domain: The International Policy Arena" *Transnational Corporations*, Vol. 1, No. 1, p. 7.

Porter, Michael (1990), *The Competitive Advantage of Nations*, New York: Free Press.

Price Waterhouse (1989), *Doing Business in Barbados*, Price Waterhouse.

Price Waterhouse (1991), *Doing Business in Trinidad-Tobago*, Price Waterhouse.

Price Waterhouse (1993), *Doing Business in Jamaica*, Price Waterhouse.

Ramsaran, Ramesh (1985*), U.S. Investment in the Caribbean. Trends and Issues*, New York: St. Martin's Press.

Robock, S H and Simmonds, K (1989), *International Business and Multinational Enterprises*, 4th Ed., Homewood, IL.: Irwin.

Rolfe, Robert J ; Ricks, David A ; Pointer, Martha M ; and McCarthy, Mark (1993), "Determinants of FDI preferences of MNEs", *Journal of International Business Studies*, Vol. 24, No. 2, pp. 39 - 44.

Rolfe, Robert J and White, Richard (1992), "The Influence of Tax Incentives in Determining the Location of Foreign Direct Investment in Developing Countries", *Journal of American Taxation Association*, p. 39-57.

Root, FR and Ahmed, AA (1978), "The Influence of Policy Instruments on Manufacturing Foreign Direct Investment in Developing Countries*", Journal of International Business Studies*, Winter, pp.81- 94.

Rubner, Alex (1990), *The Might of the Multinationals. The Rise and Fall of the Corporate Legend*, New York: Praeger.

Rueber, G; Crookell, H; Emerson, M.; and Gallais-Homonno (1973), *Private Foreign Investment in Development*, Oxford: Clarendon Press.

Rugman, Alan (1981), *Inside the Multinationals. The Economics of Internal Markets*, New York: Columbia University Press.

Sakaibara, Eisuke (1992), "Japan: Capitalism Without Capitalist", *International Economic Insights 3*, No.4 (July-August):45-47.

Schnitzer, Martin C. (1991), *Comparative Economic Systems*, Cincinnati, OH.: South-west Publishing.

Shaw, SMS and Toye, JFT (1978), "Fiscal Incentives for Firms in Some Developing Countries", in JFT Toye, *Taxation and Economic Development*, London: Frank Cass.

Schollhammer, Hans (1974), *Location Strategies of Multinational Firms*, Los Angles, CA.: Pepperdine University.

Simmon, Herbert A (1982), *Models of Bounded Rationality*, Cambridge, MA.: MIT Press.

Standard and Poors (1993), *Registrar of Corporations, Directors and Executives*, New York: Standard and Poors.

Stopford, John and Strange, Susan (1991), *Rival States, Rival Firms: Competition for World Market Shares*, Cambridge: Cambridge University Press.

Streeten, Paul (1992), "Interdependence and Integration of the World Economy: The Role of the States and the Firms", *Transnational Corporations*, Vol 1. No.3 (December), p.132.

Sturdivant, Frederick D (1981), *Business and Society. A Managerial Approach*, Homewood, IL.: Irwin.

"A Survey of Multinationals" (1993), The Economist, Mar. 27, p. 19.

Teece, David (1980), "Economics of Scope and Scope of Enterprise", *Journal of Economic Behavior and Organization*, Vol. 1, pp. 223-47.

Teece, David, (1981), "The Multinational Enterprise: Market Failure and Market Power Considerations", *Sloan Management Review*, Vol. 22, Spring, p. 4.

Thurow, Lester (1992), *Head to Head. The Coming Economic Battle Among Japan, Europe, and America*, New York: William Morris & Co.

Trevor, M A and Farrell (1987), "Direct Foreign Investment, the Transnational Corporation and the Prospects for LDC Transformation in Today's World: Lessons from the Trinidad-Tobago Experience", in *Developing With Foreign Investment*, London: Croom Helm, p. 221-44.

Tyson, Laura D'Andrea (1992), *Who's Bashing Whom? Trade Conflict in High-Technology Industries*, Washington, D.C.: Institute for International Economics. p.2.

Unipub (1991), *Directory of American Business Firms Operating in Foreign Countries*. 12th Ed. Vol 3., New York: Unipub.

United Nations (1974), *The Impact of Multinational Corporations on Development and on International Relations*, Department of Social and Economic Affairs, pp. 15-162.

United Nations (1992a), *World Investment Report, 1992: Transnational Corporations As Engines of Growth*, Transnational Corporations and Management Division, p. 65.

United Nations (1992b), *Formulation and Implementation of Foreign Investment Policies. Selected Key Issues*, Transnational Corporations and Management Division, p. 64.

United Nations (1993), *World Investment Directory, 1992. Foreign Direct Investment, Legal Framework and Corporate Data*. Vol. 7 : Developed Countries, Transnational Corporations and Management Division.

United Nations Centre for Transnational Corporations (1983*), Transnational Corporations in World Development, Third survey*, UNCTC, p. 12.

United Nations Centre on Transnational Corporations (1985), *Trends and Issues in Foreign Direct Investment and Related Flows*, UNCTC, p. 28.

United Nations Centre on Transnational Corporations (1991), *World Investment Report, 1991:The Triad in Foreign Direct Investment*, UNCTC, p. 287.

United Nations Conference on Trade and Development (1993), *World Investment Report, 1993: Transnational Corporations and Integrated International Production*, UNCTAD, p. 13-15.

U.S. Congress Senate Committee on Finance (1970*), Implications of Multinational Firms*, Wash., D.C.: U.S. Printing Office, p. 173.

U.S. Department of Commerce (1977), *U.S. Foreign Investment Abroad*, Wash. D.C.: Government Printing Office, p. 340.

U.S. Department of Commerce (1993), "Barbados Economic and Trade Policy", (Market Research Report, 24 Apr. 1993).

U.S. Department of Commerce (1993), "Jamaica Economic and Trade Policy", (Market Research Report, 24 Apr. 1993).

U.S. Department of Commerce (1993), "Jamaica - Foreign Economic Trends" (Market Research Report, 24 Apr. 1993).

U.S. Department of Commerce (1993), "Survey of Current Business", Bureau of Economic Analysis, July, pp.97-100.

U.S. Department of Commerce (1993), "Trinidad & Tobago Economic and Trade Policy", (Market Research Report, 24'Apr. 1993).

Usher, Dan (1977), "The Economics of Tax Incentives to Encourage Investment in Developing Countries", *Journal of Development Economics.* p. 119-61.

Vernon, Raymond (1966), "International Investment and International Trade in the Product Life Cycle", *The Quarterly Journal of Economics,* Vol. 1, No. 2, p. 190-207.

Vernon, Raymond, (1971), *Sovereignty At Bay*, New York: Basic Books, Ch. 2.

Wallace, Cynthia Day (1990), *Foreign Direct Investment in the 1990s. A New Climate in the Third World*, Dordrecht, Netherlands: Martinus Nijhoff, p. 177.

Walters, Robert and Blake, David (1992), *The Politics of Global Economic Relations*, Englewood, CA.: Prentice Hall.

Weekly, James and Aggarwal, Raj (1989), *International Business. Operations in the Global Economy*, Orlando, FL.: Dryden Press.

Wells, Louis (1986), "Investment Incentives. An Unnecessary Debate", <u>CTC Reporter</u>, Autumn, pp.58-60.

Williams, James Delano (1988), "The Attractiveness Index : An Investigation of Direct Investment Economic Policies of Four Newly Industrialized Countries: Hong Kong, South Korea, Singapore, Taiwan", *Journal of International Business Studies*, Vol. XX, No. 2, p. 406.

Williams, Frances (1994), "Poorer Countries Grab More Investment", *The Financial Times*, May 4, 1994.

Williamson, Oliver (1986), *Economic Organization. Firms, Markets and Policy Control*, New York: New York University Press.

Wint, Alvin G (1988), "Investment Promotion: How Governments Compete for Foreign Direct Investment", PhD Dissertation Abstract, Boston: Harvard University

Woodward, Douglas P and Rolfe, Robert J (1993), "The Location of Export Oriented Foreign Direct Investment in the Caribbean Basin", *Journal of International Business Studies*, Vol 24, No.1, p. 121.

The World Bank (1989), "The World Bank, the IFC and MIGA", *The World Bank Annual Report, 1989*, Wash., D.C.: The World Bank.

The World Bank (1992), *World Development Report, 1992. Development and the Environment*, Oxford University Press, pp. 284, 306.

The World Bank (1992), "The World Bank Foreign Investment Survey" - draft form CECTM (CECSE), The World Bank.

The World Bank (1993), *The World Bank Annual Report, 1993*, Wash., D.C.: The World Bank, p.36.

Worrell, DeLisle (1987), *Small Island Economies. Structure and Performance in the English-speaking Caribbean Since 1970*, New York: Greenwood Press.

Worrell, DeLisle; Coderington, Harold; Khan, Zorina; Lawson, Morse (1987*), Private Foreign Investment in Barbados*, London: Croom Helm.

Xiaohong, He (1991), International Tax Trends and Competition: Tax Sensitivity of U.S. Foreign Investment Abroad, Ph.D. Thesis, University of Texas at Dallas.

Yoffie, David (1993), Beyond Free Trade. Firms, Governments and Global Competition, Boston, MA.: HBS Press.

INDEX